"In this lively, engaging, and insightful dialogue, Ma and Larsen interrogate the assumptions and ideologies undergirding contemporary criminology. Eschewing a conventional textbook approach, the authors invite readers to draw upon their own experience to grapple collaboratively and critically with a wide range of topics: the complexity of crime causation; the impact of media and moral panics; and the role of power and culture in shaping the social order, constructing deviance, and normalizing social control. *Troubling Criminology* will fire the 'criminological imagination' of both new students and seasoned criminologists alike."

Greg Simmons, Department of Criminology, Kwantlen Polytechnic University

TROUBLING CRIMINOLOGY

TROUBLING CRIMINOLOGY

Michael C. K. Ma
and Mike Larsen

Between the Lines
Toronto

Troubling Criminology
© 2025 Michael C. K. Ma and Mike Larsen

First published in 2025 by
Between the Lines
401 Richmond Street West, Studio 281
Toronto, Ontario · M5V 3A8 · Canada
1-800-718-7201 · www.btlbooks.com

Library and Archives Canada Cataloguing in Publication
Title: Troubling criminology / Michael C.K. Ma and Mike Larsen.
Names: Ma, Michael C. K., 1964- author. | Larsen, Mike, 1981- author
Description: Includes bibliographical references and index.
Identifiers: Canadiana (print) 20250227525 | Canadiana (ebook) 20250227576 |
    ISBN 9781771136853 (softcover) | ISBN 9781771136860 (EPUB)
Subjects: LCSH: Criminology. | LCSH: Crime—Sociological aspects.
Classification: LCC HV6025 .M3 2025 | DDC 364—dc23

Cover and text design by DEEVE

Printed in Canada

MIX
Paper | Supporting responsible forestry
FSC
www.fsc.org   FSC® C103567   ® GCC/IBT

We acknowledge for their financial support of our publishing activities: the Government of Canada; the Canada Council for the Arts; and the Government of Ontario through the Ontario Arts Council, the Ontario Book Publishers Tax Credit program, and Ontario Creates.

Canada   Canada Council for the Arts   Conseil des Arts du Canada   ONTARIO CREATES   ONTARIO ARTS COUNCIL / CONSEIL DES ARTS DE L'ONTARIO   an Ontario government agency / un organisme du gouvernement de l'Ontario

Contents

Contents

Points of Departure

Context should matter for criminologists. Criminologists must take into consideration the social and historical context in which matters of deviance, crime, justice, and injustice are thought about and acted upon. Put differently, we could say that the socially negotiated meaning of an action or event is contingent on when and where it takes place.

Context matters for writers, as well. Our work on this book, for example, began in 2020, during the initial lockdown in response to the COVID-19 pandemic, and the disruption and uncertainty of that time—the coming-together, falling-apart, and constant reminders of inequality and stratification—certainly shaped our thinking. Our work was also shaped by the renewed and intensified public discussions about justice, injustice, and the role of legal systems in perpetuating oppression, marginalization, and racism that defined the summer of 2020 and by the spectacle of resurgent fascist and authoritarian movements directly attacking democratic processes. During this time, we saw organized efforts to change traditional responses to social problems, including widespread calls to defund police and decriminalize drug use and possession.[1] We also watched the expected push-back from police agencies and other groups committed to law-and-order politics, resulting in increased police budgets and opposition to harm reduction.[2] We spoke with our students about the intersections of justice and diversity, equity, and inclusion while observing concerted efforts to restrict the rights of transgender youth in educational settings.[3]

We had set out to write an introductory textbook that invited our readers to question the status quo, and we found ourselves drafting chapters and discussing content (socially distanced, via video chats) at a time when the status quo was being both challenged and re-asserted around us, by circumstance and by social movements.

This brings us to our first point of departure for this book: an effort to think seriously about what it means to study criminology now, and to engage with its central themes, in a context of public health emergencies, climate crisis, land defence actions, settler-colonialism, calls for justice reform, unmarked child graves on the sites of former residential schools,[4] and spiralling rates of housing and economic inequality.

A second and related point of departure is the idea that students who are studying criminology for the very first time bring with them a lifetime of engagement with some of the central issues in the field. For example, most people will have spent considerable time thinking about matters of justice and injustice, right and wrong, good and evil, and the nature of law and legal institutions before ever formally studying any of these topics. They will have been immersed in images and representations of crime through news media and popular culture. Engagement does not imply expertise, of course, and working hypotheses, misconceptions, and gaps in knowledge must be challenged. However, we take the position that our readers have a foundation of interest and familiarity that equips them to learn through dialogue and engagement rather than through the memorization of a canon. Moreover, we recognize that we cannot assume a *shared* foundation on the part of our readers, who we understand to be a group characterized by diverse cultural, geographic, social, and experiential backgrounds.

A third point of departure is that this book was produced as part of an ongoing conversation between colleagues, and our hope is that it will inspire and facilitate similar conversations between readers. We make a point of posing questions and thinking collaboratively about possible answers. Readers, especially students studying criminology for the first time, are invited to take the conversation in different directions and arrive at different conclusions. This reflects a vision of criminology as a "problem-posing" discipline. We would consider this project a success if our readers felt better equipped to ask critical questions about crime, justice, and the ideas, ideologies, and institutions associated with them.

Finally, a fourth point of departure that this book offers the reader is the invitation to assess alternating perspectives: (a) That society constructs the individual such that a subject may not always be understood to be responsible for all of their actions, (b) that categories of crime are socially constructed and should not be understood as naturally existing categories in themselves (e.g., a crime in one society might not be one in another or what is a crime today may no longer be later on because our definitions of deviance and normalcy change), and (c) that even though we understand society as constantly constructing us, we can still have hope that changes to policy or criminal justice practices (e.g., policing) can alter this construction. It is not inconsistent to think that, on the one hand, society dictates what we can be and constructs us as subjects, while on the other hand, there can be different interventions or attempts to change the way society is organizing us. That is, the social construction of self and society is not set in stone.

It is possible that this approach may frustrate readers who are seeking straightforward answers to pressing questions about what crime is, why it occurs, or what is to be done about it. There are many worthy texts that address these questions. Our hope is that this book will be received as an invitation to engage in the intellectual work of nuanced and critical thinking about ideas that are central to criminology.

age we are already being shaped by our parents as they establish "social practices" that are acceptable or unacceptable. The family is a reflection of accepted social norms and social order.

At this early age we are being taught—in the nucleus of the family—what is right and wrong, or good and bad. At this early age we are being "conditioned" about what is right and wrong, or what is good and what is not good, or what is normal and what is abnormal. For example, in the context of oral health, teeth brushing is taught as something we must do; we have no choice. It must be done. It is good for us. Parents might take lots of effort to explain why we must brush our teeth but at some point it just becomes a habit.

ML: This is a very simple example, but it is a good microcosm of the formation and internalization of social norms.

MM: Yes, even the language we use to understand what is right and wrong or what is normal and what is deviant is a "language" or code that is already being programmed into our brains and our bodies at an early age. At the level of language, this self-evident projection of good and bad is already being realized in our own intellectual or conceptual framing of the world. For example, how would a child explain that something is good? They would say it was not bad. How would you explain that something is bad? You might explain that something is bad because it is not good. In this regard, there does not need to be an explanation of why something is good or bad; rather, it has been established at a deeper unconscious level. Some might call it an ideological inscription. Good and bad are established as opposites.

In this sense of conditioning and coding, the notions of what is acceptable or unacceptable is a specific set of social, relational, and language rules. If we use the example of recreational cannabis, we can understand how our laws around cannabis have made its recreational consumption legal in Canada.[1] While we can understand that it may be illegal in other countries, we now understand it to be acceptable or normal in our county but prohibited in others. It is normal here but abnormal elsewhere. Therein lies the contradiction of norms and deviance. How can a recreational substance be good here but bad elsewhere? The physical substance has not changed its attributes based on region. The cannabis itself has not changed, but its reception differs in different regions. This shows that what we understand to be normal is socially contingent. In one country, a substance has been legislated and made "good" through law, and in another it is "bad" or illegal.

In this sense, the laws around cannabis are just like your mother telling you not to hit your brother. It is simply a family rule, but unlike the parental rule we have something that can be named the repressive state apparatus (e.g., the police) who enforce the law through some kind of kinetic or physical way. The term "repressive state apparatus" was coined by Marxist philosopher Louis Althusser as a way to describe the physical and coercive institutions of the state that help maintain established social norms and rules. Institutions like the army, the judiciary, prisons, and the police use mental and physical coercion to maintain order and to punish those who deviate.[2] When we are studying norms and deviance, we are trying to understand how norms come to be, how they have been established, how they have continued to exist, how they are currently practised, how they have expanded, how they have been altered, how they have been reproduced, and how they are changing. That is what we are doing when we are studying norms and deviance in the context of criminology.

ML: A starting point is to begin by challenging some of the assumptions that have been baked into criminology. Historically speaking, one of the points of departure that is of interest to me is this association between criminology as a field, crime as a concept, and notions of certainty that come about because crime becomes defined and reified through state law. It is *literally* codified in the language of legal statutes. There is this very categorical nature to a lot of our foundational ideas: good and evil, right and wrong, lawful and unlawful. But as we continue to examine and interrogate these things, we become much more familiar with the shades of grey and the nuance of right and wrong and how it is established through law.[3]

At the outset I want to trouble some of these notions of certainty and obviousness. I want—instead of taking for granted the notion that there are natural crimes and that our task as criminologist is to explain why people commit them—to step back and think about how we *create* certain norms. How does normativity come to be embedded in processes of social regulation? How do we come to define certain things as being normal, abnormal, deviant, or conforming to expectations? And I want to do this in relation to a sociohistorical context because the obviousness of these foundational concepts of criminal, crime, right, and wrong are a reflection of time and place, society and culture. Through the process of socialization, we (particularly as young people) come to learn about and internalize the values and norms of the society we live in. These values and norms come to be understood by us as normal and natural, and that can make it difficult for us to step back and recognize that our norms are a reflection of the way our society is organized and that these norms change—sometimes subtly, sometimes dramatically—over time.[4]

MM: Yes, for example, in terms of nuance, it could be argued that many young people today have a much more nuanced and progressive understanding of gender as a nonbinary social construction. Or, in the context of housing, in the 1970s and 1980s it was considered "normal" for young people to move away from home when they came of age. Now, this has become an exception rather than the norm, in part because of the skyrocketing cost of housing. In this regard, it is the economic parameters that have changed and affected social norms. And moreover, it is quite normal now for students or young people to move back home after going to school. And that is understood now to be normal, when thirty or forty years ago it would have been peculiar.

ML: Your examples get us thinking about the relationships between norms and the broader social conditions we live in. So often, conversations about norms refer to some notion of deeply entrenched moral imperatives. In fact, though, our expectations regarding what is normal and abnormal are contingent and influenced by a whole variety of factors. It is worth noting that the young people in question, whether in the 1980s or in our present day, would probably understand their experience to be a reflection of social norms that may seem obvious to them.

We might consider it to be self-evident that something is a crime because we know it is against the law.[5] It is a violation of society's rules. In Canada, up until very recently the prohibition of cannabis has been a linchpin of the war on drugs and related efforts to address organized crime, the operation of black markets, and all the harms that go along with it. The cultivation and possession of cannabis was treated by the justice system as inherently deviant, and the criminal law was used to prosecute people involved in these activities. But times have changed, and Canada and some US states have recently redefined cannabis as a legal but regulated substance. In a short period of time, we went from criminalization through prohibition to a situation where entrepreneurs and large corporations can apply for government grants to support their production, operations, and storefronts, and the legal cannabis industry has pushed aside the black market. Ten years ago, this kind of production and distribution effort would have had to take place "underground," involving organized crime, and it would have been the subject of massive police interventions.[6]

In criminology, we should question categorical claims of right and wrong and scrutinize how rules are defined and enforced. It is crucial to understand that not all important societal norms are formalized in criminal law; many exist as conventions in social conduct. For example, why and how do you stand in a line? It seems like such an obvious question, but consider what would happen to the "order" of our society if we did not observe the "first come, first served" and "wait your turn" rules reflected in lineups. We learn how to line up at a very young age, and we make use of this knowledge every day. It is a means through which we perform civility and fairness. This sort of foundational norm is not governed by criminal law—and yet, cutting in line is clearly recognized as deviant behaviour. What would happen to our society if large numbers of people started to reject and abandon the norms associated with lining up?

To summarize, I think we have been emphasizing the importance of understanding and embracing nuance and ambiguity when thinking about matters of crime and deviance. This may seem counterintuitive, as the very concept of crime is meant to recognize an act that is categorically wrong, prohibit it, and make it subject to proactive and reactive suppression. However, the field becomes infinitely more engaging and provocative when we start to consider all of the shades of grey, politics, and forms of contestation that really shape both rulemaking and rule breaking. To acknowledge that rules and norms are social constructions is not to say that they are unimportant or lack meaning. We can recognize that certain norms are widely shared and socially beneficial, but we should remain aware that even these norms are the products of social processes.

MM: I think this discussion of norms and rules naturally leads us to consider the nature of laws. Laws are rules and regulations created to restrict people from certain behaviour or with the goal of compelling people to behave in a certain way. I think the enactment and enforcement of restrictions, rules, regulations, and the law is based on the assumption that people act in a self-centred manner. It takes for granted the idea that people primarily act in ways that benefit themselves and so preserving order necessitates creating some type of rule or restriction to limit people's selfishness.

We must interrogate this assumption. Is it true that people are naturally self-centred or are there conditions not of peoples choosing that create a certain kind of subjectivity or a certain type of subject of the law that necessitates this kind of assumption about human nature? We return to this question in our discussion of the Locke-Hobbes debate in chapter 2: Fear of Harm. So much of current contemporary (Eurocentric) North American law is centred on notions of property and the rights to property. That may be something we want to unpack. And one last thing to question: Do we need laws to protect ourselves from each other? For example, how we share the sidewalk with one another without any rules and regulations is a perfect illustration of how individual subjects coexist or share space without any formal rules. Another example is how we share the boundary with our neighbour without too many rules or regulations. Yes, there is an existing property line, and the laws support it, but it is not the main reason we have peace with neighbours. Similarly, we are not nice to our neighbours simply because we are worried about the police watching us. It is not a worry about sidewalk surveillance that makes us share or yield the sidewalk when someone is walking down the street towards us. We share the sidewalk and we cooperate with other people not because of laws. Rather, despite the laws, we are cooperating in an *extralegal* way with pedestrians and neighbours.

ML: You have suggested that the reason you do not harm your neighbours or accost people on the sidewalk is not because of your concern about possible legal sanctions or fear of punishment, and I think that this makes sense. Most people obey most social norms most of the time because we have internalized them and we believe in them and regard them as valid. The available evidence does not support the idea that we are self-interested hedonists who are only constrained from harming others by the watchful eye of the state and the deterrent threat of legal sanctions. This is a crucial point because it relates directly to how we imagine ourselves, others, and society. Many social theorists have observed that we, as a species, are naturally inclined to cooperate and engage in acts of mutual aid and that the development of hierarchical social structures sustains and legitimizes forms of coercion that are not the product of natural human evolution.[7]

Freedom and Deterrence

MM: OK, Mike, I have a thought. When we examine the criminal justice system, the question of justice is linked to the questions of freedom and liberty. What do you think?

ML: One of the things we notice if we examine the criminal justice system is that a lot of the powers inherent in the system are variations on the ability to deprive people of their liberty. For example, the whole idea of arrest or detention is based on a coercive limitation of a person's mobility. The idea of imprisonment and remand, or pretrial custody, revolves around the very direct revocation of a right to liberty. And of course, the most severe sanctions available in the Canadian criminal justice system involve the deprivation of liberty through incarceration up to and including indefinite incarceration and solitary confinement. The deprivation of liberty begs the question: What is the importance of liberty and freedom in our legal system such that our penal system is based on its revocation? What do you think?

MM: I think the idea of "freedom" is extremely important for us to understand because, as you note, the ultimate penalty in the criminal justice system is to take away someone's freedom. The criminal justice system understands freedom as so important to an individual that it will punish a person by taking away their freedom of mobility (i.e., putting them in prison).

We should understand that the concept of freedom is at the centre of the criminal justice system. Most rules, regulations, and laws are established to govern what someone can or cannot do. And, in this sense, rules, regulations, and punishment are all used to enforce the rule. The everyday person is supposed to fear the punishment (i.e., loss of liberty) to such a degree that they comply with the law due to their fear of punishment; this is often referred to as deterrence. The subject of law is presumed to choose freely whether to comply or resist. Therefore, the issues of freedom and free choice, or agency, are at the core of the criminal legal system. Constraining someone's freedom and generating the fear of losing one's freedom is the driving force behind legal justice and our compliance with law. Or at least this is the classical notion of deterrence and why people observe laws. It should be noted that although our punitive systems of criminal justice are not inevitable, they have become ubiquitous and globally adopted. Critics (e.g., abolitionists) argue that another world is possible, where systems of response are not based on threat, punishment, and repression.

ML: One of the ways you encourage me to comply with the rules is by threatening to take away my freedom as punishment for breaking them. Does this imply that I am otherwise living in a state of total freedom?

MM: Your questions bring up two things: the effectiveness of deterrence and the issue of total freedom. First, the notion that deterrence is the primary driver behind lawful behaviour may not be supported by evidence. Although the system behaves as though deterrence is particularly important, other explanations (e.g., alignment and internalization of values, empathy, manufactured consent) may be more persuasive. Second, there is no such thing as total freedom. You can only have freedom within rules and regulations and boundaries and social conventions. The bigger question is: How can we establish limits to freedom that are equal, fair, and equitable? That is the real question.

The use of incarceration as deterrence brings up another aspect of freedom: consent. For example, do offenders willingly consent to being sent to jail for their offence? Or are they coerced by the state to go to prison? The use of armed guards and restraints demonstrate that not everyone consents to rulings that recommend prison or other forms of detention. This brings up the problematic question of whether individuals are truly free to choose all things, all the time, and under all circumstances. Or could it be that their freedoms were already curtailed?

When the criminal justice system finds someone guilty of a crime, it will sentence them to forms of punishment that may include the loss of freedom. This suggests that the subject of the criminal justice system does not actually want to go to jail but is coerced. The subject wants to continue to exercise their freedom of mobility and yet they are not allowed. So here is an example of the absolute removal of a person's freedom of choice and their freedom to consent because that person is experiencing a certain judgment or situation imposed upon them that they would rather reject. It is common to describe a system of laws as a reflection of a set of shared values and a consensus regarding social norms, but it is clear that legal processes like convictions and sentencing do not require the consent of their subjects. The resistance to legal judgments further complexifies the notion of freedom of choice. Can subjects simply not accept, or reject, a legal ruling? It is possible, in some circumstances, to appeal a court decision, but if leave to appeal is denied or if the appeal is unfavourable the legal system will still employ coercion to enforce a sentence.

ML: The question that arises for me is: What is wrong with coercion? Is coercion not a foundational part of criminal justice systems? Calls for law and order receive considerable public support, so clearly there is a widespread demand for the coercive apparatus of the state. The sociologist Egon Bittner proposed that policing can be defined as "a mechanism for the distribution of non-negotiably coercive force employed in accordance with the dictates of an intuitive grasp of situational exigencies."[8] In other words, policing is about restoring or reproducing order through the use or threat of force. Other scholars propose that policing agents are defined by their ability to use diverse means that are otherwise prohibited—including in ways that are decidedly nonconsensual.[9] This theme extends to many classical interpretations of the role of law in society. For example, Max Weber proposed that "an order will be called law if it is externally guaranteed by the probability that coercion (physical or psychological) to bring about conformity or avenge violation, will be applied by a staff of people holding themselves specially ready for that purpose."[10] At the same time, we also find that freedom and agency are deeply entrenched social values. How do we reconcile this apparent contradiction—this simultaneous desire for freedom and the normalization of systems of control?

MM: Everyone remembers being coerced at some time or another by our parents; being forced to do something that we did not want to do, and which did not have our consent, because they thought it was good for us. They made us do something they thought was beneficial to us. For example, our parents might have forced us to learn piano or to go to school when we did not want to. So there are many aspects of coercion that we can understand as actually beneficial in this framework. Can we also think of the state in this paternalistic framework, where the state is like our parent and the parent-state is acting in our defence and to our benefit? Can we understand the state as wanting to help us to become a better citizen even when we do not agree?

ML: That is an important question. I would like to approach it by asking about the evidence we would need to determine whether a state or a state agency was motivated by a genuine concern for well-being when it was limiting our capacity to exercise consent or by imposing a coercive sanction upon us. It is one thing to assume the state operates on some form of enlightened and benevolent paternalistic intent, but it is something else to have supporting evidence.[11] For that matter, we should note that coercive actions by parents can also be assumed to be *not* benign or beneficial to children. We know, for example, that child abuse is a persistent and serious form of harm in our society. There is also the added complexity of our legal system, which assumes children are not able to exercise informed consent—in many cases—in relation to the decisions of their parents. Society and its institutions operate on the notion that parents have a duty or obligation to act in the best interests of their children and are typically assumed to be doing such. However, at some point in this relationship between parent and child, we understand people to transition from being children—subject to benevolently coercive parenting—into adults imbued with liberty and a capacity to make informed decisions about their actions.

MM: We are using useful framing here. The metaphor of parents standing in for the state is so useful in this discussion! Not only could we question whether parents always act in the best interest of their children, we could also understand that sometimes parents want things the child does not want. For example, a child may want to play hockey but that wish is at odds with parents who may prefer the child play soccer. The result is that the parents might coerce a child to comply. In this regard, maybe the parents do not have the best interest of the child at heart—especially if we consider the "rights of the child." Similarly, we find this reflected in the parent-state, where government does not always understand what is most beneficial for the citizen or the subject and coercion, punishment, and/or penalty might be the wrong instrument to apply in that situation. Is there evidence that proves the government, or the state, is acting in a way that has our health and well-being in mind? If it does, then it makes sense that the state should be allowed to coerce us, to incarcerate us, or to punish us. But the problem is that there is no evidence the state is always working to our benefit, is always in our corner, or that the forms of punishment we have in society today produce healthy and positive outcomes. We can rhetorically ask: Does prison, jail time, or punitive sentencing produce a rehabilitated and more productive and socially healthy individual after their incarceration? And that of course returns us to the questions of consent, coercion, and freedom.

But this idea of coercion also makes me think of how we often make ourselves do things and the notion of productivity. It makes me think of how we compel and comply and how it relates to our idea of "human nature." To understand our framing of human nature, we can use the analogy of productivity and unproductivity.

For example, we use schedules to remind ourselves to do things; where life is a kind of problem that must be solved with external structures that must be vigorously enforced (e.g., gym workout schedule). It suggests that our natural state is one of entropy, where order must be externally applied. Otherwise, nothing would get done. We have techniques and technology to constantly remind us to do things: clocks, Fitbits, cellphone alerts, calendars, etc. Without these tools to remind us of and force us to comply to an external order, our natural state is chaos or entropy, or at the very least to be lazy and unproductive. In this sense, external control and structure could be understood as a good thing. It allows us to make things, meet people, and be "compliant" with what is good for us. In this framework, external regulation is necessary both to defeat our lazy nature and to create the rewards of productivity that we simultaneously (or secretly) desire. No one likes work. Work is a kind of punishment that we must force ourselves to enjoy because it is imperative that we work. And yet, somehow, we know that without human production we would cease to exist. Therefore, we must force ourselves to work. Unproductivity and passivity are "human natures" that must be treated or they will run rampant. We know we will default to unproductivity so we must arrange our day in such a manner so that we "become" productive. Productivity is not in our nature. Unproductivity *is* our nature. And unproductivity is a kind of offence or a self-disappointment. Our natural compulsion is to just sit around, doodle, dawdle, or watch TV. Nonproductive activity is assumed to be our nature. We must try to be the best versions of ourselves because otherwise our "true" nature will dominate. In this framework, work is both punishment and reward. Using this analogy of unproductivity, we can understand crime and deviance to be forms of unproductivity that must be vigilantly repressed. Social and individual deviance is a natural human state that must be rigorously controlled and repressed.

Are people inherently allergic to structure such that they must create external controls to make themselves comply? It could be argued that the unintended consequence of creating and applying an external structure gives rise to resistance and/or noncompliance. Are people rebelling against their own desired structures? And is resistance a product of the rule?[12] There is a chicken-and-egg circular component to this question.

A second analogy is that we treat ourselves like an addict. We know we cannot resist eating another potato chip, so we do not buy them. We keep the object of our desire out of the house. In this analogy, work and productivity are virtues that we aspire to and that we want in our lives, but our nature is constantly at odds with this desire. We really want the potato chips! So, like an addict, we must have constant self-control and vigilance over our behaviour because otherwise we would lapse and be users again. We may even want an external control to help us. A control that is out of our control. An outside force that is beyond our influence.

These analogies show us that framing human nature in this manner—where repression and enforcement of external rules (e.g., wake up, go to work, gym, or church) are understood as socially necessary—may be an incorrect framing of human nature and the artifice of society. It shows that this equation of productivity/unproductivity in relation to an assumed human nature may be wrong-headed. It is something that we will address more systematically in chapter 4: The Quest for Causation.

ML: I think this is a helpful line of discussion for us to explore and for our readers to think about. We often conceptualize issues like control and consent and coercion in very stark terms, but a great deal of the control, governance, and regulation that impacts our everyday lives is either self-initiated or part of a system that we integrate ourselves into in order to function in contemporary society. The social theorist Michel Foucault explores these themes in his work on discipline and governmentality.[13] Foucault observes that we are embedded in a variety of institutional settings—school and work, for example—that foster particular ways of thinking about the world and our lives and that function to structure our conduct. These institutions can be highly coercive, but on an everyday basis they work by enlisting us in our own regulation and governing. So, when we think about policing and control, it is important to consider formal examples and instances when we actively police ourselves without the intervention of an outside force.

I can think of three scenarios that might help our readers to think about this issue of freedom and consent in the context of criminal justice. The first scenario involves a person who is walking down the street and is stopped by police and asked: "Can I talk to you for a minute?," or "Will you answer a few questions?" The interaction seems to imply that the individual in question has a degree of liberty and the capacity to consent or not consent to that interaction because it is posed as a question. However, when we examine it more carefully, it is clear that whether someone regards that as a consensual interaction depends on a whole bunch of different factors, including knowledge of the law, power dynamics, past experiences, and trust in institutions. Similar scenarios involve police asking: "Can I look in your car trunk?," "Could you open your door?," or "Can I come into your house?"[14] There are many questions that may not actually be *true* questions by function so much as questions embedded in criminal justice interactions.

The second scenario this makes me think about is the person who has been convicted of a crime and is sentenced—regardless of their consent—to a period of incarceration. At that stage, the question of whether they will remain in prison, under what conditions, and for how long has something to do with their demonstration of remorse.[15] "Remorse" is in some ways related to this question of consent. The "right to consent" to the experience of correction involves this performance of remorse and contrition.[16] For example, we know that wrongfully convicted people—who refuse to demonstrate remorse and refuse to consent to the prescribed correctional program—are often regarded by the system as being doubly guilty because they are unrepentant.[17]

The third scenario involves the person who has not been convicted. I think of the example of the mugshot. It has been argued that the mugshot is a coerced photograph of someone the police have arrested but is not convicted of any crime and ultimately may not be.[18] But later, even if charges are dropped or the person is acquitted of charges, the mugshot photograph remains in police files. Most people would prefer that photo be destroyed because it was taken at a moment of crisis and—if not for the power of the police—they would not have consented. They are innocent but they were coerced to being photographically framed as a guilty person, since the mugshot itself implies guilt. Police can also share that mugshot in the future without your consent.[19] It is worth noting that in our current meditated digital society, images of "deviance" can be the focus of online public shaming activities that have far-reaching implications.[20]

MM: As you mentioned at the outset of this conversation, the question of freedom or liberty is at the centre of our criminal justice system and, in some respects, at the centre of our social organization writ large. It is conceptually useful to understand people as social beings who enter into a type of Hobbesian[21] relationship with other people who give up freedoms and obey rules, which might limit their freedoms but is useful or necessary because it allows you to coexist or collaborate with others in a coherent rules-based manner. But right there the first question arises: Are these rules of my own choosing? It is true that we cannot do anything and everything we want and that our freedoms are curtailed by an imagined social contract that we have signed. The social contract suggests that we cannot act in an infinite or unconstrained manner and that we are curtailed by the law or the contract we signed. For example, in North America, we cannot drive on the left side of the street. We must drive on the right side because there are rules that regulate our manner of driving. As a pedestrian, we cannot cross a road without paying attention to certain restrictions like stop signs, traffic lights, walk signs, and other traffic signals. These signs limit our freedom, but we gladly enter into those limits and we obey those limits or restrictions so we can have a more fulsome, cooperative, and cohesive interaction with other people in society. And that is how we understand what freedoms are. "Freedoms" are limited and they are restricted within a certain set of rules that we enter into freely. And so that is the crux of the question of whether individuals enter into those relationships freely or are born into conditions not of their own choosing. This is a question we deal with in more detail in chapter 8: Criminalizing Inequality and Poverty. That is really the difficult and strange question for our readers to entertain because the criminal justice system is built on the notion that every individual is free to act and free not to act, or, in that sense, to have *mens rea,* or intention. The question of free will and agency over our actions is an exceedingly puzzling question. Do all individuals have agency and is it informed agency and is it a rational agency? Because if they do not, then it calls into question what it means to freely decide something.

I should say, for the record, that I am all for rules and prohibitions so we can be safe. For example, I like rules that say we cannot just hit each other (without consent). You can hit each other in boxing because boxers consent to being hit within the context of the boxing ring. However, I am not a boxer, and in my case, I do not want to be hit while walking down the street, nor do I want to worry about being hit. Therefore, I like rules against hitting because it helps me feel safe. So, in the context of law, I like the prohibition against assault. And the prohibition against assault, which is a limitation on the freedom to act, supports my well-being. So, in this sense, I fully support prohibitions because they allow me to walk down the street without stress or worry about being assaulted. And yet, this does beg the question: Is the prohibition against assault the main reason people do not hit each other? Some would argue it is not prohibition that provides this safety but the way people are socialized or raised by family.[22] The question becomes even more complicated when we introduce police or policing. We can understand that police act as a repressive state apparatus[23] who ensure people comply with this rule of "no hitting." In this regard, the police act as a deterrent, or a threat, to people who do not comply. The concept and institution of police also raises the idea of courts and prison. You can end up in court, charged with assault, convicted, and sentenced to prison. The question for me is: Do we need a repressive agent of the state and a court/prison system to make us not hit each other? What did we do before we had police and courts? Do all societies and civilizations have a police service? Are police a necessity for all societies? Are police always organized in the same manner? Why would some police be different? Is it possible to have a different police service? Would we even name or envision them as "police"?[24]

ML: I agree, and I think this gives us reason to talk about the abstract "we" that has entered our conversation. Here we have been talking about how we have certain liberties and these liberties are potentially constrained by the social contract or law or systems. But of course society is not homogeneous and one of the things we must consider when approaching these questions is the relative ability of different people by virtue of their status, their privilege, and their marginality to exercise various freedoms and liberties. For example, feminist geographer Leslie Kern argues that the way women experience and navigate the urban environment is very different from that of men. In part, this is a reflection of urban design, which is in turn a reflection of gendered social norms and women's experience of vulnerability. Put differently, we might note that our technical equality of rights based on statutes or "law on the books" is often out of sync with the way real people experience rights and liberties in everyday life. This distinction between law on the books and law in action is one of the central topics of scholarship in sociolegal studies, and it is a topic explored in detail by Kitty Calavita.[25] As we have previously suggested, people—including us—make decisions and act in certain ways not in the abstract sense but in real circumstances. These circumstances are in turn shaped by our social context. The sociologist C. Wright Mills emphasizes this in his seminal book *The Sociological Imagination*.[26] Mills argues that effective social analysis requires the exercise of a certain imagination or perspective that considers the intersections of biography, history, and social structure. In our case, if we want to think seriously about rights, wrongs, agency, and social order, this means paying attention to the factors that differentially impact the ability of certain individuals or groups to feel and act freely in society. Two people might possess the same formal rights and freedoms but have completely different understandings, based on their identity and circumstances, of whether and how they can exercise those rights without fear of consequence.

MM: In relation to the idea of "fear of consequences," any in-depth discussion of rules, prohibitions, and social order will eventually give rise to questions like: Says who? and By what authority? Humans once had gods, but then we came to understand that we invented gods as a place marker for authority and social order. Gods and the belief in them ensured social order. In the modern era, we replaced the figure of god with the rule of law. The rule of law is based on a human-centred or humanist assertion. The assertion is this: We are different from other living things and because we have consciousness and unique identities we must have rules to organize and manage the collaboration and coexistence of all these unique subjects and identities. The rule of law allows us to coexist with each other's unique identification, actions, thoughts, and desires. Gods and the laws that descended from the heavens used to provide us with a framework but that is no longer the case due to a decline of traditional religious authority.[27] The assertion is that without rules, whether they are god-based or human-based, our individual uniqueness would destroy us because we would not be able to function as a cohesive or collective group. Therefore, this point of view asserts that laws exist to prevent us from destroying one another (see our discussion of Locke-Hobbes in chapter 2: Fear of Harm) or hurting each other. Of course, this begs the social-anthropological question: What did we have before the adoption of a supreme being and/or the invention, formalization, and writing of laws? Was it just chaos or was there some kind of prelinguistic order and social collaboration created without formal rules?[28] Do people naturally hurt each other in the absence of formal rules or laws?

ML: These are interesting points, Mike, but I wonder if we are missing some important nuance here. Are we suggesting that there has been a consistent transfer of responsibility and authority for matters of justice from religious to secular systems? Are we also suggesting that the idea of divine judgment and retribution—and the fear of consequence—is common to all contemporary faiths?

MM: I think you are right that we should be cautious when we talk about gods or divine laws because it might suggest that there is one uniform notion of supreme being or "god format" that dictates rules for all human beings on Earth. This is not the case. And yet, I would argue strongly that we are governed by an overarching regulatory system or global order—a set of beliefs in the rule of law, for example. There is a strong consensus on the legitimacy of law and this governs trade and certain norms on an international scale. In this sense, it may seem that my previous comments are somewhat Eurocentric or Western-centric, and I think it is important to acknowledge cultural differences (which can be erased by instrumental perspectives on law, regulation, and social order). However, the question of what came before is confounding because contemporary society is almost entirely dominated by the social and regulatory systems that derive from Western European ideas and practices (e.g., law and systems of government) that have proliferated since 1492 (i.e., the colonization of the "new world").[29] In fact, it is difficult to think about contemporary society and politics without using Western European notions of democracy, freedom, rights, equality, and humanism. The global and international rules that govern human interaction and the jurisdiction of law are rooted in Western European philosophy and history. This foundation gave rise to a system of liberal humanism that has established laws and conventions based on the following concepts:[30]

- Every person is free and has agency (e.g., consciousness).
- Each human is distinct and can do what they want as long as they do not hurt anyone.
- The rule of law is established to ensure this outcome.
- Individuals have free will and the state should help them enjoy their unique freeness.
- Liberty is necessary to have a meaningful life (hence all law hinges on guaranteeing you maximum freeness as long as you do not hurt anyone or limit other people's freedom).

The philosophy of liberal humanism argues that each human is unique, distinct, and in possession of free will. Free will means that each human has their own agency to act and think independently of others. In the context of liberal humanism, "freedom" is so important that if we did not have liberty or freedom then our lives would be meaningless. However, to exist in harmony or in cooperation with other unique people we need laws that limit our freedom. Laws outline what we can or cannot do. Each person enjoys their unique but restricted free-ness in society only through laws and restrictions. Freedom exists because of rules that limit freedom. And therein lies the original contradiction of law: we are unique and free in society as long as we obey restrictions. So in this sense a society based on liberal humanist principles can only offer limited freedoms or limited agency to each person in that society. We are free and unique but only to a limited extent. For example, we can do whatever we want just as long as we do not hurt anyone. In this sense, we surrender some of our freedoms and unique thoughts and desires so that we can be at peace with our neighbours. And our neighbour also complies with the same rules and regulations. What do you think about the way I have framed this idea of liberal humanism, free will, and the law?

ML: It is an excellent summary of the foundational ideas of liberal humanist perspective, which—as you rightly point out—informs the legal system we operate within. There are ideas built into your statement that are worthy of further discussion. One theme of interest is the emphasis on the individual as the central figure of politics and society who is juxtaposed against the state or society itself as this external and constraining force that works to limit freedom.

This seems like a good time to acknowledge alternative ways of understanding justice, both as a concept and as a process. For example, we can consider forms of restorative practice, many of which have roots in Indigenous traditions of justice, that emphasize community participation, repairing the harms associated with wrongdoing, and healing. Such models are less hierarchical and through their focus on participation more aligned with the idea of consensus than Western adversarial models.[31] Your framing and summary make me ask: What is the role of community? What is the role of collective action? What are collective values in this kind of context?

MM: I agree that law has been constructed around individual freedoms and individual rights and in this sense has obscured group rights or collective rights. All our laws and regulations are based on how we—as you say—enter into a social contract that limits individual freedoms but not collective ones.[32] In fact, we have no real language within the law to deal with collective rights or collective freedoms. In so doing, we have adopted a series of laws that privilege individual subjective identity, expression, articulation, and practice of their rights, but we do not have any legal framing that helps establish how the whole of society might have certain entitlements or rights. We have a regime of individual rights not group rights. We know the law is there to protect individuals, and we know the law applies equally to everyone, but only on an individual basis.

For example, in the context of property laws, we can understand that a crime may be linked to the way society creates unequal access to resources (i.e., some have more money than others); however, the law is only able to focus on one individual instance of theft of property and does not address the larger systemic or underlying economic conditions that has created the unequal situation. The law can address one instance of theft, but it cannot address, for example, the poverty that might be motivating theft. In this sense, law is designed only to punish or correct individual mistakes. It can correct one single theft. It does not correct the social mistakes that exist in society and/or that predate an individual's birth or action. For example, there is no law that says children cannot be born into poverty. Laws seek to control individual transgressions of law. It does not address the injustice of social inequality that may be at the root of those transgressions or the social agent of those mistakes made by individual social actors. Put another way, poverty may drive many crimes, but the application of law through the courts does not solve poverty.[33] Does society and its people have a right to be free of poverty or homelessness?

ML: I agree, and I think this might be a recurring theme as we try and address some of the challenges we face around issues of systemic forms of marginalization, injustice, and harm that are not easily resolved at the level of individual rights and obligations. You could make an argument that a legal system, a political system, and a philosophy of law, which are built around the primacy of the individual, are ill equipped to deal with many of the global social and macrolevel challenges of our time. There are, for example, no viable solutions to the pressing climate change crisis that are based entirely on individual actions. If and when we take climate change seriously, it will require massive social and structural changes, a reimagining of our economy, and collaborations on a grand scale. Similarly, while it is possible—indeed, essential—for individuals to strive to be antiracist in their own behaviour, this alone will not address problems related to systemic and structural racism.[34] We return to this theme in chapter 9: Racism.

MM: It is true that many "global social macrolevel challenges of our time" (e.g., poverty, access to education, wealth, housing, healthcare, and food security) are not addressed at an individual level through the court system. It is self-evident that the court system is specifically NOT constructed to alleviate or solve such macro problems because the law has no authority over "nonlegal" matters. And yet, we know that these macrolevel challenges are the social determinants leading to the mistakes the law tries to correct downstream. And if these problems cannot be resolved at the level of individuals or their rights, then we should also question the way the law imagines its own impartiality or neutrality. Are we really all equal before the law? For example, we know a rich person, or a big corporation, will have much greater access to legal representation than an individual who is poor or has low socioeconomic status. So, right away most people would be able to recognize that some people have *greater* access to the law and to legal representation than the general public. In this sense, I think many would agree that not all people have equal access to the law and justice. And yet, this is absolutely the key premise underpinning our justice system (i.e., *we are all equal before the* *law*). The wording of "equal before the law" also brings up the question of whether the phrase refers to the idea of everyone having the same "right" of access to the law because how one exercises that right might be unequal. So how could such a scenario play out in real life? A wealthy person may be able to afford a more senior or stronger lawyer, whereas a poorer person may only have access to legal aid lawyers or duty counsel. Publicly provided lawyers may be excellent, but sometimes they have less time or expertise to support such a case. Therefore, the system of legal representation may not be equal and individuals may not be "all equal before the law" in this regard.

Our system of law is hyperfocused on the individual actor. One way of thinking about "law-breaking" is to understand it as "mistakes" made by individual people. For example, we know that sometimes people make mistakes. That is, a person may do something that breaks a law. And we know that if we make a mistake, the law will not only step in to remind us that it was a mistake, but it will also act in a punitive way. The law and the criminal justice system will try to correct our mistakes through a court system and even through the correctional system. When we make a mistake, it can lead to us being sent to a house of corrections. So in this sense we have a system that corrects individual mistakes or transgressions of law. We do not have a system that punishes groups or group action. In this regard, much of our law is focused on the individual.

Another brain-melting question comes up in relation to the uniqueness of humans and the laws we create. If we are unique beings who need laws to govern us, then who exactly are we? We certainly believe that we are different and superior to animals. We have idioms like, "Don't treat me like a dog." The phrase suggests dogs are non-human or subhuman. And because of our unique humanness we need to create human-specific laws that only pertain to humans. Or do we? Maybe we do not. For example, we have laws that govern corporations in a way that treats them like a person with rights, and yet a company is not a person. In fact, despite being less alive than a dog, they possess more rights before the law than a dog. What do you think about this idea of laws restricting only the freedoms and rights of a person? It seems we have more than just a liberal humanist position. It seems we are also affording personhood to nonpersons.

ML: This may seem like an esoteric discussion at the outset, but it is fundamentally important for us, and it is an issue that is going to have to be front and centre in some of the major debates in the near future. We are increasingly aware of the capacity of nonhuman living organisms to think, to feel, and to act, and we are increasingly aware of the impact we as humans have on other lives on this planet. As such, the foundational assumptions of a "human-centric orientation" towards law are increasingly being challenged. We know that as a species we are responsible for the elimination of other species on an ongoing basis, which raises some serious ethical challenges. Historically, animals have been treated as either nothing or as property to be owned within law. There are some variations on this issue that have recently challenged the human-centric orientation of law.[35] We have rules and regulations around things like animal testing and there are categories of rights associated with nonhuman beings like the great apes and/or cetaceans. I think this is a very important and foundational issue, and there will likely be some significant developments in this area in our lifetime.

Even if we focus exclusively on humans, we should note that equal recognition before the law is something that was hard fought for within living memory; the idea of equal rights for women, equal rights for persons with disabilities, the rights of members of the LGBTQ+ community, or the equality of nonwhite people in settler societies are comparatively recent inventions. It was not long ago that various groups of humans were treated as something less than persons before the law, and today there are organized movements seeking to claw back this progress.

MM: That is a perfect segue into the next question that I have for us. The idea of humanism and the law also brings up this other question: Who is legible to the law? We know that European-based practices of law historically only afforded personhood to men, and not to women, children, or people who were not "white." For example, a municipality cannot be prosecuted for homelessness even though it is a serious breach of the social contract. In this case, a municipality or a company can be in breach of a contract, but they cannot be prosecuted or go to jail. This illustrates how the social contract of governance is understood differently than a service contract. The regime of rights also does not recognize the rights of homeless people as a group who has rights because only individuals are recognized as possessing rights. We also know that the law often refers to such individuals as the "reasonable" subject of law. Who is reasonable and who is legible to the law?

- Who is subject to the law? (e.g., the city can be guilty of breach of contract, but it cannot be prosecuted for homelessness)
- How does the law interpret us?
- When did women become subjects of the law?
- What is a child? What is a youth?
- How will we deal with AI?
- What is a "reasonable" subject?
- We have *Gladue* and a new prosecution policy (adopted Jan 15, 2021) designed to designate Indigenous adults differently. We acknowledge their "conditions" as different from others, almost treating them as disabled or challenged by conditions not of their choosing. Therefore, this calls into question the "free will" that is the basis of law. *These are policies of equity that equalize unfair conditions not of one's choosing.*

ML: The idea of the reasonable person is something that is often discussed in sociolegal research. It is the imagined character who stands in for us in the law. The reasonable subject is a legal subject only. And there has been much discussion about how Western legal systems do not deal with "subjects" as distinct humans with their own backgrounds, histories, culture, and complexity.[36] Rather, law translates them into proxies of this reasonable person standard who does not actually exist in any concrete sense but is nonetheless the central feature of law.

A criticism of this is that it tends to abstract individual cases and drains all the rich background history and complexity that gives rise to conflicts in legal systems in the first place. Abstraction disregards the specific details of an individual. In other words, the law deals with legal subjects as abstract entities rather than persons or communities with their own idiosyncrasies and histories.

Rights

MM: Before we go too far into the discussion of the legal subject let us first complete our discussion on liberal humanism. Another especially important aspect of humanism and the law is the concept of rights. We often talk about how humans have rights. We have human rights! And we are supposed to have "equal rights before the law." But I think most people do not know those rights. Why do we have these rights? Who has these rights? How do you know you have rights? How would you know if you did not? What do you think?

ML: I think this allows us to move to the second meaning of the term "rights" as expressed in the title of this chapter. We began by speaking about questions of norms and value systems and how these notions of what is right are translated into law and systems of justice. The second meaning of rights, of course, is the more commonsensical, or perhaps just more familiar, notion of legal rights. I think it is especially important for criminologists to consider rights at the outset of a study of matters of crime, law, and justice. We could conceptualize a lot of crimes and harms as forms of injustice. Violations of rights can also be understood as injustices and social wrongs. In many ways, modern social justice movements tend to be organized around the pursuit of rights or the realization of rights that exist "on the books" in some fashion but may not be applicable in reality. For example, people living in homeless encampments technically have the same rights to life, liberty, and security that I have, but what does this mean—in a practical sense—when police and private security forcibly displace them, confiscate their property, and threaten them with arrest?

For rights to be meaningful, they must be recognized, both by rights-holders and by other parties with the potential to either respect or violate these rights, and it must be possible for people to assert them and insist that they be recognized.[37] Do you think people are generally aware of their rights? And more importantly, do we expect that people understand how and when to exercise their rights? And, even more to the point, if you are aware of rights but do not feel capable of asserting or exercising them, do they really exist in a meaningful sense?

MM: You have asked some confounding questions! Let us try to examine them in relation to our own experience. In the Canadian context, we have documents that describe our rights. An early document is the *Bill of Rights,* which was drafted to counteract federal state powers that could potentially infringe on people's rights. Legislators introduced legislation that provided language to protect individual citizen rights. Later, we introduced the *Charter of Rights and Freedoms,* which offered a more detailed joint provincial and federal framework of protection.[38] However, both these protections of the individual rights of citizens were just drafts of aspirational language that tried to imagine the ways rights could be infringed. That is, their language is always in relationship to how the repressive state apparatus *could* potentially damage individual rights. Therefore, these documents are just mothering principles that describe what cannot or should not be done by a state. They never outline the specific way rights can be delivered, insured, or protected. For example, the charter states that government cannot invade someone's privacy and that if you are detained by police, then you have the right to a lawyer and access to courts. However, the language does not detail how we should deliver these rights. It just states them as desirable things. The format of the charter also creates a situation where most people are unaware of such rights because they are written in a way that is not accessible to a general public, and the legislation itself is set up in a way that is not easily accessible by the public because it must be accessed through the courts. For example, if you felt you lacked "security of person," which is one of the charter rights, how would you access the charter? Typically, you would hire a lawyer to access the charter for you, and you and your lawyer would have to go through a lengthy process of preparing arguments that would ensure your charter challenge is accepted by the courts. Not all charter challenges are accepted, and it is common that cases are not accepted or thrown out of court because they do not meet minimum requirements. So in this regard there are many barriers to accessing a set of rights, which are detailed in a specific document (e.g., the *Canadian Charter of Rights and Freedoms*) that is difficult to access in a practical manner when you feel your rights have been violated.

Let us return to the question of housing. Earlier you said that we cannot in any way hold municipalities accountable for having created homelessness; that we cannot blame them for having failed their social contract to provide housing for residents or those citizens under their jurisdiction. In the case of homelessness, we would agree that it would be ridiculously hard for a homeless person to access the charter and try to show that their charter right of "security of person," which just means safety and survival of a person, was a right that was being infringed because of their lack of housing; housing that the municipality should be providing to those in need. That is, the person without housing has a right to housing, but it is never realized—as a charter right—in the context of the municipality or city in which they live. It is not realized because the charter protections are not accessible by this unhoused person in any practical sense. The person sleeping on the sidewalk would have no access to the charter and therefore no access to their rights. Our rights, which are detailed in the charter, are rights that are only stated mothering principles and not a set of principles that can be easily realized in practical everyday life.

ML: Though they may be aspirational or vaguely written, there are some important ideas encapsulated in many of our rights, including things like the right to be free from unreasonable search and seizure, which is where a lot of the principles of privacy are grounded. We are in the middle of an important and ongoing debate about the meaning of "privacy" and our understanding of what the limits are on the capacity of other people to access our personal information. These are fundamentally important questions, but because rights are often a moving target and are indeed purposefully written in a generalist manner that avoids saying something very specific about your precise rights to be free from unreasonable search and seizure, the *Charter of Rights and Freedoms* remains broad and vague. It sets out general principles and then leaves it to government agencies in an enforcement capacity, and later the courts in their judicial capacity, to apply the principle of unreasonable search and seizure in the law.

The rights we possess also consistently fall behind current events or lag behind the times we live in. For instance, our privacy rights, codified both in the charter and in federal and provincial statutes, originated in a period prior to ubiquitous smart phones, massive social media platforms, and machine-learning algorithms that can scrape the internet and generate highly detailed profiles and biometric identifiers. These are problems of the present moment. There are "off the shelf" technologies and complex interjurisdictional practices that run roughshod over privacy rights, and this can have extraordinarily harmful effects for people.[39] For example, digital surveillance can lead to "false positives" (i.e., where people are erroneously identified as suspicious or deviant), profiling, persecution on the basis of belief, religion, gender, and sexual orientation, and chilling effects on speech and action. We are only just now starting to reform our privacy laws to attempt to address these issues, and it has taken many years and extraordinary effort to create the political will to take these steps. And yet, even as we work to put updated and relevant laws in place, there are whole industries actively working on ways to get around them.

In an everyday sense, this leaves us with an interesting mix of rights.

Some issues have been clearly defined by the courts, and current laws seem to be adequate to the task. Some issues are better understood as open questions: Can a border agent make a copy of all the data on my password-protected phone when I am crossing the border? Can someone who has a sophisticated camera that can "see through" solid walls by observing heat signatures legally peer into my home? Is it legitimate to simply scrape the internet for all sorts of personal information that has been uploaded by individuals and to use this information for profiling and investigative purposes? All these issues relate to this broad thing that we speak about in terms of privacy rights. However, it is often the case that not only do these rights have to be violated before they can be effectively asserted—as you very importantly point out—but taking a violation of rights to court is no simple matter. Even organizations that specialize in human rights and civil liberties pick their cases carefully. They often select cases that can have maximum impact in terms of the law and really change things, but it may not be particularly helpful for the individual who may be marginalized or disenfranchised or who is experiencing what we could call a "crisis of rights" in the moment.

MM: So we are really in agreement on this issue. I think our discussion has shown that we understand that for society to work there must be rules and regulations. Under our current liberal humanist framework, we surrender certain freedoms or rights to maintain peace or cooperation or a kind of a collective peace within society. This "rights" framework is also attentive to the idea of "individual" rights and has worded our rights as something that can be vulnerable to infringement. So the charter is written to protect us from potential infractions or the potential invasion of our individual rights. This language of the charter is meant to provide us muscular protection from state infringement of our individual rights. Yet the contradiction of this arrangement is that at the same time we have this muscular language to protect us we also have rights that are extremely difficult to access. It is so difficult to access the language of the charter that even organizations who defend human rights must be incredibly careful in how they select and champion cases because they know how difficult it is to fight for these rights. I think we have identified the contradiction that we have laws, which are necessary to maintain and mediate relationships between these incredibly free individuals, but at the same time, we acknowledge that those laws also limit the very rights and freedoms we want to protect. And that these principles are worded only to protect "individual" rights and freedoms. We agree that there is a tension or contradiction within the legal system that governs us. We agree that it is an imperfect system that constantly needs our attention and critique.

It should also be noted that official legislation does not guarantee changes in behaviour. For example, there are speed limits on highways, but many drivers disregard these limits. Rules are often not "effective" if they are not enforced or there is little compliance. And in this sense, the creation of rules and legislation gives rise to the need for enforcement or monitoring of rule breaking. The notion of rule breaking is not just in the realm of interpersonal conflict but also in other aspects of everyday life. In 2022, Statistics Canada reported that just under 10 percent of Canadians lived in poverty.[40] Data also shows that as many as 10 percent of the Canadian workforce may make less than minimum wage, even though there are rules prohibiting pay below the minimum wage requirement. Employers do this because they want to save money even though it is illegal. The rule does not guarantee compliance, so why are there no minimum wage officers or pay-equity police that roam the city searching for infractions? Does the lack of enforcement suggest that society does not take this rule and its rule breaking very seriously? Is the requirement for a minimum wage just an aspirational mothering principle? Why do we allow for pay that is less than the law mandated minimum? Is it OK to pay someone less than minimum wage since police do not patrol or investigate such matters? Does the lack of enforcement legitimate acts that may be wrong and does it circumvent the law?

Deviance

MM: It is important for us to unpack and give some substance to the notion of deviance because crime is often about the examination of things that are "illegal," not normal, or deviant. So, in that sense, deviance is something that has gone "wrong." Society only needs police when something has gone wrong. And when things go wrong, or they deviate from the norm, then it becomes of interest to criminology, or to policing, or becomes addressed through the criminal justice system. But this is the problem with the notion of deviance. The definition of "deviance" has no—or very little—meaning in and of itself. It only makes sense in the context of a specific social situation or context. Deviance only makes sense in the context of history or a specific socioeconomic cultural framing. That is one of the key mistakes of criminology. Often criminology, or the study of crime, fails to deliberately examine or unpack what deviance is. Some theories, or practices of examination, just simply assume that deviance can be defined as "not conforming" and leaves it at that. Or, one extremely popular theoretical framing (i.e., Social Reaction Theory) posits that society "reacts" to a behaviour by labelling it normal/deviant. That is, society reacts to behaviours perceived by society as not normal or not average through rejection. We label social acts as either acceptable or deviant. That is all well and good, but that kind of "study of crime" is elliptical and noninvestigative. It gets us nowhere because it only describes a causal effect between a social act and a social reaction. As a framework of understanding and investigation, it tells us little about the social importance of creating norms and deviance or the sociohistorical reasons for their development. Such studies remain disengaged from the historical and social reasons for such normalizing rules and behaviour. It avoids the main event of repression and control. The way a society has criminalized or made deviant certain acts is what needs to be unpacked. That is why we need to unpack how we determine what is deviant. The job of criminology, or one of its jobs, is to understand how certain acts and certain practices or social practices are criminalized and/or made deviant. The first premise of criminology should be that there is nothing inherently deviant in any social act.

ML: That is true. All conceptualizations of deviance and reactions to deviance and the transgressions that represent deviance are products of their times and their setting—or sociohistorical context. The social construction of deviance does not take place in a vacuum. This means that people studying crime and deviance need to engage with the sociology of law and the philosophy of justice, but they also need to adopt the perspective of historians. If we examine it on a purely legalistic level, then we get ourselves into serious trouble because we strip away all of this and we start thinking about deviance as something inherent, as simply a social problem to be responded to with a variety of policy measures. If we reduce it to just a policy, we lose sense of the social meaning embedded in "deviance" and where it comes from. So to me this suggests that an approach to deviance needs to be informed, for example, by the work of C. Wright Mills on the sociological imagination.[41] When we are studying any example of something that might constitute deviance, we would understand it as something that exists at the intersection of individual biographies and their broader social structure within a particular historical period. That is a good lens to bring to the study of all sorts of issues of deviance. It helps us think and provides guidelines to follow when we are trying to understand changes in the conceptualization of deviance. For example, why is this legalization process for cannabis taking place in Canada at a particular point in time, and why not in other places at the same time? Why do we have contestations around this? The approach to the study of deviance often brings us to the fault lines or the points of contention where the question of norms, conformity, and transgression are themselves under scrutiny. These are areas of debates, areas of contestation. They are opportunities to consider power and interests. The scrutinization of these questions makes for a much richer and more exciting approach to criminology than more conventional "by the book" approaches.

MM: What you just said made me think of something important. Some sociological framings—especially criminological sociology—at times attempt to divorce the social practice from the historical specificity. Such studies attempt to create an ideal universal theory of the act of deviance, or being not normal, across time and space. For example, I am thinking of "control theory," which uses a grand theory of control to explain all crime, for all time. Such theories are not profitable for us as criminologists because they are posited upon an understanding of society that is ahistorical, ungrounded, or delinked from specific social situations.[42] Rather, our field of research would be more accurate when it acknowledges that deviance is contingent, historical, embedded, or rooted in social practices. We should avoid grand unified theories of criminal behaviour. We could also very easily replace the word "deviant" with "different," asking, for example: What is different in society and why does society want to control, patrol, or arrest acts that are different? We can understand that society also applies the term to marginalized groups and marginalized behaviours because they violate social expectations and norms. Could this allow us to understand the establishment of norms as the actions of the powerful? Can deviant or not normal behaviour be understood as legitimate resistance?

What do you think? Do you think deviance is entirely relative to specific societies? Are deviant acts merely labelled as such? What would be the social function of naming certain members of society "deviant"? Is it useful for society to create or label deviants? It implies a connection between deviance, power, normativity, and control.

ML: These are important questions to pose! There is something universal about rulemaking and the establishment of norms. Groups of people seek to create norms that govern acceptable conduct and limit behaviours that cause harm. Rule breaking is also universal, and I am not aware of any examples of regimes of rules or norms that were consistently adhered to. All these activities are socially contextualized, though, and—as you point out—they are intimately connected to power and interests. A particular mechanism (e.g., prohibition through the exercise of criminal law) can be used to respond to or minimize behaviour that causes serious social harm, but that same mechanism can also be used to suppress dissent and reproduce a status quo that benefits some groups at the expense of others.

Discussion Questions:

1. Consider your own experience. Do you think it is accurate to say that your compliance with rules and laws is primarily based on your fear of punishment? Are there other possible explanations?

2. Our society is based on the premise that "we are all equal before the law"; however, we also know that wealthy people and corporations have greater access to legal representation than the average person. Can wealth or inequality upset this assumed equality? What are some examples or outcomes?

3. Make a list of five current events, trends, or social problems that are relevant now in the place you live. How do you think these things influence the way we think about crime and deviance?

4. We sometimes take it for granted that the institutions of the justice system we have inherited—police, courts, prisons, criminal law, and individual rights—are natural and inevitable. These institutions evolved over time and have become dominant around the world. This raises an intriguing question: How would we envision the design of justice processes if these institutions were absent or if we could replace them?

5. This chapter has addressed some of the ways our legal system is connected

to the legacy of settler-colonialism, to the social construction of deviance, and to hierarchies of power and inequality. Why is it important for people who aspire to work in the justice system to consider these topics?

6. Liberal humanism posits that individuals are unique and possess free will, yet the law imposes restrictions on individual freedom. Unpack this conundrum by discussing the evolution of this idea and its relation to law and critically analyze the contradictions it raises.

CHAPTER 2

Fear of Harm

In this chapter, we examine the concept of harm and expose some of the reasons that underlie our fear of certain forms of harm associated with crime. This chapter examines how some of the ways we respond to harms, such as banishment, shunning, or imprisonment, can produce unintended consequences or negative outcomes. We examine how this fear of harm can become an open-ended quest for security that in turn results in an expanding police or surveillance system. We argue that when the fear of harm is connected to biases informed by race and racism this can give rise to discriminatory enforcement practices. The chapter concludes by highlighting how an examination of police and criminal justice practices might need to move beyond individual-level responses and critically examine the institutions of criminal justice that respond to, cultivate, and govern these social fears.

Mike Larsen (ML): In the previous chapter we talked about the concepts of crime, law, and deviance. We troubled the obviousness of all these concepts and sought a deeper understanding of how these concepts are used and what they mean. One of the points of departure that criminologists have used when thinking about these things is the idea of harm. In other words, if you want to understand why things are criminalized or considered deviant, one way to approach this is to say: "Well, they are treated this way because they harm people." And that invites us to examine the concept of harm. At first glance, it appears to be obvious, but when we dig a bit deeper, I think harm is not so obvious and deserves some problematization.

Michael C. K. Ma (MM): I agree. Harm is often thought of as how an individual harms another individual in society. And it brings up the question: How do we prevent that injury and harm? I think we can understand harm as an effect of having done something that is wrong or bad to somebody else. But what if the solution to correct that harm also does bad, also is wrong, or does harm through its correction? Let us return to the useful, though imperfect, analogy of parenting. If you recall, we introduced parenting as an analogy for some of the restrictive, corrective, and governing behaviour of the state and the legal system. If a child does something wrong or bad, then we might think an effective way of correcting that wrong would be to banish them; that is, have them sit in a corner or on the stairs so they can ponder what they did. This is often referred to as a "time-out." We hope that that this time-out, or banishment, will both teach and punish the child. We hope they will think about it and then come back and apologize. So that is a kind of everyday banishment—with the hope of rehabilitated return—that we practice in contemporary society. In the context of prisons, we do something similar to putting a child in a "time-out" corner; we put people far away from mainstream society. In so doing, prisons are often located in remote areas. However, there is evidence to suggest that banishing children away from the family unit or social unit can be harmful. That is, the corrective of banishment (e.g., go to your room or go sit by yourself) may not successfully rehabilitate the child. Rather, it may do harm. Some child development experts argue that punishment is harmful to a child's emotional development and that isolation, or time-outs, are in fact forms of punishment.[1] Banishment of the child or the prisoner may have an effect that is the opposite of teaching a lesson and/or producing rehabilitation. The solution itself may be harmful because shunning or even temporary shunning are forms of rejection that may have unintended consequences (e.g., labelling, internalization, self-loathing, and suffering). That is an example of how the solution to harm might also cause more harm.[2]

ML: Is it possible that banishment could be harmful but also effective in some sense? The fear of banishment could be a very strong motivator. The threat of expulsion—through incarceration—as a response to transgression is built directly into the sentencing principles in the Criminal Code of Canada, for example. The command to "obey the rules or face exclusion" has been part of theories and systems of crime control for hundreds of years. We might even suggest that a society shows the extent of its disapproval of certain acts by imposing punishments that include the prospect of banishment. A less serious transgression carries with it the threat of a short-term internal exile in a prison, whereas a very serious transgression can result in a person being "put away" for decades.

MM: I do not think time-outs work because they do not create the kinds of outcomes the practitioner envisions. You ask if something that causes harm could also be effective. My answer is that it cannot. Banishment cannot improve society because it ultimately hurts the people it professes to help and correct. Continuing with the analogy of parenting, there is evidence to suggest that parental banishing of children, or the use of time-outs, which are forms of exile, may not produce the desired effect of better-behaved children. It may even make the behaviour worse. Some have argued that instead of banishment, parents should bring them back into the constitutional fold of the family and try to talk about what happened to cause the offence.[3] Banishment itself may cause a person to pause and think, but it may not create dialogue, and it does not work to repair the original offence. In fact, it may never help a person fully understand the original transgression because the main feature of banishment is to create an experience of exile, rejection, and maybe even self-loathing. It might not help a child understand their behaviour or develop skills to regulate their emotions.

Another thing that could also be harmful in the context of parenting is monitoring or watching a child "too" closely. For example, if you have a teenager, and the teenager feels that you are watching them all the time and correcting them on everything—well, many parents know that the teenager *hates that feeling.* They hate excessive monitoring or compulsive surveillance in the absence of anything suspicious. Parents know they cannot sustain that kind of vigilance or monitoring, and they know it could be unhealthy for you and your child. They also know they cannot sustain excessive monitoring and that they must pick their battles. So maybe they survey certain things (e.g., making sure they brush their teeth or do not bring their cell phone into their bedroom), but they do not signal to them that they are being watched all the time. As a parent myself, I try to hide any monitoring I might be doing or do it in a more nuanced or covert way. I try to signal that I am *not* watching over my kids. Furthermore, demonstrating constant and excessive surveillance would be self-defeating because it does not help teach children the lesson of self-regulation. There is ample evidence and literature that shows constant surveillance is detrimental to the person being watched.[4]

So, what does this have to do with harm? If we use the example of surveillance, we can understand that the impulse to watch and monitor is conducted with the goal of reducing harm. It is the reason for having police or CCTV cameras watch us. These services are meant to reduce harm. However, what if surveillance and monitoring create harm?[5] Using the example of parenting/teenagers and the efficacy of close monitoring, it is well known that young people very much dislike and resist being watched because they understand that as an intrusion into their privacy and an impingement on their agency. If we substitute "teenager" with "society," then we can use this analogy to understand how society might not benefit—and indeed might even be *harmed*—by a use of surveillance, even if born of care.

ML: The example you provided regarding the cell phone that is not allowed in the bedroom because of potential harms provides an interesting point of departure. Within criminology we use the concept of harm, or the concept of security, quite often to describe a whole variety of things (e.g., preventative surveillance, CCTV surveillance, monitoring of digital communications, profiling, machine-learning algorithms, even bail decided by predictive algorithms), and there is an important distinction between responses that are oriented towards harms that have occurred or can be said to have occurred and those that have not yet occurred.

The criminologist Richard Ericson wrote about this in his 2007 book *Crime in an Insecure World*.[6] He notes that societies—and especially the large and growing security industries within them—have become fixated on the problem of uncertainty. The future, in these late modern times, seems increasingly difficult to predict, despite all the efforts and resources dedicated to this objective. At the same time, there is an awareness of the potentially catastrophic nature of certain harms—acts of terrorism and political violence, human-caused disasters, large-scale disruptions of economies, and pandemics, but also forms of interpersonal violence, organized crime, and some of the traditional objects of criminological concern. There is a general belief that it is better to prevent something bad from happening than it is to respond to it once it has happened—especially when we are talking about catastrophic events. Prevention requires a degree of foreknowledge, though, and the quest to achieve this foreknowledge has been a driving force behind the growth of surveillance mechanisms. The quest to resolve uncertainty creates more uncertainty. And hence the things we do to prevent harm in turn create harm, even when we do not intend to create harm. The desire for foreknowledge and prediction of the future all plays on our existing social anxieties and fears.

On the one hand, there are harms, such as interpersonal assault, that occur between two people. One response to the harm of assault is healthcare to address any physical harm along with social mediation or social response to repair the problems arising from the assault. This response is straightforward because you know the parties involved and you can try to repair the harm that has occurred.

On the other hand, there are alleged or potential harms (e.g., possible shoplifting) that have brought about an increasing gamut of actions to anticipate and try to forestall or prevent potential future harms through surveillance. These can be understood as actions geared towards the potentiality of harm and how we try to govern uncertainty. That is, there are potential harms associated with uncertain outcomes (e.g., an employee stealing from a company, a person becoming associated with a gang, a migrant/refugee presenting a risk to a nation, or a student cheating on an exam). In these cases, we take interventions to proactively prevent or deter them. But as you point out, those actions can themselves have problematic effects for people and communities. You can with the best of intentions take steps oriented towards addressing potential harm but in so doing create greater insecurity and diminished agency for people precisely because of the surveillance and monitoring. Paradoxically, I think you can inadvertently make people's lives more uncertain by surrounding them with mechanisms of security and surveillance because it changes the nature of the social interaction.

MM: I like how you point out the difference between harms that have already happened and those that have not happened but that we fear might happen. It is the fear of future harm that is most confounding for us as critical criminologists because it is very hard to quantify fear and what kind of response it warrants. When we think about crime we often think about this very linear sequence where there is the action and then there is the harm that arises; action and then response. Our own field of criminological theory is heavily invested in such explanations (e.g., social disorganization theory, strain theory, control theory, and social learning theory). These theories try to explain the why of an action, why people harm other people, and how we should respond to it. Much of criminology now also focuses on the prediction and prevention of future actions (e.g., predictive policing). The efforts to reduce harm may be practised with the best of intentions, but these efforts that arise from the fear of harm get us into complex philosophical territory concerning prevention and a problematic imagination of future harms.

ML: I like your reference to the idea of "future" crimes. It makes me think of the science fiction movie *Minority Report*,[7] where future murders are prevented by a police service who have insight into the future and arrest people before they commit the act. The story is often cited in philosophical discussions about the limits of law and responsibility because it raises important questions: Is it ethical to intervene in someone's life because you anticipate they will do something wrong in the future? Can someone be morally responsible for something that did not occur but might have if they were not stopped?[8]

MM: What a mind bender! Thank you for offering it as an illustration of the problem of future crimes. That movie is a dystopic take on predictive policing taken to its logical conclusion. So let me build on it. *Minority Report* plays with this idea of "precrime" and it can help us think about how current police practices might have something similar going on in terms of criminalizing someone before they have done anything wrong. I can think of two very good examples.

First, Nicole R. Fleetwood argues that the mug shot, or police booking photo, has helped manufacture this fear of harm regarding Black men.[9] The suspicion and fear of Black men as criminal is created in part when these photos are released to the public. She argues that mug shots of Black men are disproportionately released to the public and thus contribute to the criminalization of Black men and the construction of fear. Some police services even agree with this argument. San Francisco's police chief, William Scott, explains, "This policy emerges from compelling research suggesting that the widespread publication of police booking photos in the news and on social media creates an illusory correlation for viewers that fosters racial bias and vastly overstates the propensity of Black and brown men to engage in criminal behavior."[10]

So, like your illustration of *Minority Report* and future crime, we already have a form of predictive policing that instead of being based on perfect information, as depicted in the movie, is a flawed technique and database that creates bias. The mugshot database helps create the bias that future criminals will more likely be Black. It is a bias even the police themselves admit. And all this comes about precisely because of the efforts to prevent and/or respond to potential future crimes through the creation and dissemination of the database of mugshots. This inadvertent social harm of bias and racism comes about because our fear of harm led us to create a database and publicly share its information as a way to respond to harm. It is an unintended outcome.

Second, is the example of predictive profiling used in Florida by the Pasco County Sheriff's Office. The sheriff's office uses a machine intelligence system that generates a list of people it thinks might break the law based on history or contact with police services. Then it sends sheriff deputies to find and interrogate the identified people. In each of these interrogations there is no probable cause or the use of a warrant. The machine intelligence or algorithm merely uses past contact to identify people it recommends should be bothered and intimidated by a deputy. It forecasts future behaviour before the behaviour occurs.[11]

ML: I think this discussion has highlighted some of the serious challenges and ethical tensions animating this area of criminology today. On the one hand, most people would probably agree that it is better to prevent harm from occurring rather than simply reacting to harm that has already happened. I would rather reduce victimization and trauma than respond to them. On the other hand, preventative and predictive practices can lead to what Ericson aptly refers to as the "criminalization of the merely suspicious."[12] We are living in a moment when the science fiction of yesteryear is fast becoming the reality of our technological present, and these are serious issues that publics and policymakers will need to resolve. Whether the mechanism is a database of mugshots or a machine-learning algorithm, these technologies function to shape our understanding of what—and who—should be considered suspicious or potentially harmful, and they introduce the potential for bias, stereotypes, and "false positives."

MM: Yes, in the context of mugshot databases and machine intelligence identifying potential harms I think these technologies only help whip up fears, not diminish them. I think you and I both believe there is less to fear in society than most people think. There is probably an exaggerated sense of fear, or the fear of being harmed, and that is why people seek the safety of police. In some cases, even just the image of the police will suffice. That is, some individuals might value a police squad car driving by their house or a beat cop walking through their neighbourhood. The very image of police presence might alleviate fear. Some people have a fear of becoming a victim of crime even without having had any previous experience of being a victim of crime.[13] Could we propose that fear of harm is really a paranoia, an anxiety, or insecurity that people have? Since fear of harm does not match the actual levels of crime a person has personally experienced, or even could expect to experience, could we propose that fear of criminal harm is an ungrounded anxiety?[14] What are your thoughts on that?

ML: I think there is not a simple and direct relationship between any measurable likelihood of becoming a victim and the perceived anxiety or fear of crime. This has been a consistent finding in a lot of research for many years.[15] In other words, whether and to what extent I am afraid of crime or afraid of my own likelihood of becoming a victim, or potentiality being victimized, is decoupled from, or not in step with, our statistical likelihood of experiencing crime. And I would go a step further and state that the kinds of fears we have reflect our cultural and social mythology about crime, and it is that insecurity, rather than a clear understanding of the likelihood of experiencing harm, that drives our understanding of crime.[16] For example, a lot of people are afraid of what we call "stranger danger," or predatory victimization involving an imagined figure actively out to find a victim.[17] And we know the anxiety about being that potential victim can be hugely impactful. It can have an enormous impact on how people go about their lives, how they live their lives, whether they choose to do certain things or go certain places at certain times, and whether they choose to surround themselves with security products (and all sorts of things like this) or call for more intensive policing to alleviate this sense of anxiety about this inchoate "other" they perceive to be a threat. At the same time, we tend to ignore things that have a much higher probability of occurring. For example, we are less fearful of exploitation in the workplace, wage theft by employers, or fear of the harms associated with just living in an urban space, such as the dangers and risks associated with impaired driving. These more everyday forms of fear or risk do not tend to register in the same way, and they do not generate the same kinds of intense social reaction as fear of criminal victimization or attack.

MM: OK, but are you unfairly minimizing the general public's fear of stranger danger or potentially being a victim of crime, even when their likelihood of victimization of violent crime or attack is very low? Low is not zero. Are you suggesting that people should not be afraid?

ML: I do not think it is our role as criminologists to tell people that they should or should not be afraid of things or that they are wrong for being afraid of things. It is a strong starting point to recognize that if somebody is afraid or has anxiety about something, then that is a genuine feeling. Now, whether it is connected to a constructed vision of threats or fear is something we can examine, interrogate, and discuss. What criminologists can examine, for example, is how people's genuine fears transform, or are transformed into, policy actions. A lot of criminal justice policies are based on fear of crime as opposed to the actuality of crime, so it is clear that a lot of symbolism is being projected. For example, a police initiative to eradicate child sexual exploitation or child pornography might symbolize that these practices are running rampant in society or that police are working overtime to stamp out these crimes.[18] Campaigns to stamp out such behaviours might symbolize that it is a huge problem. It may even signal to the public that pedophilia is an issue best handled by police rather than medical or mental health practitioners. If fear itself is something that generates panic and concerned calls for someone to do something, then a lot of the *responses* to fears are also symbolic. This is where a community might experience calls for things like more boots on the ground—to use military policing terminology—or more visible signs of surveillance by police or more intensive reaction and/or punitive responses to address those fears and calls for more public safety. That is a key point to bear in mind.

Fear and crime are not directly correlated phenomena and there is something distinct about fear and how it is decoupled from victimization. That also helps explain why some people in communities characterized by low levels of victimization (if we are using any reasonable measures of likelihood of victimization) may have extraordinary fears of crime, particularly crimes associated with notions of a stereotypical "other" or threat to the order of everyday life, that allows a community to take extreme efforts to address those fears. Whereas people living in a much more potentially hostile or insecure environment may have less fear of crime as part of their everyday experience. Looking at neighbourhoods where people have a greater likelihood of victimization, you tend to also find a lower level of perceived fear of crime or risk of crime.[19]

MM: OK, I have two comments. First, I like what you said about the fear of becoming a victim and how fear of harm is mismatched with actual crime and how it drives a certain type of anxiety-produced policing.

You use the word "symbolic," which is appropriate because you are suggesting policing is also a theatrical performance that signals to the public—in sometimes quite spectacular ways—that they are protected from harm. I am thinking of drug seizures that make frontpage news, with a big photograph showing the seized banned substances, guns, money, and paraphernalia. These become symbols of public safety and how the police are securing us from harm.[20] And yet, for example, we also know intellectually that there is an ongoing opioid overdose crisis that cannot be solved by these symbolic drug busts—only harm reduction and addiction treatment can combat overdoses. How safe from harm is a drug user who might overdose from a contaminated and illicit drug supply? Does the drug bust protect them from harm? Drug seizures do little to keep non–drug users safe from overdosing since their risk of overdose before the seizure was already zero. As nonusers they are not directly protected by police actions that reduce a drug supply. The drug seizure only acts as a symbol of safety for the non–drug user. It is meant to signal to the general public that the drugs themselves are being eradicated and therefore the drug addict will no longer have any drugs to use, thereby making society safer and free from harm. But that would be magical thinking; research has shown us that deep-seated addictions are not solved by a simple temporary obstruction of drug supply.[21]

Second, you used the description of "boots on the ground" and how the presence of a peace officer or public safety officer can negate or lessen a person's fear of victimization. I am wondering, are we "naturally" afraid of things like walking alone at night because it goes back to our fears of being alone in the dark or being chased by a tiger? Are people somehow biologically hardwired to be fearful of being alone or of the unknown?

ML: I think what you are getting at is the idea that there is something essential or human about fear and responses to fear that characterizes part of our social and our human condition. That makes good sense if you are in the forest and are uncertain about what is around you because a lot of fear is connected to uncertainty. In that case, it seems perfectly reasonable for someone to experience elevated levels of fear. But I do not think it is necessarily a good idea for a criminologist to say that your fears are laughable, or you ought not to be afraid of things, or that you are afraid of the wrong things. It does, however, make sense to think critically about the sorts of things that are—and are not—recognized and responded to as "legitimate fears." For example, there are well-documented and commonplace sources of risk and harm associated with an intensive work week, stress, lack of sleep, food insecurity, and particular jobs. We do not tend to have the same policing response to the types of things that are baked into our social organization of every-day life. In this regard it is understandable why our fear of harm is strongly associated with the danger and threats of the unknown and not with our workplace.

MM: It sounds like you are suggesting that there are aspects or situations of modern life that give rise to specific fears. Is there an author or area of research you are thinking about?

ML: Nicole Rader has explored the ways fear of crime is shaped by "crime myths" that are highly gendered and reproduced through family and educational settings.[22] She notes that myths about crime impact the way people—particularly women—experience public spaces, how institutions perceive and respond to victimization, and how media frames crime and public safety issues. Sociologist Zygmunt Bauman has emphasized that it is a characteristic of our late modern context that we are surrounded by not only sources of personal uncertainty and precarity (e.g., worry about whether you can afford healthcare, your house next week, to take these kinds of chances, to get an education), but we also experience "terrors of the global," which relate to things like pandemics, war, climate change, and terrorism.[23] He argues that people are increasingly anxious just as an aspect of our present social condition. Bauman ties this social anxiety, or contextualized uncertainty about the present and the future, with this politics of insecurity, which taps into this anxiety. Promising to address this fear and insecurity—or, more specifically, a desire for these things to be alleviated—becomes a resource that certain institutions can use to expand their mandates.

This gives rise to an interesting question: Who benefits from fear of crime? The intuitive response to fear is to say, "I would prefer not to be afraid of things," or "this here is not a good feeling unless it's controlled." (This is different from our entertainment interests in haunted houses or horror movies, which are controllable fears.) But if I am feeling anxious and uncertain about going about the city, then we can understand that that is not a good feeling, and I may want it to be alleviated in some way. While I might seek ways to do that, we must remember that not everybody would regard my fear as something to be gotten rid of. Rather, it might be a resource; it might be something that would compel me or make me more likely to do things, buy things, vote for a party, or endorse certain ways of being.

MM: I think what you are getting at is how fears can be monetized or commodified as products or services. I agree that fear is a resource for those who are in the business of public safety, and that includes both public and private security. Our private fears become public resources for policing, surveillance, and control. And sometimes those solutions can be excessive and lead to new problems that did not exist before we introduced the solution (e.g., surveillance leading to the anxiety of always being watched). Bauman's work points out that contemporary fears are in fact socially contingent or socially constructed fears.[24] And these fears change as society changes. That is, it turns out that our personal fears are not so much individual and personal ones as they are widely shared social ones. For example, fear can also get mapped onto what we eat or consume. It is not just about police and public safety. For example, we may buy organic food because we fear pesticides and the contamination of our food. Or we may buy bottled water because we fear the contamination of our drinking water. The key point is that we are not experiencing these fears of harm as individuals but rather as a cohesive group experiencing a unifying fear. We are a social group and not just individuals who are acting independently. In the case of organic food and bottled water, these items only become something we can buy precisely because we, as individuals, become a market. They exist as products because our fear of contamination has become a resource for marketing and commodities. This train of thought makes me think of the concept of moral panics. Do you think it is connected to this idea?

ML: This makes me think of the work of filmmaker Adam Curtis, who did this fantastic documentary series in the early 2000s called *The Power of Nightmares*.[25] Curtis points out—and this is consistent with a lot of research on media moral panics—that contemporary politicians and leaders of all stripes recognize that articulating people's fears and nightmares and then offering some kind of response is a conduit for power. We need only think about some of the more intense political campaigns of recent years to understand how fear plays a central role (e.g., fear of the other, of anarchy, of disorder, of political violence, of migrants). One point worth bearing in mind is that we experience fears differently, as we talked about previously. We know deviance is in some ways in the eye of the beholder. If deviance is a social construction, then you can have different notions of conformity, norms, and deviance across different groups at the same time, and the social responses to fear also share those idiosyncratic elements.

MM: OK, so, we have touched upon the notion that our fears are not always just our own unique ones but are, rather, socially shared ones. We have given lots of examples of how they are socially shared across the board, but we also know that some fears are not shared or experienced in the same way. Can you think of an everyday example of these shared fears, our response to fear, and how there is differentiation?

ML: We can use a hypothetical scenario that reflects a common pattern: Let us assume there have been reports of a number of shootings in my city over the last couple of days. In response to my knowledge of this, I might feel insecure, and I might feel that my sense of safety could be improved by an increased, visible police presence—police cars patrolling the streets and parked at major transit stations or public hubs—and maybe even a heightened level of uniformed foot patrol, because all of these things make me feel reassured. The installation of more surveillance cameras might make me feel that I am being watched over by some kind of a security apparatus. These kinds of measures may alleviate my fears of crime whether or not those fears of crime were founded in the first place.

However, my neighbour might experience the exact same visible efforts to address fear of crime as a source of greater insecurity. It may become a source of anxiety or uncertainty for them. They may experience the increased police presence on the street, police officers patrolling around transit stations, and particularly armed police officers as deeply intimidating and as a much greater, more visible, and more tangible and everyday source of fear and anxiety than my hypothetical concern about being shot because there is some gang conflict in my city. The increased surveillance may hugely impact their quality of life and their everyday experience going about the city. It is not just a matter of having different tastes. I do not want to make this seem like it is rooted in preferences. There are groups in society, for example, who because of historical and contemporary practices of racialization, discrimination, and overpolicing, would experience a heightened presence of security in a deeply intimidating way. Other groups, historically insulated from the more repressive aspects of formal social control, might have a completely different perception. So, when we talk about insecurity and responses to insecurity, we must examine them in a broader social context and consider how this connects with the politics of race, class, and gender.

MM: Yes, the question of race and racism is a key issue for us to explore in relation to the question of harm and the fear of harm. You bring up the issue of race, class, and gender, and I agree that our social experiences are not all the same. For example, an Indigenous man with low socioeconomic status might experience police as less of a public good and more as a repressive authority who poses a potential danger to him because of the known practice and/or fear of police racial profiling. For him, the police may pose more danger than safety. And this is an issue we will examine throughout the book. But let me return to the issue of victimization and fear. We can understand police, or the criminal justice system, as a response to the public's (mis)perception of their risk of victimization. But is there a way of thinking about fear in a non-psychological manner? When we think of fear, we often think of it as something unconscious or something that is individually embodied. Is there another way of thinking about fear that is external to the subject or to the notion of an unconscious or an unconscious fear? Is there another way of thinking about fear that is less based in psychology?

ML: It is probably impossible for us to completely decouple the discussion of fear from the individual subjective experience. I will use the word "subjective" instead of psychological because I am not a psychologist, but there are subjective and emotional elements to fear and there are intersubjective ones. Perhaps "fear" is actually the wrong term for us to be using. We are talking about this broader phenomenon while using a term that is adapted from this psychological and individualized vocabulary to describe something that is deeply social. When we use the lens of criminology, we are using it to describe and unpack how social anxieties—both socially constructed and experienced forms of uncertainty—are interpreted and their meaning negotiated and managed by groups, by professions, by organizations, and by politics. So that is certainly more than just a subjective experience. It is social.

MM: So how do we redefine fear so that we do not make this mistake of using a psychological or subjective term of reference (i.e., fear) to refer to a sociological or social phenomenon?

ML: Instead of redefining fear and saying, "this is our definition of fear," perhaps we want to propose that fear is a broader phenomenon that could manifest at an individual level and inform fears and anxieties that are more subjectively or psychologically rooted. The broader phenomenon of interest to us is this social management of uncertainty, insecurity, and perceived risk and this is something that is done at a higher social level, a symbolic level, and at a political level. Fear is a driver of a lot of relationships within the criminal justice system in terms of the allocation of resources, the passage of laws, and the responses to crime. Fears are generated and shaped not only by our lived experience but also by the media we engage with and by our interactions with institutions.

MM: OK, you are unpacking how personal fears are harnessed by public policy, but often only at a theatrical, performative, or symbolic level. And you are also saying that these personal fears are being produced by media. It seems to me like you are describing a feedback loop of fear leading to public policy, which leads to symbolic performance, which leads to media generating the materials for our anxiety. Is that correct?

ML: Yes, we can say that just as the concept of security may have this very individual character—where my security is what makes me feel safe or free from fear—what we are interested in is the much larger social character of fear, and that opens up some interesting conversations. We can examine the kinds of fears that are recognized and officially sanctioned. What are we supposed to be afraid of and what is reasonable to be afraid of? Think about contemporary politics, where people who are afraid of climate change and its effects on themselves, the next generation, and the world itself are often belittled as naive or concerned about frivolous things—or at the very least, told that their fears do not fall under the purview of the criminal justice system. On the other hand, people who express fears about gangs and guns—traditionally recognized crime issues—may find their concerns legitimized and seized upon by authorities and responded to through major criminal justice interventions. You cannot make an argument that those fears of crime are more important or legitimate than the fear of climate change in any objective sense. But you can socially explain why certain fears are elevated to this level of recognized actionable fears, whereas other fears, other sources of concern and uncertainty, are considered peripheral and not reasonable issues for social policy to address.

MM: I wonder what it says about our society that our fear of street crime and gangs dominates the public's threat landscape and its imagined dangers, while the very real existential threat of global climate change goes unchallenged? Do you think street crime has been framed as something very solvable by increased policing, whereas climate change is not presented as something that can be solved at a local or individual level? You suggest we should move beyond the individual-level response. Can you expand on what you mean by this suggestion?

ML: Yes. I think individual psychological or subjective experiences of fear are attached to responses that are also individual in character. That is, we are not always calling upon the state to respond; rather, we are recruited to personally take responsibility for our perceived risk. For example, we might begin thinking: What can I do? What should I do to make myself feel more secure? And this individual response has led to the creation of a massive multibillion dollar industry that markets to exactly this insecurity. Have you taken tactical training for your concealed carry weapon? Have you installed the right security cameras? Do you have the right security service? These are all individual-level responses that are meant to alleviate some of those fears. One of the curious aspects of this is that the more we invest in these kinds of technologies of security the more aware we are of uncertainty and potential risk to ourselves.[26] If I go about my day-to-day business with a bunch of weapons on me, wearing a bulletproof vest under my jacket and driving my armoured car, or what have you, I am much more aware of fear and uncertainty because I feel them physically on me. It then creates this self-perpetuating cycle.

MM: OK, let me make sure I understand you correctly. You argue that we should understand fear not just psychologically but in a social manner or with a sociological framing. The example of private security and having cameras to make you safe is certainly born of an individual's fear of potential victimization, but it is also the case that the homeowner is not the *only* homeowner in the world that has this fear. That is, your neighbour and your neighbour's neighbour and the whole community might have that fear. That is why there is a whole industry to serve this social fear. You might be expressing it as an individual instance of fear of harm, such as fear of robbery, but many people have that fear. So, you argue that it is no longer an individual unconscious or individual subjective feeling but has become a social phenomenon or a social practice that is catered to by a company or a service. The very fact that there is a security service called "private security" demonstrates that these are not individual fears but social fears that are expressed privately.

ML: Indeed, and we should note that this is not necessarily a simple linear process. It is not necessarily the case that I—as the hypothetical homeowner—have concerns and anxieties and therefore seek out these various security products and technologies to alleviate them. Just like any other kind of industry or marketing process, if I am in the business of selling, let us say conducted energy weapons like Taser International, which is now called Axon, or if I am in the business of selling you a home security system, I have a vested interest in cultivating your fears. I have a vested interest in making you aware of them and in advertising my responses to potential fears you did not even know you had—if I am doing my job well. That is an easy argument to make when we are talking about someone who is selling a security gadget or gizmo.

Where it becomes more provocative is when we consider how this relates to public policy, policing, and the creation of law. Do lawmakers, police organizations, and security organizations also have a vested interest in cultivating particular fears and anxieties so there is a market or a demand for a greater response to your fear of harm? Surely if the entire objective of these institutions is to reduce crime, prevent crime, and alleviate fear of crime, then—if these things were measurably reducing—there would be a corresponding reduction in investment in these kinds of resources and institutions. That is, a reduction in policing. However, there seems to be a perpetual push to expand the reach, power, and scope of the security apparatus, always in response to new, evolving, or resurgent forms of fear.[27] There is an escalation built into our politics around the response to uncertainly and it is cyclical because the more we are surrounded by images of insecurity and by commentary on fear, the more likely we might be to support police-based solutions.

Discussion Questions:

1. Why is it important for criminologists to study "fear of crime" as a distinct topic?

2. In both this chapter and the previous chapter, parenting is used as an analogy for exploring aspects of rulemaking, social reaction, and criminal justice. In what ways is this a useful analogy? In what ways is it limited or imperfect?

3. Erin and Gurpreet have both lived in the same neighbourhood for about five years. Recently, they both filled out self-report surveys on fear of crime and sense of safety. The results show that Erin is significantly more concerned about crime, potential victimization, and their own personal safety than Gurpreet is. What are some factors that might explain this difference in perspective?

4. Using web searches, locate two or three products or services that are marketed as solutions to insecurity, fear of crime, or fear for personal safety. Briefly describe these products and comment on the language and images used to market them.

5. What is meant by the proposition that fear is a social phenomenon and not just an individual feeling or insecurity? How does this relate to the issue of policing and/or private security?

CHAPTER 3
Media Representations

We open this chapter with a conversation about why criminologists find it important to study the representation of crime, justice, and injustice in news media, emphasizing the role of news media in the social construction of our knowledge and opinions about crime and deviance. Criminologists also study media—both news and entertainment formats—because they are interested in the ways media engagement may affect behaviours and attitudes and because media products about crime and deviance are an important feature of popular culture. It is also the case that certain crimes and social reactions to crimes are heavily "mediated." This chapter introduces the idea of focused, intense explosions of concern and distorted coverage of certain issues, which criminologists refer to as moral panics, and discusses their impact on public policy. We then address some of the important trends shaping the media landscape and considers their role in the representation of crime. To emphasize the idea that crime news is socially constructed, the chapter draws on a case study to critically consider the role criminologists sometimes play as claims-makers. The conclusion emphasizes the importance of media literacy as a competency.

Michael C. K. Ma (MM): Why do you think it is important for us to include a discussion of news media representation in our exploration of criminology? Why would news or the construction of news stories about crime and deviance be of interest to criminologists?

Mike Larsen (ML): Good question Mike. A straightforward response is that I think these are fascinating issues, and I have enjoyed exploring them in my own career. But, more importantly, we have set out in this book to discuss the social construction of crime and to consider all of the ways our understanding of crime and deviance is shaped by social context. It would be impossible to do this without incorporating some consideration of the way most people get their information about matters of crime, justice, law, deviance, and disorder, and that is through various forms of media including news media.

MM: Are you suggesting that media is creating the reality of crime for its viewers or its readers and that media itself is the only access to crime or deviance available to the average person. Is that what you are saying?

ML: Throughout this text we have discussed the ways deviance and norms are in many ways connected to issues we encounter in our everyday lives and how notions of fear and security, and right and wrong, are embedded throughout social systems. So, in this sense, no, I do not think media is the only way we access matters of crime and justice, but I think it is a very important one. Even criminologists who are professionally involved in the study of these issues do not spend too much time in court, nor do we spend a lot of time dealing with serious crime. Like everyone else, our understanding of these issues is shaped by the media that we consume. Let me pose the question to you: Why do you think it is interesting or important for criminologists to study media as part of the broader exploration of crime and justice?

MM: OK, but before I answer that I want to get back to something you just said. You said "media is not the only way we access matters of crime, but it is a very important one." I think differently. I think that media is really the only way most people access their understanding or knowledge about crime. For example, if I consider my parents, I can say with great certainty that they have little to no contact with police services, courts, or corrections and that their entire knowledge about the Canadian legal system, about policing, or about prison has been through their consumption of media. Their knowledge of crime only comes through reading newspapers and watching television news, movies, and TV shows. They are an example of how most people have very limited access to the criminal justice system.

The example of my parents demonstrates why it is important for us to study the effects of media on people's perception of crime. It is precisely because it is the key, and sometimes only, mechanism by which they access the criminal justice system. It may be true that some people might have contact with police services when they are pulled over for a minor traffic violation or with the courts because of some minor civil or municipal matter concerning property or municipal bylaw, but I think even those contacts with the police or courts is so limited that it would really give the average person little or no insight into what counts as major crimes, what police do, or how the court system works. Media representations of crime are internalized by consumers, and they then get expressed as personal opinions. Media representations are recycled as subjective positions.[1] That is why I think it is important for criminologists to study the effect of media representation of crime, deviance, policing, courts, and corrections. Media is the main vehicle by which the public comes to understand our criminal justice system.

ML: We are actually closer in viewpoints on this than it might seem. I absolutely recognize and emphasize the important role of media in shaping our understanding of the meaning of crime and justice, including the kinds of issues we consider to be important and what we think is appropriate to do about them. But I also want to recognize our earlier work in this text, about some of the ways discussions of right and wrong, justice and injustice are shaped by things like socialization, our interactions with others in everyday life, and our own experiences of harm, victimization, and transgression. I think we can agree that any study of these issues that fails to take into consideration the mediated nature of our knowledge is necessarily limited.

But if I may, perhaps I can offer a few ideas about why criminology as a discipline has incorporated the study of media as part of its framework in the past. I think there are four major branches in criminological exploration of media, and as we will explore, they overlap and intersect. One branch has concerned itself with what we could call media effects, and this connects with your own comments about the influence and impact of media on us as people. Specifically, media effects research and scholarship has concerned itself with the question of how our engagement with certain forms of media might directly shape our behaviours.[2] The forms of media of interest change over time, of course, but a consistent theme has been the question of whether the consumption of violent media, including books and comics, films, and video games, increases our likelihood of engaging in violent or antisocial behaviour.

A second branch focuses on themes we have already touched upon in this chapter: the role of media in shaping our understanding of the world, our perspectives, and opinions, particularly with respect to matters of crime, justice, and security. It is now widely accepted that media content, including both "factual" news and "fictional" entertainment products, plays an important role in the social construction of crime and deviance.[3] Scholarship in this area often focuses on what we can call the "social production of media" (especially news media). Researchers examine the processes, institutions, and interests that play a role in the selection of issues for representation and the packaging or presentation of those issues. Through an analysis of these processes and the media content they generate, we can come to understand the operation of news values that act like filters, sifting through the diverse happenings of everyday life and selecting certain happenings for emphasis and representation. We can also come to understand the role that formats, frames, and labels play in the construction of stories about crime and justice. Media producers constantly make decisions about what is newsworthy and how to depict or emphasize it, and these decisions are informed by observable norms.[4] While these phenomena are interesting in and of themselves, researchers are also attentive to the ways the social production of news contributes to agenda-setting and the legitimation of certain forms of social reaction. What kinds of issues should be considered priorities? Who gets to define the nature of these issues? Who do we turn to for solutions? These questions are directly connected to the ways issues are represented in the media.

A third branch of criminological scholarship considers the role that "crime media," broadly understood, plays in the shaping of our popular culture. The media that we produce, consume, and engage with are important parts of our shared culture. We create art, tell stories, listen to music, and play videogames for many reasons, including an ongoing effort to make sense of our world.[5] We have a curious and often idiosyncratic relationship with crime and deviance. On the one hand, we regard crime as something bad or harmful, and we hope that it does not directly impact us. Indeed, we take active steps to avoid crime, for example through changes in our behaviour or through the purchasing of security technologies and services. On the other hand—and at the same time—we are *fascinated* with crime and deviance and we actively seek out, consume, and produce media about it. Consider the popularity of "true crime" podcasts and video channels. Consider the central role that deviance and injustice play as themes in some music genres. How many popular television shows or films are murder mysteries, police procedurals, psychological thrillers about serial killers, legal dramas, or stories about heists, kidnappings, or organized crime? Take a walk through a toy store and think about how many toys represent policing and security.[6] The ubiquity of crime and deviance as themes in popular culture tells us something about our society.

Finally, there is a branch of criminological scholarship that is concerned with the use of media as a means to facilitate crime. Participatory forms of media, including internet forums or image boards and social media are of particular interest. Consider phenomena such as organized hate movements, the sexual abuse of children and the production of child pornography, and stalking and harassment. All of these phenomena predate the emergence of the internet and social media, but message boards, chat rooms, social media accounts, blogs, and user-generated content sites have fundamentally altered their nature. Today, criminologists seeking to understand the growth of neofascist and white supremacist hate groups, for example, must pay attention to the role of online forums and social media platforms—and algorithms—in hosting, distributing, and amplifying content and sustaining communities. Criminologists seeking to understand incel culture and school shootings must examine the ways certain online communities glorify previous acts of violence and transmit a "vocabulary of motives."[7] With some phenomena, there is no distinction between act and mediated representation. "Sextortion," online public shaming and vigilantism, and doxing are noteworthy examples.

As you might have realized, the study of "crime and media" is a thriving subfield in criminology, and we have only scratched the surface!

MM: Your mention of the fear that people might have because of books, films, or television shows and how they make us fear being made a victim relates to the concept of "moral panics" and how there are sometimes widespread fears that preoccupy an entire population. You are right that the question of whether consumption of media leads to violent or identifiable behaviour has been a principal question for behavioural science and other types of psychological and social psychological research over the last hundred years. The term "moral panic" is so useful because it very quickly describes this notion that there are some assumed things to be fearful of that lead to a widespread panic. So, if there is a "panic," then the word itself suggests it is actually something *not* to be worried about since "panic" describes an irrational response imbued with fear but without cause. The word "moral" relates to things that we understand to be right, wrong, good, or bad. When we put the words "moral" and "panic" together to describe an elevated and irrational concern about standards of behaviour, then we must challenge whether it necessitates a criminal justice system response. If it is an irrational panic, then should we be using our police, court, and correctional resources to address it? What do you think?

ML: I am glad you raised the concept of moral panic. It is one of criminology's most enduring contributions to our broader public discourse about crime and media, and it straddles the "media effects" and "social production of media" branches of scholarship we outlined earlier. While there is a vast body of scholarship on moral panics, we should first draw on the work of Stanley Cohen, the originator of the concept, to briefly make sense of it.[8] Cohen proposes that all societies at different points in time become subject to periods of moral panic. This occurs when a particular issue, problem, or threat comes to be regarded as posing an existential threat to society, and particularly to the values and moral underpinning of society. Media plays an important role in this process. During a moral panic, the issue becomes distorted, oversimplified, and amplified by media coverage and political reaction. Crucially, moral panics involve the juxtaposition of folk devils or enemies and the hypothetical threatened public. They often involve calls for officials to do something, and this tends to take the form of intensified regulation and criminalization. Cohen points out that moral panics are often volatile in the sense that something can flare up briefly, become the intense focus of public concern and outrage, and then fade into the background as other issues take centre stage in public consciousness. Cohen's work on this was based on a case study in the late 1960s of a massive social reaction to two particular youth groups in the UK, the mods and the rockers. However, the concept of moral panic is enduring and broadly applicable though. What are some current or recent examples of moral panics that come to your mind?

MM: A good example of a moral panic is the not-too-distant social preoccupation with video games and their corrosive effects on youth. At the beginning of the 1990s, when video games became more mainstream and involved first-person shooters like *Grand Theft Auto*, the public and the media became quite concerned with whether playing these violent games would normalize violence, causing people to enact it in real life. The fear was that this violence would seep into your consciousness, encouraging you to try it in real life. For many of our readers, that might seem an absurd connection; just watching or playing something that we understand as fiction or fantasy does not translate into enacting it. However, media and especially right-wing media in the United States, was concerned about the standards of moral behaviour and what is understood to be right and wrong or good and bad. Conservative critics argued that the violence depicted in video games like *Grand Theft Auto* was something to be extremely concerned with. The concern with violent video games was so acute that organizations like Common Sense Media were created to push back against and present a strong conservative critique of violent video games.[9] However, such critiques do not cite studies that deny such connections. For example, a study of thirty-nine thousand gamers by the Oxford Internet Institute suggests that "time spent playing video games is unlikely to impact well-being."[10] There has also been much speculation that engaging in a game is very different from and more corrosive than simply watching a movie or a TV show because video games are much more "immersive" than watching a movie or reading a book. So, the moral panic around video games was based on the notion that if you are controlling an action on screen as a game player, then that has a much stronger effect on your psychology or your behaviour in real life. However, many studies have found no such link.[11] What do you think?

ML: The entwined history of the "behavioural effects" question and moral panics about violent video games is fascinating. This is connected to campaigns to censor media to restrict access to video games, and it gets a lot of attention because media is ubiquitous and also a massive and popular industry, so there are high stakes associated with questions of regulation. However, the behavioural effects question is not exclusively reducible to questions of moral panic. I think there are some important research questions for criminologists and other researchers to ponder. Anyone who has ever become fearful, upset, passionate, excited, or otherwise impacted because of the media they have consumed, and I do believe that is probably everyone who has ever consumed media, would agree that the cultural artifacts and processes we engage with have a profound effect on us. You mentioned the concept of immersion, and I think that it is fascinating and that many producers of media seek to create immersive experiences for their audiences. Many audiences seek out immersive experiences in their media. Drawing and holding people's attention is one of the great quests in capitalism. With regards to violent video games, I think this is a good example of how interesting and important questions can be subject to oversimplification and distortion and how these questions can be difficult to research effectively. For example, empirical research on behavioural effects often involve experimental settings. This might take the form of placing subjects in a room and observing them while they playing video games, measuring physiological, emotional, and neurochemical changes. But such experiments have little resemblance to how people engage with media in real life. Many first-person shooters are also massive multiplayer online games, so studying how playing them impacts people in isolation makes little sense. Some research has shown that problematic changes in attitude and behaviour associated with playing video games has less to do with the substantive or thematic content of those games and more to do with the online cultures that surround them. So, for example, while the research does not show that playing *Call of Duty* turns people into violence seeking antisocial villains, there is much to be said for the ways the social cultures around certain games reproduce forms of hypermasculinity, misogyny, and homophobia.

MM: It is interesting to note that when we use the words "violent media" our minds go directly to fictional media such as movies and video games. But what if we redirected that gaze at violent media in relationship to news? For example, there has been quite a lot of coverage in news media concerning the war in Ukraine. It begs the question, does the consumption of these violent war images lead to viewers becoming violent themselves in real life? We could also extrapolate that question and expand our scope to include multiple wars and their media coverage. For example, we could question whether the consumption of violent news media of the Iraq War(s) and conflicts in Afghanistan, the Middle East, or North Africa has given rise to a more violent society. Many would say that watching news coverage of war does not make people more warlike, believing, rather, that it might make them more informed and engaged with global affairs. However, that is not what is understood when we use the phrase "violent media" in relation to behaviour and consumption. What do you think, Mike?

ML: These are crucial points. Violent crime has traditionally been considered to be almost inherently newsworthy, as have other forms of violent conflict, including war. This connects to debates about the behavioural effects of media in a variety of ways, as well as two important questions about the ethics of media production. For example, we have all had the experience of being immersed—to use a term we previously introduced—in a news cycle that is driven by coverage of an act of terrorism, mass shooting, or other horrific violence. When these kinds of events occur, they push aside other stories that might otherwise have been covered in the news, and the public gravitates towards these issues and regards them as important. Some criminologists have raised the important question of whether the way we cover news may give rise to copycats or create a form of publicity, fame, or infamy for those who enact violence and whether this might provide an incentive or inducement for others. This, again, is a complex question.

MM: This brings us back to the question of cause and effect and the question of whether consumption leads to practice. For example, if I read a lot of news stories about corporate crime, does that mean I will then engage in corporate crime at a higher rate than the average population? I think we asked this question in our chapter on counting whether there can be cause and effect or correlations between an act and its effects. I think this question of cause and effect is the critical question. Can we make the claim that reading something, viewing something, or playing something then leads a person to act in an antisocial manner?

ML: We spend a great deal of our time and energy engaging with media, and so in this sense it forms part of the broader social and cultural context in which we live. While I think we cannot say that there are straightforward and direct links between certain forms of media engagement and certain forms of problematic behaviour, we can say that our behaviour is in part shaped by the cultural setting in which we operate. There are some examples of the ways specific connections between media consumption and violent behaviour have manifested. For example, the horrific massacre in Christchurch, New Zealand, was live streamed by the shooter on Facebook, and they included a musical track, carefully selected and curated to fit with a particular ideological message, and they specifically referenced previous perpetrators of mass violence in both their manifesto and in markings on the gun they used. This was an action that was intended to connect with an audience. In this sense, there was little distinction between the reality of the massacre and its representation, as they were taking place simultaneously. But there is a great deal of difference between acknowledging that and drawing the conclusion that media consumption directly steers behaviour. As you point out, this connects with the broader criminological question of causation.

MM: Your example of the massacre in Christchurch is very evocative because it brings up the question of new media. I think when we typically think about media we think about news media as print, radio, and television. And increasingly all three of these news media are consumed via the screen and online. So newspapers are no longer consumed as paper and television is no longer consumed on your TV set. The contemporary consumption of news media brings up this question of how it is consumed via the screen and online. How does the delayed consumption of news media on a platform like YouTube or the live streaming of content news media through Facebook Live or the live microblogging of news through X (formerly Twitter) affect the contemporary production and consumption of news?

ML: This is a great question, and I think we should focus the remainder of this conversation primarily on this issue of production and consumption of news. Let us proceed by thinking about some trends that are shaping the contemporary news media landscape. The first is how we are in an unprecedented moment in human history where we are surrounded by media. Many people are never further than a metre from some form of media-connected device, and we engage with these devices constantly. This relates to the second point, which is that we are in a media producer society. We are not simply passive consumers, and we never were, but in the contemporary context we are expected to engage with media to create it and to share it, so the boundaries between production and consumption are blurred. A final vital point to consider at the outset is that our media landscape is shaped by the logic of speed. This relates to your question about instantaneous versus delayed platforms and forms of media. Our classic understanding of news media—as you pointed out—is the nightly news broadcast, or the morning paper, or the news radio that plays during our commute. These still exist, but they exist in a world where it is possible to record media and instantly have it broadcasted around the world and where the competition for viewership and engagement is so persistent that media organizations cannot afford to wait until all the details are clear before covering a story. All these factors create the context in which news, including news about crime, is produced.

MM: The question of news media production and what you have just described is even more complex than we assume. For example, an everyday person might produce and shoot a YouTube video, record a video image, or report on weather and post it on YouTube, Instagram, or TikTok. These are examples of how new media intervenes into a space of news where it previously was not located. However, that is not where the consumption ends because those social media forms of news reporting can also be repackaged as longer YouTube videos for streaming or for mainstream news media. For example, mainstream news can reuse social media reporting of extreme weather. Social media images of hurricanes or typhoons can be rebroadcast on a nightly news broadcast. So the question of authorship, the question of how citizen reporting can be repackaged or recycled, illustrates how complex the news landscape is today. I can even think of recent news programs where the story was based completely on reporters commenting on Twitter posts. So, the question arises: What type of news are we producing and watching today? Are we now asking television reporters to read the newspaper on air. Is that news?

ML: This connects to the concept of a media producer society, and to the unending demands to create content and fill airtime. In some cases, as you point out, this can lead to a self-referential media loop. As criminologists, it is important for us to underscore the impact of citizen reporting on the representation of crime and justice. So much of our conversation about issues of policing, systemic racism, and injustice in recent years has been driven by what criminologist Andrew Goldsmith refers to as policing's new visibility.[12] Discriminatory and brutal treatments of racialized people at the hands of police is as old as the institution of policing, but there is a qualitative difference in how these events are interpreted and acted upon by members of the public when they are recorded by people and shared via social media.

MM: The examples that come to mind are of course the killing of George Floyd, whose murder was recorded by a young bystander on her phone; the killing of Eric Garner by police was also filmed by a bystander as he was detained and illegally choked to death by a police officer; and the Facebook Live recording of Philando Castile by his girlfriend after they were pulled over by a police officer and Castile was shot dead.[13] Those video images became extremely important in both the legal prosecution of the case and the public's prosecution of the case in the court of public opinion. This brings up the question of citizen reporting and the notion that everyone can be a news reporter, or at the very least document a crime that can then be used to support or defend the case at a later date. We should not think that citizen video journalism is just a recent invention of the camera phone; the 1992 case of Rodney King's beating at the hands of four LA police officers illustrates that video evidence of police wrongdoing is not just a practice of the twenty-first century.[14]

ML: In some ways, it has become difficult for members of the public to push for change when that push is not backed by some kind of video evidence of a specific instance of wrongdoing, which is both interesting and problematic. The role of the participant observer or citizen journalist in the news coverage of crime also extends to the way breaking news or ongoing events are covered. I think many of us can recall news coverage of events where reporters have, in real time, asked for witnesses or participants to call the news station or share their video. I recall that you and I spent a good deal of time talking about the January 6 insurrection in the United States, and we were able to watch it unfold in real time not only on mainstream news channels but in the live footage of the events that was being broadcast by those participating in them. In the aftermath, that same live footage played an important role in investigations and prosecutions. At the time, I thought this was reminiscent of the way the Vancouver Stanley Cup riot was livestreamed by many of those present and how this documentary evidence in pictures and videos shaped social reaction to the events.

MM: At this point, I think we have introduced some important observations about some of the unique characteristics of how news is produced and by whom in the current context. Let us back up a bit though. We are talking about the production of news about crime and justice and related issues. These are topics that receive an extraordinary amount of news coverage in the current context. Criminologists often refer to crime as newsworthy. So, Mike, what does it mean to say that crime is newsworthy, and is this a recent phenomenon?

ML: Let me respond by providing a hypothetical example. Imagine that it was possible for us to create a list of all the various events and happenings that have occurred in a particular city on a particular day. I am talking about everything from people going to work and school, to the construction project on the edge of the road, to a pickup game of hockey, to a cat stuck in a tree. Let us then say that we are tasked with producing the news for that given day in some form of medium like a newspaper or broadcast television. We are faced with the task of filtering all the diverse happenings of everyday life into a much shorter list of happenings that we can fit into our format. How would we determine which happenings are important enough or interesting enough to cover? This filtering process is an important part of the production of news, and it relates to this concept of newsworthiness. Not all issues or phenomena are regarded by news media producers or by the public as being equally newsworthy. We can study this by examining historical and contemporary news products and identifying consistent patterns in the types of issues that are selected for coverage. Criminologists who have done this have described particular sets of "news values" that shape this process.

As it turns out, and this answers your second question; crime has historically and in the current context consistently being regarded as disproportionately newsworthy. Indeed, there is an old saying in the news business: if it bleeds, it leads. This speaks to both the newsworthiness of crime and the disproportionate newsworthiness of violent crime and other forms of violent transgression. At a news site today, we are likely to find that a significant proportion of the available stories deal with matters of deviance and wrongdoing. And we find a similar pattern going back to the archival records of early forms of media.

MM: When you say we could examine early forms of media, archival records, and news, my mind immediately goes to the Christian New Testament and the notion of gospel. "Gospel" means the "good news." The good news of Jesus Christ's birth, his death, and his resurrection. The notion that there can be good news, where we will be saved by a Messiah, means that there is also bad news, or the opposite of the gospel. And it makes me think that most news is not gospel but rather the other kind of news. As you said: if it bleeds, it leads. Maybe news does have a preoccupation with crime and deviance and not with good news but with the bad.

ML: That is interesting, and unsurprising when we consider our earlier discussion of intersections of crime and questions of morality and justice, themes that are also at the heart of many faith traditions. When I was referring to archival materials, I had in mind something like the illustrated police news that was published in England in the late 1800s. The publishers of this periodical recognized that there was a public fascination with violent crime, moral corruption, and policing, and they focused their coverage on the most outrageous and scandalous cases. Unlike the broadsheet newspapers of the time, which were considered the main news source for the wealthy classes and included text only, the illustrated police news included graphic illustrations of crime scenes, victims, and the police and courts—including such infamous cases as the 1888 Jack the Ripper murders. It was accessible to a broader audience and it both drove and fulfilled a demand for this type of tabloid news. Now, over a century later, the same types of stories would likely be covered via blog, YouTube channel, a subreddit, or a special section of the newspaper. So, it is fair to say that there is an enduring fascination.

MM: We could also find a more local example of tabloid police reporting in the publication named *Allo Police*, which was published from the 1950s until the early 2000s in Quebec.[15] It was a tabloid format newspaper that reported on murders, assaults, violent crimes, and police investigations in Quebec. The publication had a fascination with police actions, crime scenes, photographs of murderers, and murder scenes. These were very interesting and titillating to a broad readership in the province of Quebec, other Canadian francophones, and those who had an interest in Quebec crime.

ML: Crime and deviance have been considered newsworthy in various forms and formats throughout history. This is reflected in the content of news media. There is an important distinction between studying media content and the production of that content, though. I think we should try to lift off the lid of the media production process and consider how these issues of newsworthiness, news values, and features of modern media have come to shape the coverage of a particular story.

MM: One good example is something that recently happened to both of us when we were asked to appear as criminologists on a CBC Radio morning show to discuss and opine on shootings that occurred on July

22 and 25, 2022, in the BC lower mainland. There was one shooting in Whistler, which is a tourist and vacation destination, and another in Langley, which is a community outside Vancouver, that targeted street involved or homeless people.

This news story involved members of Kwantlen Polytechnic University's Criminology department in the following manner: CBC Radio contacted Lisa Freeman, who is a past department member, and asked her if she would be willing to comment on the recent shootings. When she declined, she was asked if there was anyone else she could recommend. She recommended her past colleague, Mike Ma, because of his long-time commitment to and involvement with the Social Justice Centre.[16] Mike Ma declined and suggested Mike Larsen (but agreed to be a backup if Mike Larsen was unable to do it). Mike Larsen was contacted, agreed, and did the interview the next day.

Lisa Freeman, union researcher, describes her invitation to speak on CBC:

> Responding to a media request is a choice. Sometimes an easy one to make, sometimes not so easy. When I was asked to speak to the recent shooting of homeless people in a nearby suburb, I was very open to it. Once I heard they wanted commentary on public safety in the suburbs, I realized I wasn't the right person to speak to this. Still, I wanted the response to be critical in nature, so I contacted my former criminology colleagues. Criminology is complex. It is a discipline without a well-defined identity. Scholars are drawn to it for multiple reasons. At that moment, I wanted a critical criminologist to speak to the complexity of the issue, not just point fingers at a fictional "bad guy." This event was tragic, there is no doubt. It required commentary from a critical thinker with a social justice perspective. Sometimes, it is hard to say no to requests that can flatter one's ego. But finding the correct person to add thoughtful and critical commentary to the public debate is needed. And, that is what I did.

Mike Ma's description of this engagement with CBC:

> At first, I was flattered that I was asked to do interview on CBC on the topic of the shootings, but I was hesitant to say yes because I am not an expert on issues of gun control, gun violence, or homicide. I also, naturally, did not know what agenda they had, but I could guess

given their request for a criminologist to opine on the two shootings. I suspected that they wanted to confirm their assumption that these shootings must point to a rising escalation and pattern of violence that was dangerous to the public. I know that all evidence opposes these kinds of knee-jerk reactions and hence I hesitated. And yet I also thought I could contribute because grouping the shootings from Langley and Whistler together was perhaps not a good way to parse the events. The shooting in Whistler was allegedly an organized crime targeted shooting and the shooting in Langley was an alleged attack on the homeless. So, these events are radically different, even though they both may involve guns.

I thought I could redirect the narrative to talk about the way the media helps construct notions of South Asian gangs, in Surrey in particular, because the shooting victim was Mahinder Gill (who is known to police) and to talk about the racialization of gangs, organized crime, and the way it is often reported by media and addressed by the police. And then to compare that with the way in which violence against the homeless and people who are drug addicted are misunderstood and/or maligned in society. That is, I would have wanted to explain how the way we understand violence against the homeless is very different than how we understand violence happening in a tourist area like Whistler.

In my ideal thinking, I thought I could introduce this question of race and class into the conversation and that would have been my contribution, but I knew that the short time of a radio interview would not have permitted that type of interaction, nor is it something that the producer or the radio host was looking for. I knew or I assumed that they were looking for an expert who could talk about gun control and whether gun violence was on the rise in Canada and whether we should be alarmed by an assumed increasing rate of gun violence. They wanted someone who could comment on the rate of increase or pattern of violence as dangerous to the public.

And I thought I—as a different kind of criminologist—would in that sense be an inadequate or unwelcome guest, because I would be contradicting the desired narrative. I would be presenting on questions of race and poverty and not on the preferred talking points of the news producer and the interviewer, who I assumed would have preferred to have someone comment on violence and not race and class. I didn't think I was the kind of criminologist they were looking for. So that is why I was hesitant to do it and didn't really want to do it. I was skeptical of whether you can dig into these complex issues within the short five-minute time frame of a radio interview. So that was why I declined.

Mike Larsen's reflections on this story:

After giving this matter some careful thought, I decided to participate in the interview. A few factors informed my decision.

First, I subscribe to the idea of "public criminology," which, among other things, involves engaging with publics outside the classroom or professional settings, responding to questions and concerns, and contributing to public conversations. Participating in media discussions can be part of this.

Second, when I spoke with the producer who was arranging the interview, I learned that they were specifically looking for a guest who was not a police officer and who could offer some context in their comments. The news cycle about these events had, at the time, been driven by police alerts, news releases, and press conferences, coupled with a small amount of eyewitness testimony. This is consistent with how "breaking news" about crime is typically covered. I felt that I was in a good position to speak to historical and current trends and to offer a different perspective on the events in question. It is important to bear in mind that a commitment had already been made by the news organization (CBC) to proceed with this story. The open question was which voices and perspectives would be included.

Finally, as someone who both teaches about crime and media and often contributes to media programs, I had a good sense of the types of questions I would likely be asked: "Are these events part of a worsening pattern?," "Should people be concerned or frightened?," "Are officials and politicians responding accordingly?" All these questions lend themselves to responses that mobilize anxieties about safety and justify calls for more intensified police and legal system actions. I was prepared to respond to these questions—which were indeed asked—in a way that acknowledged public concerns without lending support to a politics of "law and order." I should also note that I enjoy the format of live radio. Its unscripted (but not unplanned) nature means that guests can sometimes "trouble criminology" in ways that might be filtered out of a print or television format.

ML: I think that this is a fascinating opportunity for us to reflect on a specific case of media engagement. It leaves us with the question: What can we learn from this?

MM: I think being a guest on the radio broadcast showed me that I was right to be hesitant in accepting the invitation. It reconfirmed my own bias that news story reporting and requests for interviews aim to bring in an expert witness with a professional voice who can provide an assessment—in this case—of patterns of violence, patterns of homicide, and whether rates of crime are increasing or decreasing in society. Many news programs are driven by these types of factual requests and requests for professionals, and I think in the eyes of the press, academics are somehow these professional experts who can provide expert knowledge that will add clarity to a situation, but always within a small timeframe of just a few minutes. I think the news wants to have the complexity of a field of research distilled into very small sound bites and into very short digestible pieces of information. The CBC invitation reconfirmed my allergy to being interviewed because university research and teaching is often nuanced and complex and does not lend itself to short sound bites. For example, in a classroom setting we might spend three hours just skimming the surface of a subject. The requests for interview confirmed to me that I should not be on the radio because I am not able to deliver the short, concise, and exciting chunks of information that I believe news interviewers and producers seek.

ML: Your observations remind me of Marshall McLuhan's famous comment that "the medium is the message."[17] Live news radio is a place where the evolving issues of the day are packaged for rapid consumption, often with repetition every half hour or so, and the overarching narrative is that the happenings of the world can be subject to meaningful but brief and compartmentalized analysis and explanation. In this case, the seven-minute segment on the shootings was preceded by a conversation about an upcoming sports match and followed by an update on traffic and weather. So, you are correct in the sense that live radio is definitely not a forum for the kind of nuanced critical and in-depth analysis we would expect to find in our own classrooms. However, it does reflect the public fascination with issues of violence, deviance, and transgression that we have previously spoken about and there is an opportunity for criminologists to provide brief contributions that offer some insight and, perhaps more importantly, an antidote to other narratives that emphasize questions of fear, insecurity, and social reaction.

The story also offers an excellent opportunity for us to identify a number of enduring themes in the way news media covers issues of crime and violence. For example, this was of course a great illustration of the concept "if it bleeds, it leads" in the sense that gun violence and homicide are treated as inherently newsworthy and worthy of continued coverage. It is a good opportunity for us to reflect on the role source selection plays in shaping the narrative surrounding crime and deviance. By this, I mean that the people who appear on the news in whatever format are playing the role of claims-makers. They are given space to make factual comments about what is happening or has happened, trends, and applicable laws and policies, and they are able to make interpretative comments about why things are happening and what ought to be done about them. The overarching themes and tone of a story are very much a reflection of who is treated as an authoritative source within it. For breaking news stories about crime, it is almost always the public police who are in the position to provide the initial framing of what is happening, and media is ordinarily reliant on information and context provided by police organizations. This was certainly the case here, where the news coverage of the shootings was based primarily on police alerts and news releases.

MM: You are right to point out that the police are key claims-makers who control the initial breaking news regarding gun violence. They are the officials who are first on the scene and tasked with investigation and documentation, and they are the first to be contacted by the media for the "facts" of the case. They are indeed a key claims maker featured in the medium of live news radio when covering a crime. I am glad you mentioned Marshall McLuhan's famous 1964 comment about the medium being the message. It suggests that the medium of live news radio is not neutral but that it directs or constructs a specific news narrative by virtue of its format. What is perhaps not completely visible to the radio listener is that the news item, which seems to be so immediate and of the moment, is something produced and vetted with pre-interviews. The producers look for characters who they believe can support a narrative. In our case, we were first contacted the day before the interview occurred. The news radio program or interview was a highly constructed story and they were looking for willing partners to support a clear narrative. And one of the narratives that live news radio wanted to construct was that the two shootings were somehow linked as a connected pattern of violence relating to the use of guns. So even though you and I may both resist that type of type-casting, it is still very difficult to resist the medium because the medium of live news radio does not allow for a nuanced or alternative message. We could not go on the radio to argue that there was no pattern of gun violence here; that these were two unrelated shootings, which happened to involve guns, but in no way illustrate the cause-and-effect conclusion the producer and interviewer were constructing. They wanted to mould these events to illustrate that gun violence is increasing in society.

ML: An important lesson we learn from this is that the way issues are framed in the news media plays a powerful role in the social construction process. Framing involves circumscribing a particular issue, identifying a handful of key themes for inclusion in the discussion, and crucially excluding, or at least marginalizing, other themes. One of the ways an issue can be constructed is through the posing of questions. This is important because in this very text we are actively encouraging our readers to pose questions and think critically about matters of crime and justice. However, in the context of news media, the posing of a question, regardless of the response, invites a particular framing of an issue. So, if I am a journalist or a news personality, and I ask a guest, "Do these events illustrate a worsening pattern of gun violence that is making our communities more dangerous?" then I am making those themes part of the public narrative.

MM: The very nature of news media, or, in this case live news radio, is to report on current and emerging news. The production of news already begins with the idea that violence is titillating and sensational. In our case, the request for interviews occurred the day after the shootings. The goal of the news interview was to get an expert to explain to listeners why this new development is important and why they should be concerned about it. Therein lies the non-neutrality of the story; it is premised on the idea that within these developments there is perhaps a new pattern of gun violence that can be revealed. It is framed as a potential danger to the public that the public should be aware of. In our case, the medium of news was not neutral in how it acted upon us as "content" because it was looking for an expert to confirm the danger of gun violence. The news program constructs the conversation around these two shootings and asks a criminologist—who is assumed to be a professional in demeanour—to provide expert and definitive knowledge concerning gun violence. The hidden assumption of the programming is that there is a new pattern of gun violence related to ineffective gun control and that the listener should be attentive to this new pattern and potential threat. The expert is recruited to confirm this danger.

ML: To draw on concepts we have introduced in this chapter, the criminologist-as-expert is typically not involved in the social production of news at the outset. Determinations of newsworthiness, the application of news values, and the initial filtering of a story to align it with established narratives and frames all occur before the criminologist is invited to comment. This does limit the space or field for potential discourse. Some criminologists respond to this by actively avoiding this kind of reactive interview, focusing instead on formats that allow for more careful preparation, greater nuance and diversity of voices, and a more detailed discussion. It is important to note that not all mediums are equal in the way they handle the exploration of content. Often, there is a trade-off: An hour-long podcast will almost certainly provide more opportunities for critical analysis and debate, but it will reach a fraction of the audience of a live radio segment, and so the latter may play a more important role in the public construction of an issue.

There is a final observation I think we need to make about this particular case and the story. The news coverage of these events, including in the radio interview in question, included several phrases or concepts that carry a lot of conceptual baggage. I am referring to comments like the shooter was "known to police," or this was a "targeted shooting." Or, in the case of the Whistler events, that this was a "brazen crime." Coverage of both the Whistler events and the Langley shootings included comments that referred to the actions as "senseless." These terms, which are familiar to us, are intended to convey a great deal of meaning, beyond the obvious and literal.

MM: The use of terms like "known to police," "targeted shooting," or "brazen crime" suggests that the people involved in the shooting were not part of the general public but rather part of some external subcategory of society that matters less. It is shorthand for criminal and "not us." The use of these terms already shows that the construction of the news story is not neutral despite being framed in the guise of neutrality. I think that is a good illustration of the medium being the message and also that the medium of news must report on the exceptional and the unusual—and often those are activities that are criminalized.

ML: I agree. These are terms that warrant critical reflection and translation. Reference to a "brazen event" is particularly interesting. We often find this term used in the same context as the observation that "this sort of thing doesn't happen around here." In a literal sense, to say something is brazen is to say that it is bold and perhaps without shame. Not all shootings are described in this way in the news media. The term seems to be reserved for situations in which a shooting is presented as incongruous with the setting, typically this refers to a wealthier or commercial space. To say that someone is "known to police" does not literally mean they are known to the police. If either of us happen to be the victims of a serious crime that was reported on, this phrase would not be used, despite the fact that both of us know and have worked with many police officers. As you say, the term implies criminal involvement, and it is interpreted as a caveat on the victim status of a person impacted by crime.

Let us step back from our case study and consider some important "takeaways" for our readers. The key lesson that comes to my mind is the importance of being a thoughtful and critical consumer of media. This is what is meant by the concept of "media literacy," and I think we have demonstrated here that this is an essential competency for students of criminology. What are some key components of media literacy, in your view?

MM: You are correct to point out that a main takeaway of this chapter is the importance of media literacy, or perhaps even just attentiveness to the fact that our social and cultural attention is always being constructed by social institutions like news or entertainment media. That is, media institutions are making and informing our choices of what to "choose." The stories constructed by media are always in the background of our own personal interests, choices, and concerns. In this chapter, we have discussed how news and entertainment media are not just invested in the object of crime, but that crime or deviance are key objects commanding our attention. In this regard, I am reminded of Guy Debord's seminal work *Society of the Spectacle*, in which he argues that real life in modern society is always mediated by its representation and that, as a result, we may no longer have access to the real.[18]

ML: Indeed, and when it comes to media literacy, we need to inform ourselves about the interests and perspectives that shape what we view and how we engage with it. We also need to be attentive to absences and silences: Which perspectives are not represented in media coverage of crime and justice? Whose voices are absent from the conversation? Which aspects of crime and justice are considered unworthy of representation and why? Ultimately, media literacy involves consciously asking questions about the media we engage with.

To use a metaphor, I think we could agree that it is important for us to take an interest in the food we consume, in terms of ingredients, the way it is prepared or processed, and its implications for our health and well-being. The same principles apply to our "media diet," and this is particularly important for criminologists, given the prevalence and popularity of media related to crime and justice.

Discussion Questions:

1. Think about the news coverage of crime and justice issues. What are some examples of types of crime or aspects of the criminal justice system that are given extensive coverage? What are some examples of types of crime and aspects of criminal justice that are rarely represented in the news? How might we explain these trends?

2. There has been considerable debate and concern about the idea that playing violent video games like *Grand Theft Auto* or *Call of Duty* can encourage players to act violently in real life. Explain the hidden hypothesis behind this idea. Is there merit to this concern?

3. Facebook and other social media platforms have been called upon to increase their monitoring and regulation of content that might be deemed harmful, hateful, or toxic. Social media companies have often responded by claiming that they are not producers of media content and are not in the business of "policing" the content produced by their users. In your opinion, should governments or social companies take a more active role in regulating online expression?

CHAPTER 4
The Quest for Causation

Attempting to explain and describe the causes of crime is one of the most vexing problems of criminology. In this chapter, we describe criminological approaches that attempt to explain crime causation. We suggest that many conceptualizations of crime do not adequately account for the social and environmental factors that shape human activity—including criminalized behaviour. We emphasize the importance of understanding social structures and social causes of deviance rather than focusing exclusively on individual behaviour. We caution against simplistic explanations, and we reject singular causes and instead focus on how there is always a confluence of individual and social factors that contribute to wrongdoing. Without rejecting the importance of individual agency or choice, we call for a more nuanced approach that moves beyond individualizing explanations and treats criminal behaviour as an expression of social and environmental conditions not of one's own choosing. We present evidence that shows criminal behaviour can be linked to social, economic, and environmental factors that are often beyond the control of specific individuals, and we discuss the policy implications of these ideas.

Michael C. K. Ma (MM): A main preoccupation of criminology is to explain what causes crime. It is one of the driving forces behind our discipline. But before we dive into "causes of crime" we should briefly comment on the types of crime that we discuss. When we try to explain the cause of crime, our conceptualizations of crime often goes to the idea of street crime or crimes such as property theft or assault. And this makes sense since these are unlawful acts that are understood by the general public to be the most disturbing or disruptive for everyday society. But perhaps this also suggests that we, as criminologists, are inadvertently promoting the same idealizations of crime. And also, these idealizations and preoccupations—or crimes that are understood to be the most important ones to address—come to be reflected in our criminal justice system and policing practices.

Mike Larsen (ML): I agree, Mike, and it is important for us to be reflexive about this. I think our continuous referral throughout our discussion of the examples of street crime, interpersonal crime, and crimes associated with conditions of poverty is itself a reflection of the preoccupations of criminology. The purposes of criminology—as a body of scholarship, theory, canon, and ideas—was developed by people in positions of social power studying people at the margins of society who are subject to criminalization within a deeply stratified and unequal society.

MM: But wait, are you saying that the study of crime and the practice of crime prevention is out of balance because it only represents the perspective of those who are in positions of power? Or are you being even more provocative by arguing that a criminologist—by virtue of their privilege, social power, or esteemed scholarly position—can *only* have a skewed or unbalanced position? How can such criminology recover from this bias or blindness?

ML: It is good for us to introduce these provocative questions at the outset. I do not think criminologists are destined to have skewed or unbalanced positions with regards to foundational questions and concepts. However, to use a metaphor, we are often working on systems and using tools that were designed by others. Over the years, our conceptual tools and our understanding of the nature of the system have become normalized. This happens in many subtle ways. For example, the rich and useful statistical information collected and published by the Canadian Centre for Justice Statistics focuses on a particular range of offences, and it does not incorporate regular reports about things like wage theft, environmental crimes, or official corruption. This reflects a certain understanding of the priorities of a criminal justice system—and, by extension, criminology. And so, our notions of deviance, and what we need to explain, are themselves a reflection of this preoccupation and power relationship. When we step back however, we find that some of the ideas and concepts of traditional criminology are ill equipped to make sense of things like crimes against humanity, organized state violence, systematic repression of groups of people, institutionalization of groups in residential schools, and so on. The Canadian Centre for Justice Statistics is not collecting statistics for these offences and therefore by extension these are not understood as important or legitimate crimes. For some criminologists, this is reason enough to question the canon in its entirety and to think differently about questions of right, wrong, and transgression.

MM: But are you sidestepping the question of whether criminologists are still part of a status quo and cannot escape their complicity in recreating the existing system or framework of crime and justice? Can criminologists get out of this bind?

ML: If we can agree that foundational issues in criminology—the nature of crime and deviance, our understanding of human behaviour, our approach to the law—have been shaped by systems of power and priorities that reflect vested interests, we can consciously and reflexively approach the field in a way that avoids the pitfall you are referring to. The key is to question taken-for-granted concepts, practices, and axioms. There is an excellent tradition of critical criminology that seeks to do this, approaching the study of deviance, harm, and power from a different perspective and with different interests in mind.

MM: I think we have to go beyond the tactic of "questioning" existing practices because it may never do anything to change those practices. For example, we can question burning fossil fuels, but that is not going to affect climate change. How the prevailing practices of criminology can be radically changed is the real question. This puts a spotlight on the internal problem endemic to criminology, which is: What is the purpose of describing or examining criminal behaviour? Is it to better understand criminal behaviour so we can prevent it from the point of policing? Or is it to understand the problem of society and how it criminalizes certain acts and certain people? For some criminologists, the question of behaviourism becomes their central analytic lens and object of analysis.[1] I think it is our job to understand that society is flawed, or that society and its social structures can be improved and changed, rather than to focus on fixing behaviour or behaviours that deviate from norms. So, that is really the core of this discussion. As criminologists, we want to understand the multiple social causes of deviance and control. We both agree there are no final causes for deviant or criminal behaviour. And we agree that it is the examination of the problem of law, the problem of policing, and/or the problem of surveillance that is important; we regard these as the primary objects of investigation for the criminologist. It is not so much about trying to improve policing or to make people more compliant citizens.

ML: This is a chapter about causation. In many criminology texts, this is the primary focus of the entire book, a series of explanations or models that approach the question of causation from different angles or traditions. Before we get into this, we should clarify what we mean by "causation." Simply put, if one or more things come before something else and make it happen, we could say they have caused it. In practice, causation is extraordinarily difficult to prove or demonstrate conclusively when we are dealing with complex issues. It is also often confused with correlation, which is an observed pattern or relationship between two things. It is often interesting and useful to identify correlations, as they tell us that "something is going on," but we should not jump to the conclusion that correlation equals causation.

MM: The whole thing about cause-and-effect explanations is that any two things can appear to be causally joined. This reminds me of a jokey sign I saw in front of a bookstore. It said: "Dinosaurs did not read. Dinosaurs became extinct. Not reading made dinosaurs go extinct." The premise behind the joke is that these two things are in fact not causally linked but can be made to appear so in an argument or statement.

ML: So, we should be wary of grand claims of causation. At the very least, they warrant careful examination.

MM: Yes! In a similar vein we can ask: What causes climate change? What causes cancer? What caused the French Revolution? What caused the Air India bombing? These are all questions of causation, and we ask them because we are curious why things happen. In the field of criminology, we ask the same kinds of questions, which often get expressed as: Why do people commit crime? What makes someone steal something? What causes someone to break a law? Why does someone hit another person? Why do people commit fraud? What causes crime? The thinking behind this line of questioning is that if we knew what caused individual acts of deviance, then we could prevent it from ever happening. But it is not easy to answer these questions because causal questions and answers are extremely complicated and not black and white. They are almost too easy to ask but terribly difficult to answer.

ML: Absolutely. Despite this, the quest for causation drives many studies in our field. For example, researchers ask questions about the innateness of deviance, the transferability of deviance through association, and the role of parents, video games, and communities in shaping offending behaviour. All of these are variations on the "Does X cause crime?" question. Criminological theories can be understood as systematic attempts to answer this question, drawing on concepts, hypotheses, and data. The question of why we are interested in causation is so important. You point out that one of the primary reasons is concern about prevention. This is true. In criminology, there is a close connection between the pursuit or quest for causation and the correctional impulse. That is, the notion that if we understand the root causes of deviant behaviour, then we could fix the people who exhibit it. A great deal of thought and energy has been dedicated to this aspect of applied criminological thinking. Both the question of prevention and the question of correction have, historically, tended to focus on individual actors.

MM: Yes, the example that comes to mind are the two criminologists from the 1700s, Cesare Bonesano Beccaria and Jeremy Bentham, who both exercised the perspective that criminals are rational beings who choose to commit crimes. For them, the cause of deviant behaviour is free will or rational choice because individuals choose to commit crimes that benefit them (e.g., stealing). For these two criminologists, it is the individual actor who is under scrutiny for their behaviour and motivation. Many of these kinds of questions in criminology are based on the idea that one person acts and that act causes harm. I, too, am skeptical of formulas that frame criminal acts as simply rational choices that individuals have made. For myself, I am not so much interested in what causes individual free will decisions leading a person to "choosing" criminal behaviour; rather, I am much more interested in understanding how conditions—not of our own choosing—give rise to who we are. I am much more interested in the problem of society and how we can investigate the way society predetermines our choices as individuals. I am more interested in asking questions about how we are socially constructed than I am in searching for reasons or causes that explain individual behaviours that are coded as negative, bad, antisocial, and/or criminal. In fact, I do not think people are all that free to make any decision they want. For example, in this regard, I am much more a product of social conditions beyond my control (e.g., male, immigrant, middle class, nonwhite, English-speaker) than an independent decision maker. I did not "choose" my social conditions. Rather, my inherited social conditions have a powerful effect on what I can choose. Some authors go so far as to argue that we cannot even counteract our given social conditions.[2]

ML: That is a provocative claim, and one that I think challenges our inclination to regard ourselves as the people in the driver's seat of our own behaviour and by extension our destinies. Could you unpack the idea that we may be unable to counteract our given social conditions?

MM: Yes, for sure. For example, it is easy for me to "choose" not to steal because I am employed, have stable housing, good health, and education. Why would I risk committing a petty crime when it is not necessary? I have plenty of money and status. In this regard, it is true that I made a choice, but it was an easy no-brainer choice. Is that really a choice? It seems like my choice was already predetermined by my wealth. Whereas if we consider instead an Indigenous youth who fled a foster home and is now living on the street—and living on the street is already "illegal"—then it might be more difficult for that person to make the decision *not* to steal because they are already in an adverse environment. They are already perceived to be out of order. You could almost say that it makes sense for them to *choose* to steal because their choices are so limited. Some authors might call that a "criminogenic environment" because society has impoverished the person who chooses to steal.[3] On the surface, we have both made "choices," but if you dig beyond the surface, you will come to the realization that these choices are not equivalent at all. Did we really make these decisions freely (i.e., to steal or not to steal) or did our social conditions already predetermine what was possible? This is why I do not think the question, "Why did this person choose criminal behaviour," makes much sense—unless it is asked to point out the lack of decision-making agency possessed by many individuals. Our choices are often circumscribed, or caused, by external factors and circumstances. What do you think?

ML: I appreciate these examples, and I am thinking about a scenario in which both you and our hypothetical youth are walking down the streets in downtown Vancouver and how both of you might navigate the choices presented to you by this environment. The idea that your social and economic circumstances shape your choices in ways that you might not even be aware of or think about is very important. One way to think about this is to consider how you and our hypothetical youth might go about trying to meet your basic biological needs by gaining access to a restroom in downtown Vancouver. Many restrooms are "for paying customers only." For you, the idea of hopping into a cafe and purchasing a coffee so you have access to the restroom or simply asking for the key and expecting your social status to convey the legitimacy of that request is something we take for granted. The youth, however, by virtue of their circumstances, might be denied these opportunities and be forced to find some other means to meet a basic biological need. It would be hard to explain this exclusively as a matter of individual choice.

MM: Yes, it is also true that the homeless youth might already have an experience from a cafe owner of being denied access to the washroom, or they may already have been profiled by the owner of that cafe in the past, or they might be easily profiled by their clothing or their appearance. So those aspects are beyond their control. I should add that in the hypothetical scenario of stealing/not stealing, the homeless youth can always choose to return home and comply with the state-ordered foster home; however, that choice might be the more harmful one because that foster home might not be safe or appropriate in the eyes of the youth. How should we understand behaviours or choices that are illegal but which might be the informed and correct ones to make? Sometimes people act intuitively, and they are not wrong to do so, but it might be illegal.

ML: The important thing about your question is that it invites us to move beyond a simplistic or binary conceptualization of legality and illegality. We often think that what is legal is obviously natural and right and what is illegal is clearly wrong and harmful and that the deterrent of sanction will guide us towards making the lawful choice. But, as your example invites us to consider, sometimes, and particularly in situations of marginalization, that compliance with legal and regulatory regimes (e.g., state-ordered foster home) presents their own risks and indeed their own deterrents. To return to our example of the cafe restroom, entering and asking permission, in other words following the rules, would present negligible risk to you. But that same action might expose the youth to profiling sanctions, or even simply negative attitudes, on the grounds that they would be visibly out of place in that setting.[4]

MM: So, if we use my example of stealing and your example of the cafe, they clearly illustrate that it is not a simple matter to ask what caused a crime or what caused certain behaviour or what causes people to behave. Both these examples illustrate how extremely difficult it is to understand decision-making or the choice to commit crime. I should also add that the example of me versus a homeless youth may not be a very fair illustration of "choice" because the differences are so extreme. That is, our subject positions and social entitlements are so far apart that it makes the example perhaps too extreme. The extremeness of the example may serve a function of illustration, but it may be even more revealing and complicated if our situations were the same. For example, what makes two similar people (e.g., middle-class, white, educated, employed) take on two very different decisions? In this scenario, we could ask: What causes one to commit a crime while the other does not? That is the trickier question to parse because the overt social conditions are identical, but they give rise to different decisions or outcomes. Therein lies the confounding situation of "cause" and social conditions.

ML: This is an important point. I think one of the greatest pitfalls of criminological thinking has been the quest for singular causes and straightforward explanations for complex and highly contextualized events and behaviours. When you think about it, we understand that other kinds of social phenomena, for example our preferences for our favourite foods, are shaped by a variety of factors: geography, culture, upbringing, experiences, resources, health conditions, the preferences of those around us, and so on. Now if we understand this intuitively in relation to something like food preference, surely we must recognize that harmful, antisocial, or otherwise criminalized behaviours must also be the product of a confluence of factors.

MM: It is great that you brought up the example of food because we all know that not everyone enjoys the same foods—even people who come from the same social group or society. What makes a person like or dislike ice cream or french fries? It is not apparent. The cause for liking a food is multifactored, logical, illogical, obvious, obscure, or maybe even mysterious. In this regard, all human actions must be the product of a confluence of factors. And yet, our field routinely rejects this insight and focuses on one explanation. For example, in asking what compels a person to act in a particular way or what gives rise to their deviant behaviour, there are also attempts to use only science and biology to explain the cause of behaviour. Biology—as an explanation of why we do things—is attractive to some scholars because it offers a singular empirical explanation of the fact of our bodies. The individual is reduced to a knowable physical thing that is examined through an objective method of science. Subjects are turned into objects. Our bodies—as external systems or objects—are understood to be beyond our free will and, as behaviour, beyond our control. For example, our beating heart or our ability to sleep can easily be understood to be beyond our conscious control. And if these uncontrollable things exist in our bodies, then maybe we can find other uncontrollable things in our bodies that give rise to other behaviours (e.g., criminal behaviour). This perspective is very attractive and seductive for explaining crime and deviance because it links behaviour to a biological cause.

ML: This concept of uncontrollable biological factors is so interesting. Much of criminology has focused on the issue of control and controllability. When we say that behaviour is controllable or uncontrollable, we are implying that there are certain ways of intervening, or modifying it, and diverse ways of understanding blameworthiness associated with that behaviour. Another way to think about blameworthiness is to use the concept of guilt or responsibility; concepts that are understood to be absolutely foundational to criminal legal systems. After all, a criminal trial is essentially an effort to answer the question: Can we blame this person for this thing and hold them responsible for it?

Criminological theories also take up this question of blame and responsibility, but they do so in ways that differ from the approach often used in courts. For example, as you have suggested, there is an entire school of thought in criminology that focuses on biological explanations for crime causation. Early biological theories associated "criminal propensity" with physiology and body shape. More recent theories focus on neurotransmitters and genetic factors. Heredity is a common thread. There are also psychological theories. For example, a large subfield has explored the relationship between factors that influence personality development and patterns of deviant or antisocial behaviour, while other research has examined how behaviour is learned through various forms of conditioning and modelling. There are also distinctly sociological theories of crime. For example, strain theories have examined how people adapt—sometimes in criminalized ways—to pressures created by the social and economic structures they are embedded in, and subcultural theories have explored how criminal behaviour can arise from socialization into groups with "unconventional" or deviant values and norms.

These are only a few examples. Before digging into any of these ideas further, I think we should talk about the notion that biological, psychological, and sociological approaches are distinct and separate. This is how they are often presented in textbooks—a chapter on biological approaches, one on personality, and so on. You can imagine the attraction: it helps to keep things organized, and it is true that many contributions to the history of criminological thought were based on specific disciplinary approaches. Is this an effective way to organize our thinking about the causes of crime today, though? We have already noted that singular explanations for complex behaviours are too simplistic. Would we be better off if, at the outset, we acknowledged that all human behaviour is shaped by biological, psychological, and social factors interacting?

MM: I could not agree with you more. But it is more than just a question of integration. It is a question of accuracy. Our field of study would be stronger if it were not segmented into these discrete fields of biology, psychology, sociology, and economics. In part, we do not have a unified theory of deviance and crime precisely because academic disciplines have been historically organized in silos that are alien to one another. Each field holds up their method of analysis as the superior one, and this gets in the way of interdisciplinarity or more complex and connected explanations regarding the cause of crime and deviance. Each field has its own seductions. For example, if we return to the question of biology and cause, we have Caesare Lombroso, an early pioneer of this method of explaining causes of crime, and his use of the scientific method to measure the human body and reveal the biological signs for deviance. His work led him to believe that all criminals are born and not socially made. He adopted a Darwinian or evolutionary approach that allowed him to search for deviant traits in humans. He believed that criminals were less evolved (i.e., atavistic) and had leftover traits from an earlier stage of human development. It was based on the premise that humans evolved from a more primitive state but that criminals had somehow retained and inherited some of these less desirable and less evolved traits. And this desire to measure the less evolved human being also had a racist component. Lombroso also speculated that nonwhite humans were also somehow less evolved.[5] And this line of thinking was adopted from other biological theories about a superior "Caucasian" race, such as that developed by Johann Friedrich Blumenbach and others who were interested in theorizing human races a century before Lombroso's work.[6] In this regard, Lombroso is following a social and biological Darwinism that also takes on a hidden racial component. It is a racial component that is embedded in the history of the science of criminology. So, when we investigate biological theories of causation, we do also have to acknowledge that they are connected to the history of race and racism and the work of Western European scholars. So, that is something that needs to be investigated as well.

ML: These are excellent points, and we can go a step further: not only did these early biological approaches connect with racist ideas in circulation at the time, but they also functioned to provide empirical justification for a politics of racial superiority by purporting to describe assumed "natural" differences between categories of people. For example, these ideas provided intellectual cover for the institution of slavery, and for settler-colonialism, and indeed for the eugenics movement. What is interesting to me is that this entire quest for biological explanation was driven by the idea of some kind of objective scientific understanding of human behaviour, and the early proponents, including folks like Lombroso, thought that what they were producing was distanced from the perhaps problematic sociological and philosophical traditions of the day, and yet when we reflect back at this so-called objective empirical positivist science of crime, we find that it is deeply infused with all of the assumptions about normalcy and deviance that were taken for granted at the time. I think what this does for us is gives us reason to think skeptically or at least critically about all claims to establish a definitive causal model of criminal behaviour rooted in some form of objective science. It invites us to consider how all the ways we think about crime and its causes are shaped by the social context from which they emerge.

MM: Yes, it does give us, as you say, a reason to think skeptically or critically about efforts to establish a definitive cause for criminal behaviour, but as you also point out, Lombroso understood the previous work of Bentham or Beccaria to be unscientific. That is, for Lombroso, their theory that criminal behaviour was the product of rational decision-making could not be correct because it did not employ scientific methods. He saw their entire framing of criminal behaviour as wrong. And so, he began to measure people's bodies. He used calipers to measure people's noses, ears, eyes, mouths, foreheads, and skulls to determine if there were tells or signs of deviance that could be observed. In this regard, we must applaud Lombroso's goal because he sought to improve our understanding of what causes crime. However, we also know that his research was deeply flawed and that crime does not come about because of evolutionary throwbacks or less "developed" humans. Lombroso's scholarship was certainly guided by a desire to better understand the cause of crime, but in so doing, he produced some very unscientific notions of race and behaviour. This is a case where the search for a cause led to research that *caused* harm.

ML: I think a conversation about causation is incomplete if it does not also touch on the issue of justification or rationalization. Let us acknowledge that there are many factors that can influence our behaviour and our actions and shape the circumstances within which they take place. Bearing this in mind, I think we can also acknowledge that we, as human beings, are constantly involved in a process of making sense of our own behaviour. We ascribe meaning and intentionality to our actions and we work to justify (to ourselves and sometimes to others) the choices we make. Sociologist C. Wright Mills introduced the concept of a vocabulary of motives to describe the ways we make sense of our own motivations for our actions and the motivations we associate with other peoples' behaviour. The idea is that we are constantly faced with the task of explaining why people act the way they do (including ourselves), and we develop a set of explanations or provide satisfactory responses to these questions, given the circumstances. This helps us to navigate the everyday social world.

MM: So, are you saying that we make up stories to explain our actions? Is C. Wright Mills's concept of a "vocabulary of motives" something we make up after the fact? Is it a reinterpretation of our behaviour and action?

ML: Sometimes, yes. We all have the experience of acting impulsively and then attempting to make sense of our own behaviour after the fact. But there are two points worth briefly emphasizing. First, it is sometimes the case that we find ourselves able to act only after we have made sense of both what this action will mean for us and how we might explain it to others. In this sense, the vocabulary of motives we draw on proceeds our actions and makes them possible. Second, it is sometimes the case that we will use different rationalizations or vocabularies of motive to make sense of our actions depending on our intended or anticipated audience. So, this is very important because it suggests that "motive" is not a singular thing. I craft my motive, or at least my explanation for it, in relation to my audience.

MM: So, are you saying that we are both an unreliable narrator of our own actions and lying to ourselves or making stuff up because we must make sense of our actions?

ML: I think most social interaction involves making stuff up. In a way, it is the idea that there is some definable singular authentic cause for behaviour that gets in the way of understanding social phenomena. I would consider myself authentic, truthful, but also unreliable. I spend a lot of time thinking about what I have done and what I will do, but I might not explain my actions the same way to all people precisely because there are different ways of explaining them—and, I have come to learn that different audiences are more or less willing to accept certain explanations.

MM: OK, so I understand your answer as relating to the notion of social norms and our need to comply with them; or if we violate the norm, then having to work hard to explain ourselves.

ML: Yes, within the field of criminology, researchers Gresham M. Sykes and David Matza noted that one of the common features of most crimes—especially those that directly harm others—is that they violate widely shared values and norms.[7] When we knowingly act in ways that we understand to be wrong and consciously choose to violate norms, most of us experience feelings of guilt or shame. These are not good feelings! Even if we "get away with it" and avoid some form external detection or punishment, it can still feel bad to break our internalized sense of values or our own moral code. Sykes and Matza pose an interesting criminological question: How do people who understand their actions to be wrong or harmful go about suppressing or circumventing the guilt that comes with this? They propose that we use "techniques of neutralization"—denials, rationalizations, and excuses, similar to vocabularies of motive—that allow us to simultaneously recognize the validity of social norms and values and justify breaking them in a given circumstance. For example, a person might honestly claim to believe that it is wrong to hurt other people but also choose to beat someone up because "they deserved it" or "they had it coming to them." Sykes and Matza would call this "denial of the victim," a common technique of neutralization. Importantly, Sykes and Matza emphasize that techniques of neutralization are not just post hoc excuses for our actions. Our actions are made possible by the rationalizations and justifications we apply to them.

I find these theories, and other theories and concepts that help us to understand the ways we "make meaning" and interpret our actions, to be vitally important when thinking about causation. They help us to move beyond the problem of the actor as automaton, shaped entirely by forces (biological, psychological, or sociological) beyond their control, and beyond the idea of the actor as "homo economicus," guided by dispassionate rational calculation and cost-benefit analysis. We are beings with subjective (internal) lives, and we strive to make sense of our world and our place in it. This idea is particularly important because it "scales." We can think of the role that vocabularies of motive and techniques of neutralization play in a student's decision to plagiarize an assignment or in a police officer's decision to brutalize a person in custody. Provocatively, we can apply the concept on a macro-social scale to explain how a society can engage in the systematic repression of minority groups.

MM: I love that you used the phrase "actor as automaton" and that you introduced the concept of us, humans, always making up reasons or excuses for our actions. It really calls into question the whole idea of rational choice vs. social conditioning vs. physical being. On the one hand, we all know that we are not automatons or robots that have been preprogrammed. And we know this because we feel we have consciousness and subjectivity. That is, it is self-evident: we know who we are! On the other hand, maybe we *are* just robots made of meat! We all acknowledge that we did not invent the language we speak, we do not control our heart rate, we do not control our eyes blinking, we do not control our sleep or the need for sleep, we cannot control when we wake up, we cannot control cancer if it grows inside us, our hair and nails grow without our choice, we digest food without conscious effort, we use language without really understanding how it works, thoughts some-times pop into our heads without our conscious effort, etc. These are things that just exist for us and are predetermined. They are not chosen. Even "falling in love" suggests there are forces beyond our control. And if they are not chosen but rather things we "fall into," then this calls into consideration our personal volition and human agency and our control of our own destiny. We do not instruct ourselves to fall in love or be infatuated with a hobby (e.g., skiing, stamp collecting, or beer making). Why do Canadians love hockey? Did we choose these hobbies, or did they choose us? And even when we choose something, these "things" are within a very narrow range of choices.

The Hungarian Marxist Georg Lukács theorized that there is both an objective and subjective quality to the way people are trained by a capitalist society.[8] They are made into worker units in a system not of their choosing, but one that simultaneously produces perceptions and feelings for the worker that are completely different from those of the employer. For example, a worker will begin to perceive their interests as being different from the employer (e.g., better wages vs. better profit margins). So, even the things we like or want are limited or predeter-mined. There is not an unlimited number of ice cream flavours. Yes, you can choose one, but you cannot choose one that has not yet been invented. For example, in the context of our current opioid epidemic, an addict can only choose fentanyl if it is the only synthetic opioid avail-able to them in the context of an illegal or prohibited drug market. If I am an addict, then did I want fentanyl before it was invented? Perhaps I *choose* it because I have a twenty-year addiction to opioids that I am failing to control. Did I "fall into" addiction? Is the addict in control of their choices? Maybe addiction is the true me, and it controls all my actions, and I am not free to choose. As a long-term addict, I know that without the continued use of opioids, I will become "dope-sick," or drug withdrawal sick, and I might feel like I am physically dying. My desire to avoid the feeling of dying drives my drug use. So, am I an automaton? Am I a robot? Am I a robot made of meat? Is the addict an automaton or have they made informed and rational decisions during each session of drug use? What causes drug use?

ML: These are fascinating questions for us to consider, and the kind of thing I enjoy talking about with a friend over a coffee. But there are serious implications arising from these questions for how we approach matters of deviance and crime. For example, a legal system treats people as free choosing agents who are both capable of controlling their own actions and by extension responsible for them. So, what happens to our legal system if we come to understand that most behaviour is shaped or conditioned by forces beyond individual control? To take it one step further, is it ethical for a society to operate a legal system that assumes and presumes individual agency in a world where circumstances strongly constrain and influence our behaviour?

MM: This is a great point you are making about the way legal systems are constrained by the very rules of only searching for the facts and searching for specific individual offenders or perpetrators or criminals and not being able to address the larger social context. And this is something that we will investigate and examine in Chapter Seven: Systems of Response, which examines law and the legal system. But I want to return to your use of Sykes and Matza and how their work examines how people understand their own behaviour. You mentioned neutralization, denial, and/or the use of excuses, and this points to the very crux of the question of causation. Causation of deviant behaviour is multidimensional, and some of those dimensions may include poverty, housing, health, education, trauma, and/or inequality in society. Wealth and poverty are often conditions that you did not choose because, if it were a choice, everyone would choose wealth. The conditions that you were born into—not of your own choosing—predetermine so much of what your life can be.

Even the person who is framed as the offender or the criminal does not necessarily understand why they themselves acted in a deviant manner. For example, if you asked a homeless youth—who has nothing—whether they rationally decided to steal something from the dollar store, they would probably admit they acted in a rational manner and that no one twisted their arm. However, that is only because they do not have the social analysis to understand their own social conditions; a condition of homelessness in which they never made a conscious choice to be homeless. And to be homeless and very young are the key precipitating factors allowing for those actions of theft or deviance. So, when we think about the work of Sykes and Matza, I think you find that this vocabulary of motive is not especially useful for understanding crime or criminal behaviour or criminal deviance. In fact, one can argue that the criminal is an unreliable narrator. The homeless youth cannot explain their situation. They themselves have no insight into the cause of their behaviour. This throws us for a loop because the "agency" of the individual is at the core of much legal reasoning. But when we examine this through the framework provided by Sykes and Matza, we find that it is pointing us in this different direction; that even the person who is acting deviant may not understand their deviance or why their actions are understood to be wrong or deviant.

ML: I think the value of the vocabularies of motive, techniques of neutralization, and tools we use for thinking about behaviour and its causes is not that these are accurate reflections of some true causal essence of behaviour. Rather, the value is in recognizing the importance of the motivation to narrate in and of itself. Regardless of whether my interpretation of the causes of my actions, my behaviour, or my circumstances is accurate or reasonable, I feel a desire to make sense of the way I act. Furthermore, I may want to make sense of the way others act in relation to me and to feel that my behaviour is consistent with the way I understand myself or my circumstances. And this is extremely valuable for us because it tells us that criminological theories of causation should attempt to incorporate some elements of people's subjective understandings of their lived experience. It is true that our understanding and explanations may be deeply flawed, but that does not mean our rationalizations, justifications, excuses, and vocabularies of motives do not work.

One of the central insights that Mills has in his work on vocabularies of motive is simply that we are constantly expected to explain why we are acting in certain ways. This will be familiar to our readers, who have surely been asked why they think what they think, why they are doing what they are doing, or why they are behaving in certain ways on an ongoing basis. I think we can speak from this experience and recognize that the answers to these questions (i.e., the vocabularies we draw upon to explain our motives) will be different depending on the setting and the questioner. The question: "Why are you studying criminology?" when posed by a professor may elicit a quite different response than the same question when posed by a parent or a friend. The objective is not to identify some true, singular, an essential motive for actions but to recognize that the very question of motive is socially contextualized. We construct narratives about our lives and actions with an awareness of audience.

A narrative does not have to be effective or successful. For example, a child who is instructed not to take a cookie from the cookie jar and who does so anyways will likely be asked by a caregiver to explain why they have done this thing. And speaking from experience, they will probably attempt to craft a narrative that will produce a desired outcome. That is, to get them out of trouble. This is unlikely to be successful, but the usefulness is in recognizing the expectation and desire to produce rationales.

MM: Well, it seems you were a naughty kid! But that is the perfect anecdote because if the child who gives an excuse for stealing a cookie feels that they must explain themselves in a rational way that can be understood by mother or father, then it helps us understand that being caught gives rise to our need—in ourselves—to make up a story about why we did it. That is, our rationalization is not from within but is stimulated from outside us. And that again goes back to this notion of narration and telling a story and making sense of why we did something, or why we did not do something, as external to our own thinking or the original offence. This is the key issue in the study of crime and our desire to explain why a criminal act has happened. So, what is "outside us"? Social conditions and social formation are outside us. If it is true that society is something we did not choose, and that many of us are born into conditions not of our own choosing, then it stands to reason that even the way we can explain our actions has already been decided for us by the time we were born into, the place we were born into, the language we speak, the communities we live in, and the schools we attend. We choose none of these things, and so we can begin to understand that the environment is a key overdetermining condition beyond our control. It is a key condition not just for deviant behaviour but even for behaviours of excellence. Great wealth and success are also dependent on being born in the right place and at the right time.

When you stand back, you may begin to understand that people are simply floating in a sea of life where there are currents, waves, or forces beyond our control pushing and pulling us. We maybe wash upon shores that we cannot control. For example, you can watch any science fiction alternate-reality show for proof. Such TV shows or movies often present a scenario where a single turning-point—that can go in any direction—gives rise to multiple and quite different lives. That presents a huge problem for the study of crime because the study of crime is so tied to the desire to explain "why" crime happens. And the current and most popular framework for explaining why crime happens is tied to a classical notion of the rational actor. The explanation is that the criminal decided to act in a deviant manner. Therefore, if we punish them, that will deter future criminal behaviour. It suggests that we simply adopt an economic model of rational choice in which the person has an array of options that are linked to associated outcomes and the perfect information to weigh the outcomes.[9] And yet, if you understand what I just said, then this type of response to crime is irrational because we just agreed that people are born into conditions not of their own choosing. So, you are caught in a loop of illogical cause, effect, and response. In part, that is what criminologists are studying: the flawed problem of criminal response that we have today. In some respects, as criminologists, we are not even studying the criminal, we are studying the response to the criminal or trying to understand how society gave birth to the criminal.

ML: I agree, and the imagery of waves and currents and shores is extremely useful for thinking about matters of crime and deviance. It certainly invites us to think about powerful forces that shaped the world around us. As an individual, I can navigate a current, but I cannot change it. But I wonder if our conversation about social factors and forces that shape behaviour might leave our readers with the impression that individuals who cause harm to others knowingly and deliberately cannot or should not be held personally responsible for their conduct. Are we denying the concept of free will? Are we suggesting that people cannot choose to act differently in a given situation?

MM: Great question, Mike. If we return to the illustration of robots, I do not think I am a robot made of meat. I think I am a person. I think I have free will. I think I decide what I want to think, do, eat, read, or watch. I believe I have complete control over my decisions and destiny. And yet, if I step back, I can also understand that I am kind of a robot made of meat because there are so many things that I cannot control. As I said earlier, my heart rate, the number of times I blink a minute, my rate of digestion, my rate of sleep, etc., these are already predetermined for me. I have no control whatsoever over these things, even my breathing is controlled for me. I do not consciously make those decisions. And similarly, I think we can all agree that our social conditions have been predetermined, as we have covered already. We have established that our wealth or our poverty—into which we are born—are not our choices. People start at different starting lines, and they end up at different finish lines. I was lucky enough to be brought up in a middle-class, intact, and supportive family who valued education and the health of their children. That was my starting line! So, to answer your question, "Are we suggesting that people cannot choose differently?" or that they have no free will; my answer is, "Yes, I have free will," but when I think about the criminal justice system and the way the law interacts with, names, detains, or punishes people, then suddenly I want to give more weight to the conditions that gave rise to their criminal deviance, their criminal profiling, and/or their criminal framing. And I understand these actions, on the part of the state, as things that are external to the individual. So, in this sense, there is a moment in this logic when the individual is not free because they have been captured by society. And then I want to connect this examination of the state with an examination of the individual's socioeconomic background.

ML: I think what you are getting at is the idea that the very question of free will, or agency vs. determinism, is an oversimplification and unproductive. Agency is always subject to structure. We do not make decisions in a vacuum. And the fact that we make decisions at all does not invalidate the mosaic of factors that shape our circumstances.

One of the starting points I often use when introducing criminology to my students is an article written by Stan Cohen in the late 1980s. Stan Cohen was a South African criminologist and originator of moral panic theory, and he describes how the media helps create a threat to society and then fuels its proliferation. Cohen conducted a survey of the field of criminology titled "Footsteps in the Sand."[10] In this essay, he says there is a lot of diversity within criminology, but generally, the academic fields can be summed up with three questions: Why do people break laws, why do people make laws, and what can/do we do in response to law breaking? He argues that these are the three fundamental questions for criminology. And there is no doubt that the question "why do people break laws" (i.e., why do people commit crimes and what causes crime) is a central question for us. So, Mike, how would we answer the question of what causes crime?

MM: Great question. The simple answer is that people cause crime. People disobey or break laws. One law that we can use as an illustration is the law against theft. People steal and in so doing they break the law. If a person steals, then they have caused crime. But what causes a person to steal? That is the real question. Some would say avarice, greed, or coveting other people's possessions or money. They want other people's money. But why is a law breaker missing the thing they covet? Why do they want that thing the other person has? The real question is: Why is the person stealing somehow deprived of or missing a resource? Why are they missing money? Why do they not have enough money to buy the thing that other person has? Why does the wallet of the poorer person who steals have less money than the wallet that is stolen? The simple answer is that the economic system is not working for the thief in the way that it should. They break the rules because the system of wealth creation is broken or not well designed. There is inequality of wealth between the thief and person from whom they are stealing. And that inequality is not the fault of the thief. Inequality and the rigid structure of law cause crime to occur.

ML: It is also interesting that it is easy for us to frame the thief's behaviour in relation to the criminal law as "stealing," but the person at the top of the economic pyramid—the 1 percent of the 1 percent who makes billions of dollars on an annual basis—is framed as innovative, bold, successful, and even inspirational, but certainly not criminally.

MM: Yes, and that speaks to the reality of work for the other 99 percent. In our economic system you are supposed to get a job to make money. But what if that system of getting a job to make money is not working for you? Maybe you do not have a good job and cannot get access to good jobs. And you need more education to get a better job to get more money. But if lack of education and a lack of good jobs is fuelling your behaviour, then the crime of theft must be linked to social conditions. Maybe individuals are not completely responsible for their situation in life because you might be born into conditions not of your own choosing. It is social conditions such as not having a good education or not having a good job or not being able to access education that would allow you to get a better job or a higher salary that is the cause of crime. The answer to your question "what causes crime?" is the economic system into which you were born, and because you never asked to be born into it, we can understand these conditions not to be of your own choosing. Maybe the social and economic system is flawed because it is giving rise to these types of behaviours (e.g., theft).

ML: That effectively speaks to one of the main approaches used by criminologists to address the question of causation. You immediately put this into a framework of social structures and historical context. What does it mean to live in a society with particular constraints and norms? I also think that the idea of "being born into conditions not of ones choosing" is especially important to understand when thinking about this. But maybe we can further extend this line of thought by considering that many people are born into conditions of absolute, or we could say relative, deprivation and face significant social and economic pressures and lack the resources and means to achieve desired social standards and expectations, but not all of those people will engage in theft to acquire things. Not all people will seek to address those kinds of deprivations through means that are criminalized. One of the questions this raises for us is if there is a structural basis to crime, and to the question of causation, then, why do we find so many people in positions of deprivation who struggle but nonetheless adhere to laws that manifestly do not benefit them *and* do not engage in crime? In other words, why do so many people not commit crime?

MM: That is a great question, and I will answer it first in a backwards way by giving the example of someone who has been arrested for being homeless or having a mental health crisis in the middle of a street. This is a person who has not done anything wrong and has not committed a crime and yet has now been arrested for vagrancy or having a medical condition because they have disturbed the peace. They have been criminalized because the prohibition against acting in a disorderly manner in the middle of a street is what causes the criminal offence. It is not the act of a mental health breakdown, which may be linked to being homeless, that is the crime but rather the strict adherence to an ideology of peace that creates the action for a police officer to arrest someone and charge them for a crime. The rule says you cannot have disorder. The arrested person did not commit any crime in the classic sense of the term (e.g., theft), but their disorderly "existence" or behaviour is criminalized. That is a perfect example of a person not committing a crime and yet being detained, arrested, and/or charged for one. To have mental illness is not a crime; it is a disease or a health issue.

But I have dodged your question. You asked why so many people do not commit crime. The answer is simple: if you are socially and economically secure, then you do not commit crime. It is that simple. That brings us back to the issue of social conditions. If your social conditions are bad enough, they can give rise to criminal behaviour. But you asked about someone in a position of deprivation. I think a person in a position of deprivation (e.g., a person in extreme poverty) who does not act in any way to break a law does not exist. Their very being is in a state of illegality. For example, the unhoused person who is passive, nonthreatening, and nonviolent is already committing the crime of vagrancy. Once you are in a position of deprivation you are already criminal, or at the very least "out of order." If you are unemployed or unemployable, then I think society has already put you in a box labelled "unproductive" and of "less value" to society. That person might neither be breaking a law nor resisting social order, but they are still labelled as broken or not useful. They submit to this identity of deprivation. That in itself is a form of social damage. They are damaged by this labelling. They have not been served or recuperated by society. Society's response to the person in a position of deprivation (e.g., extreme poverty or homelessness) is one of erasure or temporary detention. The policing solution resolves neither deprivation nor poverty.

But I have still dodged your question. You asked: Why do so many people who are in positions of deprivation continue to adhere to laws that do not benefit them? I will answer that question in two parts. The first part is simple and is related to the repressive state apparatus[11] or what we call the "police." Our society has a mechanism, called police, that has been given an extraordinarily strong mandate to surveil the streets and keep them free of homelessness, vagrancy, mental illness, poverty, disorder, etc. The person who lives in a position of extreme social and economic deprivation and lowered social class is already afraid of arrest, detention, prison, and general contact with police. They do not want to call attention to themselves and do want to avoid contact with police. In this regard, they are compliant and behave accordingly even though the social system is absolutely not working for them. The second part of my answer is related to the ideology of "possessive individualism."[12] Through socialization people come to believe they are wholly responsible for their own social and economic condition. It is a pervasive way of thinking in society. We are taught that our lives and our destiny are in our own hands. And so, even people who are extremely poor will continue to understand their situation of deprivation as wholly their own responsibility. Therefore, if you have a deep attachment to the idea that your identity, fate, and success is not dependent on anyone else, then you may believe, live, or act in a way that reflects this ideal. You might not engage in any deviant behaviour precisely because this ideology is so strong. So, to recap, I think people adhere to laws that do not benefit them because (a) people want to avoid contact with police and (b) people understand their life conditions as something they created for themselves and by themselves; they accept it as a product of their own faults and do not resist or blame the social system.

ML: This points to the importance of being able to understand social reaction to crime and disorder as a phenomenon connected to but not directly overlapping with transgression and violation of social norms. There are certainly situations where you have enforcement despite a lack of transgression, as you point out, such as the policing of people by virtue of their social status. I can think of another example—and I will invite your thoughts on this one. What about the person who is well financed and privileged and who engages in acts that are harmful and clearly transgressive? Here is a situation where a person is perfectly capable of meeting any standards of expectation in society and has by most perspectives achieved success, people who run corporations for example, but also engage in acts that are grossly harmful. We know there are a lot of people who are engaged in, let us say, white-collar professions who commit offences to further their accumulation of wealth and resources. How can we explain this kind of offending?

MM: White-collar crimes are often framed by the criminal justice system as victimless crimes because they are crimes of finance (e.g., embezzling from a bank, defrauding an insurance company, or tax avoidance). There is a notion that there are no victims in this crime because no one was assaulted or physically harmed. It is just a financial loss. In this regard, white-collar crimes are framed as a safer crime and a crime that is punished in a less severe manner than theft or burglary. But then we also must ask how our society views such white-collar crimes. It reminds me of something my brother-in-law has stated. While philosophizing about sports, he said, "If you are not cheating in sports, then you are not trying hard enough." And it made me think. Is this the kind of mantra that is espoused in the corporate and business world? There is a consensus that one of the ways you can succeed in business is by finding loopholes, for example in corporate law, tax law, or accounting. That is why corporate tax law is such a highly regarded form of legal practice. Even past US presidents are famous for having boasted about how they pay almost no tax because they are smart enough to find loopholes in tax law that allows them to, lawfully, not pay any tax owing. The manipulation of the financial system and the finding of weaknesses in the system, or in tax law, is understood to be good corporate behaviour. Here, we can again use Sykes and Matza's framework to understand how easy it is neutralize and explain unethical behaviour as legitimate, or even good, corporate behaviour.

ML: I think that is a fascinating response, and it makes me think about the differences in the way we respond to these different kinds of transgressions. We have the example of a person experiencing serious mental health challenges in the street and the expectation that this is a police matter though it may not initially be a crime matter. It is certainly regarded as a symbol of disorder that is routinely subject to policing. By contrast, the white-collar professional who is knowingly bending and breaking rules in an effort to game the system is highly unlikely to ever find that behaviour patrolled by any kind of law enforcement. There are no police beats that encompass Bay Street towers or Wall Street financial institutions. This disparity in policing is useful for us in thinking about the relationship between these notions of causation and our expectations of enforcement. Our explanations for causation so far have focused on structural factors and this gives me reason to ask: If structural factors are important in shaping the causation of crime—as we have suggested—what role is there for agency and therefore responsibility? Is it reasonable for us to hold people personally responsible for behaviour that we understand has strong structural determinants?

MM: I think that is a crucial question to ask. In the context of asking what causes crime, can we then say the social conditions into which a person is born is the cause of deviant or criminal behaviour? That is a strongly true statement because human beings are completely shaped by their social context and by their social habituation and social conditioning. People are social constructs, and they are social constructs of a system not of their own choosing. It behooves us to think of ways to address behaviours that transgress social norms other than using a criminal framework that criminalizes and makes something deviant (or not normal) because that practice of criminalization is not useful as a social tool. It is too simplistic to simply state: Deviant behaviour is the cause of crime.

ML: As a starting point for studying criminology, it is vital to consider social structure. There are lots of approaches to the study of crime and criminology that follow a more historical evolutionary narrative. In terms of the history of the field, which very much begins with individual agent choices and very positivistic questions of pathology, deviance is a product of difference starting from a structural perspective. It yields us more fruitful outcomes and invites us to ask better questions. However, we can be left with the challenge of explaining crime as a social construction determined by structural, social, and economic forces while losing capacity to account for individual choices, moral agency, and efforts by people to change circumstances, and that is something to be wary of.

MM: I agree with you that individuals have agency and that we can act as independent actors in society. However, it is quite clear that there are many things in society that we have not chosen. Not just social ones; we also do not choose nature (e.g., the weather or when the sun will rise). So, similarly, I did not choose that I *must* go to work to make money. I did not choose that I *must* live in a particular way that complies with social norms otherwise society will frame me as deviant. It is both true that individuals have agency and can make active informed decisions *and* that those decisions are always circumscribed by existing or pre-existing social structures. For example, the removal of a law (e.g., prohibition against recreational cannabis consumption) can then make the choice of consuming a substance a legal recreational practice and not a prohibited practice. I can choose to obey the law—while consuming cannabis—because the law protects, rather than prohibits, consumption. I can choose lawfully to consume. But I only have this individual choice because the Criminal Code was changed and recreational cannabis was made legal. As an individual, I had very little input on the changing of the law. But the law has a giant effect on what I may choose. Similarly, if I steal money, then I have made a conscious decision—without duress—to steal. But what are the social factors that brought me to the point of stealing? Those are external social structures not of my own choosing. Those are external causes of crime.

Discussion Questions:

1. Consider your own experience and behaviour. Discuss whether what you "choose" or what you "do" are the product of your own actions and can be understood as the result of your agency and free will. How might your actions be influenced by circumstances beyond your direct control?
2. Offer three possible answers to the "what causes people to commit crime?" question. For each answer, briefly discuss the implications for social reaction (response, prevention).
3. You and your colleagues have been asked to propose some significant social and legal reforms that would result in a considerable reduction in the amount and seriousness of crime within the next ten years. What kinds of reforms would you recommend, and what effect do you think these reforms would have?

CHAPTER 5
The Counting Conundrum

In this chapter, we are concerned with how and why crime is measured, quantitatively and qualitatively, with a particular emphasis on the production of official crime statistics. Public opinion about crime and state crime control policies are, in part, tied to knowledge about the nature and extent of crime, and a variety of data collection and reporting mechanisms have been devised to provide this knowledge. A key theme in the chapter is the idea that measurement can be valuable and informative, but that it is necessarily also flawed and limited. We discuss the differences between action, perception, reporting, and recording and the ways these actions connect to official measures like the crime rate and crime severity index. The chapter also considers the role that certain crime measurements—for example, the homicide rate—play in shaping public debates about crime and public safety. We then turn to the important idea of statistical overrepresentation as a means of measuring bias and discrimination in criminal justice processes.

Mike Larsen (ML): Is crime going up or down? Is crime getting worse? Is the criminal legal system efficient or fraught with delays? Do the people who are "in" the system represent a cross-section of the public or are certain groups over- (or under-) represented? Are certain groups more likely to experience victimization? Is crime spread evenly across different regions, or is it concentrated in certain communities or parts of the country? Are most offenders "one-time" actors, or do repeat offenders account for multiple cases over time? These are important questions, and you can understand how the answers to them tell us a great deal about the phenomena of crime, deviance, victimization, and social reaction. Many criminological theories are based on efforts to explain observed patterns involving relationships between variables (called correlations). For example, a theory might attempt to explain the relationship between gender and violence, based on the observation that the overwhelming majority of violent crimes are committed by men.

Michael C. K. Ma (MM): These are great questions, and they bring up the thorny issue of "responding" to crime. The issue of factual clarity is the main reason society is so preoccupied with statistical counting of crime. Statistics deliver us the promise of objectivity. That is, the promise of counting is that it will allow us to understand the way things really are if we only count correctly. Measurement is supposed to allow us to understand something objectively and clearly. But the "thorny" part of the equation is: What if we do not know what to count or how to count something? In your example you mentioned violent crime as something important to measure; however, what if a violent crime occurred but was not reported or underreported? If it is not reported accurately, then the accuracy of the counting is immediately in dispute. And if the patterns of crime cannot be accurately measured or counted, then it makes it difficult to know how to effectively respond to the crimes we seek to count. If a pattern cannot be accurately observed, then what does this mean for the efficiency of a criminal legal/police system? You also mentioned that the majority of violent crimes are committed by men, so I could provocatively suggest that one way to reduce violence would be to reduce the number of men in society. Even accurate counting could lead to unreasonable responses.

ML: Thorny question, indeed, and you pose a provocative response. I think you let me off the hook a bit there in the sense that you did not problematize my use of the term "violent crime." This is one of the main categories of crime counted by governments, and they have very specific criteria that determine what counts as a violent crime. But are these appropriate criteria? Are there different ways to determine what counts as violence? We find that in addition to the problem of gathering information and accurately and effectively responding to it, even the categories that we use to organize our understanding of crime reflect very specific choices. We should also acknowledge that counting occurs not just in the criminal justice context but in many governmental uses (e.g., in a population census or in the preparation of economic budget). Counting is understood to be straightforward and a vital tool of government that is not much problematized.

MM: OK, so we both agree that counting crime is a difficult endeavour. And that it could even be a flawed aspiration. Is there a better way to count or measure crime? Is there some way we can improve the legal or criminal response to crime through objective measurement? Are the mechanisms and categories we use to count inherently flawed?

ML: This is a good opportunity for us to recall our earlier observation that crime and deviance are socially constructed. If we take that as a starting point, then we can acknowledge that the categories we use to count crime are also constructed. They reflect priorities, choices, and even political motivations.

How we respond with our legal system is closely tied to the question of how we collect information about crime. Before we can start to explain trends, patterns, and correlations, we need to collect and consider data, and this brings us to the question of counting. How do we count or measure crime? This may seem like a straightforward question, but it is quite complicated in practice. As we have established, crime is a multifaceted phenomenon, and this means that it can be measured or counted in a variety of ways. For example, if we want to know about assault, we might begin by examining the statistics collected for the number of assaults that have occurred in a given jurisdiction; however, this presents us with the challenge of determining when something has "occurred." In many jurisdictions, an offence is considered to have occurred when—and only when—it is recorded by police. We can imagine a number of scenarios in which something that could be considered assault occurs but is not reported to police and therefore is not counted. We might also note that the colloquial understanding of assault—nonconsensual physical contact towards another person—may be legally interpreted in a variety of ways by our legal system, and this will impact how it is counted.

Furthermore, an assault could involve someone pushing someone or spitting on someone, or it might involve striking/hitting someone, kicking someone, or punching someone. It can also encompass threatening or attempting to assault someone. All these acts of assault are very different and have different outcomes and harms. But they would all still be categorized and counted as "assault." This brings up the question of whether the counting of these assaults as the same one thing helps us understand the severity or harm of each assault or even the nature of the assault.[1]

For a more complex example, let us assume that we are interested in learning about hate crime in a given province over a given year.

Consider the questions we would need to answer to develop a measurement tool or method:

- How should we define a crime motivated by hate?
- How will we decide when a hate crime has occurred? Will we rely on police reports, which recognize hate crimes based on motive as opposed to offence type? Or will we count only specific offences that are designated as hate crimes in Canadian criminal law? Both?
- Will we attempt to gather any information about cases that are not reported to the police?
- Will we attempt to gather information about court cases, convictions, and sentences?
- Will we focus on counting incidents and types of offence only, or will we gather information about victim and offender demographics?
- Will we gather information about the types of motives that inform hate crimes? How will we collect this information?

There are many ways to answer these questions, and it is important to recognize that the choices we make when answering them will have a profound impact on the data we collect and in turn on our understanding of the issue we are examining. In other words, the instruments we use to *measure* a phenomenon like hate crime play a role in *constructing* that phenomenon. It is possible for five different criminologists to develop five different approaches to the measurement of the same phenomenon, each valid and justifiable from the perspective of the researcher. Different criminologists may be interested in different facets or aspects of an issue, and some researchers will have more time and resources to spend on data collection than others.

MM: You have really upped the ante here, Mike. You went straight to the incredibly contentious issue of hate crime! But you are right to point out that the named crime of "hate" itself is extremely amorphous or ambiguous. As you know, there is no such thing as a "hate crime" in the Criminal Code. There is only a provision in our sentencing guidelines allowing judges to give out stronger sentences if the judge believes the crime (e.g., assault) was motivated by hate. So, before we can even answer your first question, we are stymied by the fact that there is no Criminal Code violation named "hate crime." The question arises: How should a researcher count this type of crime when the crime itself does not exist in the current Canadian Criminal Code? It also makes it difficult to compare different regions if comparison is one of the needs of counting and measuring. Does Canada have more hate crime than, say, Japan? It is unclear because Japan does not have the same hate crime (or hate speech) legal framework as Canada. Even our own data collected by Statistics Canada, since 2006, suggests that the collected data of "police-reported hate crime" may only be one-third of all incidents. To further compound the problem of counting, we have no collected data on how the courts have used the sentencing provision related to hate crime because we do not track hate/bias sentencing. It is true that in the case of specific hate related offences (e.g., advocating genocide or public incitement of hatred) the consent of the provincial Attorney General must be sought before the case can proceed; these cases are then counted. However, any judge may determine if hatred was an aggravating factor in deciding the severity of sentence to be given, but this use of hate by a sentencing judge as an aggravating factor is not counted by Statistics Canada.[2]

It is also true that the very definition of the word "hate"[3] is quite unclear. In its use in the legal forum, it is typically used to refer to hatred perpetrated against racialized peoples, nonheterosexual people, nonbinary people, people with disabilities, and/or those who hold particular religious beliefs or practices. There are no written guidelines for a judge to refer to when deciding to assign a harsher sentence; the judge is meant to use their legal knowledge and discretion. We are dependent on individual judges to decide the presence or absence of hate, and we rely on them to decide the severity or mildness of the penalty, but the term "hate" is not defined by the Criminal Code. Criminologists are also dependent on such judgments when collecting data on hate crimes. Statistics Canada does use the term "hate crimes" to refer to police reported incidents that were motivated by hate, but the Criminal Code itself does not have a crime named hate crime. This in itself can be very confusing! For example, in case of assault, there is no Criminal Code violation named "assault motivated by hate." The Criminal Code violation is recorded as "assault," but the penalty assigned by the judge may be more severe than an assault not motivated by hate/bias. Our Criminal Code only has three sections pertaining to hate (e.g., Section 318, Advocating genocide; Section 319, Public incitement of hatred; and Section 320, Warrant of seize) and none of them refer to the phrase "hate crime." So, to get back to the original question, how would we count "hate crimes" in the context of criminal justice?

ML: We have certainly complicated this, and that is OK—important issues are often complicated! I think most of us would agree with the idea that hate and hate crime—however we may want to define it—are bad things, and they ought not to happen. And when they do happen, then we ought to do something about it. This brings me to the question: Bearing in mind all the very real difficulties we find when trying to conceptualize what is categorized as hate crime, is there merit in the desire to measure or track it at all? Do we want to be able to say hate crime is getting worse and here is how we know this?

MM: I think this conversation would be easier if we were just talking about bicycle theft, and it makes sense for us to ask the question: Is bicycle theft going up or down or remaining the same? But since it is about the very contentious issue of hatred, hate crime, motivation of crimes through bias, or crimes motivated by hate, then it becomes a much more contentious question. We will talk more about this issue especially as it pertains to race and racism or racialization in chapter 8: Race.

ML: So far, one of the points I take away from our conversation is how reliant the very idea of counting crime is on the definitions that are created and employed by the criminal legal system. In many ways it is criminal law that creates the boxes that the disparate, complicated, and messy events of everyday life that we call crime are sorted into. In actuality, it is the activities of the police, courts, and corrections, which are part of the criminal legal system, that are documented. It is these documents that serve as the main way we count crime. This is important because it is a window into understanding how we, as a society, respond to crime with our criminal justice systems. Importantly, the justice system provides the "legitimate" means through which we count crime, whereas, in comparison, alternative ways of understanding, measuring, and responding to criminalized issues are readily dismissed. For example, police might use resources to investigate and document bicycle theft one year but not the next. That policy change would alter the number of bicycle thefts counted and could be interpreted incorrectly to show that the thefts have decreased from one year to the next.

I think we should be extremely critical about the methods we use to count crime. We do not need to reject them out of hand as being biased or problematic—although there is a lot of that to it—but we should understand that measurement methods reveal things to us while at the same time obscuring them. Most people are familiar with the concept of a "crime rate," and this is often used in media discussions as a substitute for just saying how much crime is taking place. But the unspoken and unproven assumption of the crime rate is that it is somehow possible to measure crime like you would measure liquid in a beaker. It is like saying, OK, according to our measuring cup we have thirty litres of crime this year and that is down/up from last year. That tends to be the way the concept is used, but that is not what the crime rate shows at all.

The crime rate really does not measure crime, which we have already problematized as a concept; rather, it measures the activities of the police. It measures questions of reporting, recording, and relative trends for that process. On the one hand, it is a particularly useful measure because it provides insight into what police organizations are doing, what they are prioritizing, and what kinds of issues police are likely to follow up on. It measures the kinds of things people are likely to report to the police because most police activity is still responsive to public reports. On the other hand, the statistics around crime rates and the crime severity index[4] may be highly useful, but not in the way we might initially assume because they have not accurately provided a true measure of crime—a concept that we have already indicated is nebulous and socially constructed. In this regard, if you step back, it does seem bizarre that we could say crime is a social construction but then assume it can be accurately measured like a physical object. The term "crime rate" is used precisely to evoke that kind of scientific certainty or statistical clarity.

MM: I agree that it is useful to be able to measure what is happening in the real world using mathematical measurement. But you have shown that the way we are currently doing it is also deceptive because the crime rate does not measure crimes that are unreported or unknown. What about murder? Can we successfully count or measure how many murders are occurring in a given country and how that murder rate can be compared with the murder rate of another country? Such comparative analysis is useful for showing whether one country is doing as well, or not as well, as another country. What are your thoughts about things like the usefulness of the murder rate as a form of empirical measurement of a specific crime?

ML: The homicide rate ends up being one of those statistics that media and policymakers tend to focus on as a bellwether or as a general indicator of public safety. At the end of every year, in December, news media outlets begin to feature the kind of end-of-year stories that focus on the crime trends for the past year, and these often focus on the homicide rate and whether it has gone up or down. It is presented as a demonstration of whether we are safe as a society. But as an indicator of general public safety it is problematic for a couple of reasons. I will start by saying it is an interesting measure because we tend to find that homicide statistics are more accurate than other kinds of crime statistics. In part, the severity of the crime means they are more likely to be reported than, let us say, the theft of my bicycle. You are going to find that you are getting closer to an accurate representation of social experience with your homicide stats than you are with some other kinds of crime. In this regard, there is a value in that comparison both year to year and region to region. But homicide is exceedingly rare as a phenomenon—and thank goodness for that—even though so many people come into criminology and are interested in murder, serial killing, and things of this nature. I mean, it is extraordinarily rare as a phenomenon and accounts for such a small percentage of overall crime. You could have a situation in which people became demonstrably less safe in a city over a given year for a variety of reasons that might have to do with things like homelessness, poverty, addictions, and/or the current toxic drugs crisis, but they would not command the same attention as the homicide rate. Homicide has less impact on public safety than these other more chronic issues but commands greater attention.

So, there are a variety of things that massively and negatively impact public safety, but if these all occur during a year when there were, for example, three less homicides in the city as compared to the previous year, the decline in your homicide rate can then be misrepresented as the city getting safer. It also works the other way around. You could have a situation where people's lived experience of safety and fear of crime has improved, but if there are several homicides in that same place, then public safety is understood to be compromised because safety is understood through the lens of homicide. I think homicide statistics can be useful, but we must also put that information into context. We must ask what this is showing us and what it is not showing us. One of the things we do not find in homicide statistics is any question of causation or the underlying contributing factors. These numbers are often decontextualized, and that makes them problematic and inaccurate as a window onto overall safety and security.

MM: Our discussion of homicide, causation, and statistics makes me think about an alternative way we can use official statistical measurements as a form of critique. That is, although statistics can be misleading, they are also useful in demonstrating the limitations of the system. For example, we know that Indigenous Peoples and people of colour are overrepresented in their contact with police services and rates of incarceration in Canada. That is, their contact with police and corrections is disproportionately high in relation to their population size. Official statistics can be used to show, in a critical manner, how the system is perhaps biased, unfair, or unequal because it is statistically improbable that you would have such a disproportionate statistic. In this regard, numbers and counting are useful when you can use the official numbers to demonstrate to the public, or to police services, that there is something wrong in their criminal justice practice and that there is something unequal or unfair in the conduct of justice in Canada. What are your thoughts about that?

ML: That is a great point, and these are important concepts regarding overrepresentation and disproportionality. One of the things we can start with here is acknowledging that our crime statistics are telling us something. But the question is, what are they showing us when we are talking about this skewed proportionality? They are clearly showing us that there is a systemic basis to a trend. If you have a group that represents—according to census data—5 percent of the population but 52 percent of incarcerated people in a given jurisdiction, that shows something is going on and that it is a remarkable outlier. This is what is meant by "overrepresentation." It means there are far more people represented than should be given the small size of the population. If you make up only a tiny fraction of the population but the bulk of the prison population, then your demographic is overrepresented. Put another way, if we take as a starting point the idea that every person over the age of twelve is understood to have the capacity to commit a criminal offence, then we might expect the statistics on offending to roughly match the demographic makeup of the population. However, we find massive disparities regarding involvement with the legal system based on age, ethnicity, gender, geography, and income level. This is what criminologists are referring to when we speak about disproportionality and overrepresentation.

MM: I agree. For example, we know that Indigenous and Black people are statistically overrepresented in their contact with police and end up incarcerated in prisons at a much higher rate than the average population.[5] Such statistical imbalances illustrate the existence of social inequality. When trends have that kind of disproportionate representation, it gives us an opportunity to start asking questions, like: What has caused this? What is the explanation for this? How do our systems produce such unbalanced outcomes? It makes us think of the criminal justice system as if it were an assembly line in a system producing specific unbalanced outcomes. It takes in raw material like social inequality and social conflict and it outputs specific outcomes, one of which is incarceration. And if a certain population experiences that disproportionately, that is reason for further investigation. However, we should also remember that we do not collect information about everything, and we should be wary of thinking it is an adequate trace of all things unequal in society and policing. Our crime statistics are not a complete capture of the way our legal system functions.

ML: Another issue in Canada that has been very contentious for over twenty years is the issue of the collection, or lack thereof, of race-based data around criminal justice processes. Communities of colour have said: "Hey, we are disproportionately stopped by police. My lived reality and everyday experience include being stopped, harassed, questioned or street checked." And these are the communities of colour who testify to this fact. In this instance of data collection, the decision not to collect this on-the-ground information is a failure of the state. And there might be a prejudice of data collection in this instance because anecdotes and first-person testimonials are understood to be qualitative data and do not have the same traction with policymakers as quantitative data. And yet, if we do not collect information about these trends, then it becomes exceedingly difficult to unpack how they are unfolding on a day-to-day basis. In terms of statistical counting, it is a quandary because the incarceration rate is all we have. What happens before, or leads to, incarceration becomes a blind spot. The racial disproportionality tells us something is going on that requires further examination. We must step back and think about what we are counting and what we are not counting.

MM: Yes, without the hard data preferred by policymakers, our state agencies and government bodies cannot propose the future changes necessary to address systemic problems. By not reporting existing racial disproportions we may be willfully disregarding the way social stratification has been congealed in the criminal justice system. We may be concealing its systemic problems regarding race and bias. It is a conundrum because we know our methods of counting are flawed, but we also rely on that same (flawed) data to hold government to account. Are there other ways our counting methods are flawed or inexact?

ML: Most of our crime statistics tend to correspond to what we might call street-based interpersonal violence or street-based property crime. We do not collect official crime statistics on things like injuries and deaths in the workplace through negligence, as pointed out by Jeffrey Reiman in his classic book *The Rich Get Richer and the Poor Get Prison*.[6] Many of the major forms of social harm are not measured through crime statistics. This bias is reflected in both the uniform reporting system (Uniform Crime Reporting, or UCR) that gives us the crime rates and in the crime severity index. In our recurring General Social Survey on Victimization, we ask questions about critical issues like family violence, perceptions of safety on the street, assault, and vehicle theft, but we do not ask any questions about what we might consider white-collar or corporate crime. These absences allow us to think about what statistics are telling us while also inviting us to interrogate what we choose not to count.

MM: Just to follow up on that thought, we also know that the burden of proof, or the level of proof, for a criminal conviction is often higher than the burden of proof in civil court. That is, it may be easier to get a conviction in civil court than in criminal court. So, a criminal case might not progress to court, but a victim could proceed with a civil charge. Thus, the case never appears as a criminal case, nor will there ever be any criminal sentences given or recorded. That is another way some "crimes" might be undercounted. Another instance where this undercounting might happen is in regards to white-collar or financial crimes. White-collar crimes are commonly dealt with in civil court as plaintiffs seek financial reparation for damages—not prison time—and these transgressions are not recorded as criminal offences. We might even rhetorically ask: Are white-collar crimes even "crimes" since they are not addressed through the Criminal Code or criminal prosecution and are instead "civil" disputes?

ML: This is a good opportunity for us to note that the streaming of cases into criminal vs. civil court is not as straightforward as it may seem. Many activities that are or could be criminalized are dealt with in civil court, with one party suing another for damages. Sometimes, this takes place in addition to the criminal prosecution of offences. For example, if a corporation or organization is responsible for creating a toxic work environment that exposes employees to sexual harassment and assault, that organization could be subject to both criminal investigation and individual or class-action lawsuits. Perhaps counterintuitively, it is often the civil proceeding that ends up being the main forum for justice, and financial reparations for damages in these cases and the criminal portion of the charges are dropped or never filed in the first place. This is something we saw recently in the case of a major class-action settlement by the RCMP in response to a systemic pattern of sexual misconduct against women members.

To introduce another layer of complexity, we can point to practices such as "civil forfeiture," which police and prosecutors use to confiscate property that they allege to be linked to the proceeds of crime, without necessarily having to secure a criminal conviction beforehand. All of which is to say that while our primary statistics around crime are attached to the activities of police and the criminal courts, these present only a partial picture of how offences and harms are processed through our legal systems. As the examples above illustrate, many cases that we might think are "criminal" are rerouted or processed through noncriminal channels.

MM: I like how the examples you have given bring up the issue of sexual misconduct in the context of civil cases because it reminds us of the undercounting of sexual offences or sexual assault. What are your thoughts?

ML: Sexual assault ends up being one of the most important issues or topics to use as a vehicle for exploring the counting of crime and the challenges that arise with it. With any kind of offence things only become statistics when they are detected by, and then reported and recorded by, police organizations because in Canada our official crime statistics are police-reported crime statistics. Crimes occur all the time that do not come to the attention of police and therefore are not part of our official crime statistics. The police do not count it because the public does not report it, and this in turn means that it is not counted by the Canadian Centre for Justice Statistics as part of the routine UCR survey. For example, there are consensual or transactional offences where it would be rare for people to report themselves or other parties involved to police. In such a scenario, I could sell illicit drugs, which are prohibited, but it is not likely I or my customer would report to the police. So, there is a lot that does not appear in our crime statistics, and this is a reflection of how and what they measure.

But let us come back to sexual assaults. We know through a lot of research that part of the traumatizing nature of sexual assault is the perception and very real risk of revictimization through contact with the criminal justice system. The victim must relive the assault through the police reporting and legal processing of the case. The lack of an effective response by police and legal services demonstrates that people are often made to relive trauma. The very reporting and the litigation itself become a disincentive to report such crimes, and so we have lower rates of reporting sexual assault.

Additionally, when people do report sexual assaults, they run into a situation where they may not be believed by police organizations. We have seen this for years, and in Canada some recent groundbreaking investigative reporting has documented the depth and scope of the problem. The research was done by journalist Robyn Doolittle for *The Globe and Mail* newspaper in the series titled Unfounded.[7] Doolittle systematically investigated how police organizations across Canada—in every province and territory—responded to people coming forward with allegations of having been victims of sexual assault. She found that whether a claim of sexual assault was treated as legitimate, and therefore recorded in statistics, had much more to do with the police organization and geography than any factor related to the crime itself. In other words, people were believed, or not believed, based on the cultural and organizational values and experiences of police organizations and not by the strength or truthfulness of their claim.

That tells us something. It tells us that statistics have this veneer of objectivity that comes with numbers. It is one of the reasons they are so valued by policymakers. The numbers appear to result from objective raw data and a detached counting process, without political or social pressures. In the context of sexual assault, for something to become "raw data" it must first go through this deeply interpretive process that is infused with a complex set of politics around gender, patriarchy, misogyny, organizational culture, rape myths, police culture, etc. before something becomes a number; before an experience is translated into data. That is a very instructive example for which we now have some fantastic recent research.

The last thing I will say on this is that Doolittle's research was so impactful and so effective that Statistics Canada, which coordinates the data around crime rates and crime severity, changed its mandatory reporting practices around these phenomena after the report came out. There have been attempts to address this serious gap in recording and a lot of police organizations were required to take action to change the way they dealt with this issue.

MM: I could not agree with you more about the question of sexual assault, the problem of reporting, and the lack of confidence in the legal/social system that many women might have when confronted by sexual assault and what to do in response. One of the last things that most women want to do is approach police services because they fear not being believed. It is not surprising that they may be doubtful of the usefulness of the law and its application. As you mention, the victim can be revictimized by having to tell their story again, in addition to the risk of not being believed by police services. In cases of sexual assault there may not be physical evidence, physical proof, or witnesses. All these factors would affect accurate measurement and counting of sexual assault.

ML: So, I think we can conclude by noting that there are a variety of reasons we seek to measure crime and that we have developed, implemented, and continued to use a variety of specific techniques that get at things like crime rates and crime severity. These measurements have their uses. But perhaps the main theme we have explored here is the idea that measurements are always complex and partial and must be understood in context. There is truly no way to measure crime as though we were measuring liquid in a beaker. Nonetheless, the measurements we do use are meaningful in their own way, if we understand what they are—and are not—showing us. To return to the example of bicycle theft, we can gather statistics about bicycles that have been reported stolen in a given jurisdiction over a given period of time. But these statistics will tell us nothing about bicycles that were stolen but *not* reported, and more importantly, they will tell us very little about the reasons bicycles may be stolen. Rather than thinking about official measurements of crime as *answers* to important questions about prevalence, trends, and causation, it is more helpful to treat them as starting points for asking questions about these things.

Discussion Questions:

1. One of the ideas discussed in this chapter is that official government crime measures like the URC survey do not actually measure crime; they measure the activities of the criminal legal system. Explain what this means and discuss its implications for our understanding of the nature and prevalence of crime in Canada.
2. What kinds of illegal activity do you think are most—and least—likely to come to the attention of the criminal legal system? How can we explain this, and what are some implications?
3. Consider the chart on the next page from the Canadian Centre for Justice Statistics. It shows police-reported crime rates, measured over a period of sixty years. What are three important observations that we could make about the trends shown here?

Police-reported crime rates, Canada, 1962 to 2020

Rate per 100,000 population

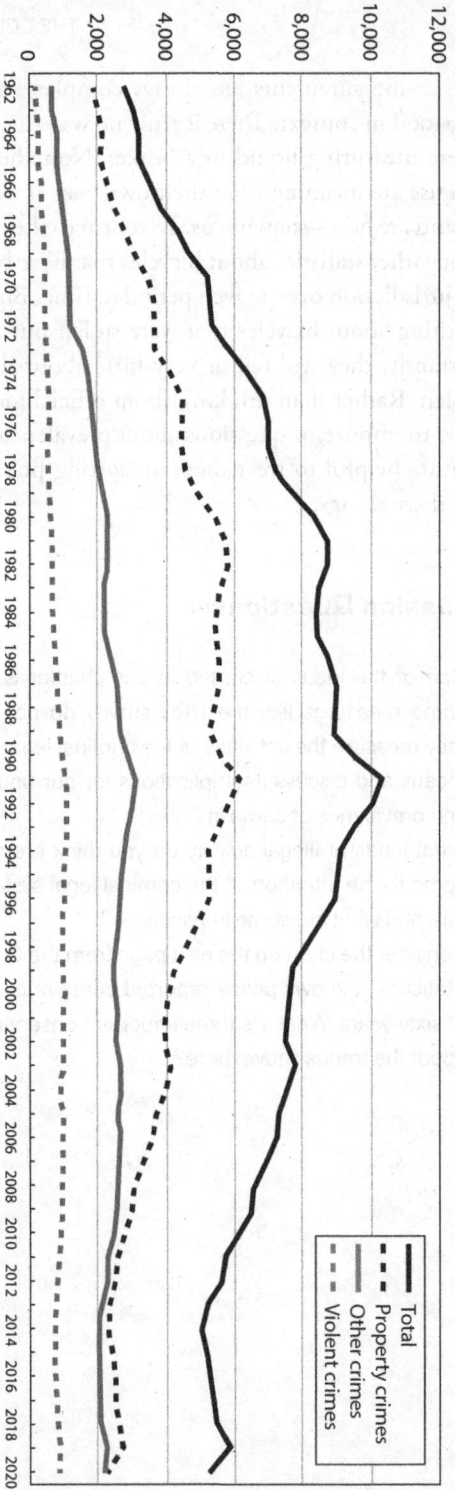

Legend:
- Total
- Property crimes
- Other crimes
- Violent crimes

Note: Information presented in this chart represents data from the Uniform Crime Reporting (UCR1) Aggregate Survey, and permits historical comparisons back to 1962. New definitions of crime categories were introduced in 2009 and are only available in the new format back to 1998. As a result, numbers in this chart will not match data released in the new UCR2 format. Specifically, the definition of violent crime has been expanded. In addition, UCR1 includes some different offences in the "other crimes" category. Populations are based upon July 1st estimates from Statistics Canada, Centre for Demography.

Source: Statistics Canada, Canadian Centre for Justice and Community Safety Statistics, Uniform Crime Reporting Survey.

Source: Greg Moreau, "Police-Reported Crime Statistics in Canada, 2020," *Juristat,*
Canadian Centre for Justice and Community Safety Statistics, 2021, gc.ca.

CHAPTER 6
Consent

In this chapter, we examine the concept of consent and how it relates to our society and its institutions. While there may be some debate about whether we truly give our consent to be governed, our institutions of justice are predicated on the assumption that we, as legal subjects, consent to our laws and are therefore responsible for complying with them. Further, whether a given action is considered lawful or unlawful is often determined by whether the parties involved consent. The core discussion in this chapter tackles the difference between tacit, deliberate, coerced, and manufactured forms of consent. We ground this discussion in the debate between John Locke and Thomas Hobbes about limiting individual freedoms through a social contract; a social contract that produces and make possible forms of social safety and prosperity that are otherwise unattainable. In so doing, we interrogate how police powers and the criminal justice system all hinge on concepts of consent.

Mike Larsen (ML): There are several concepts that are well recognized as being standard and a part of introductory discussions about criminology that include questions of justice, norms, and deviance, but we have added the concept of consent to this to this cluster of issues. Why do you think consent is an important topic for us to consider as part of this discussion?

Michael C. K. Ma (MM): Consent is important to the discussion regarding the criminal justice system because we consent to being governed by laws. As citizens, we consent to the will or authority of a government to establish and invoke rules and regulations that curtail or control our freedoms. In so doing, we are consenting to losing some of our liberty or ultimate freedoms. Our consent allows the state to limit our freedom to do whatever we want. We consent to limits. We accept these limits with our eyes wide open—or so it is assumed.

ML: I wonder if we do in fact consent to these limits, or if perhaps our society and its institutions and laws are organized around the assumption, or maybe even the fiction, that we consent? What do you think?

MM: I think we have already come across our first roadblock before we can even get this conversation started. I think individual citizens, residents, or the general population are not individually asked to give consent to being governed. Their consent, and indeed yours or mine, is already tacitly understood to exist simply because we are not rebelling, fighting against, or resisting these rules. In this sense, I understand our consent not as deliberate consent that is freely given after consultation but rather as an unspoken consent or maybe even consent that is arrived at through sheer inertia. We comply more than we consent. For example, we may be asked to elect a party to run government, but a voter can only pick among the existing choices. That kind of sounds like coerced consent. On the one hand, the ideal of consent refers to an agreement that is arrived at rationally and deliberately and without coercion, and it implies that the subject has the potential to say no. On the other hand, the opposite of consent is coercion, and it is arrived at through influence and pressure to accept someone else's will. It is achieved without free and open consent. Consent is also connected to our understanding and practice of freedom, and that is probably most well-known publicly in relation to our *Charter of Rights and Freedoms*, but that might be something to discuss later. So, that is why consent is at the heart of our social rules, political conduct, and laws.

ML: That is provocative. I wonder if we could then conclude that the absence of pervasive resistance or outright rebellion is interpreted as the presence of widespread social consensus.

MM: Yes, the question of consent and resistance is very complex, and it comes with a deep history. But let us back up a bit and sketch out the broad outlines of the debate. There is a theoretical debate in Western philosophical thought between John Locke and Thomas Hobbes in which they represent the view that all societies have an implied social contract that both limits and ensures our entitlements, privileges, and/ or rights.[1] The social contract is a "consent" that people in a society freely give to an external group to form government and to govern society in a way the benefits everyone. The framing of this debate proposes that we give up certain freedoms and we consent to being ruled by a set of rules or laws or regulations because it guarantees us greater safety and prosperity. It is assumed that agreeing to these limits will lead to a more cohesive social order. For example, I consent to the law that neither my neighbour nor I can kill each other. I consent to a law that makes it illegal to do so. The law offers each person some type of social protection from violence. But then this means I am no longer "free" to do whatever I want, whenever I want. I might also consent to the rule that we are not allowed to steal someone else's stuff, and other people consent also not to steal my stuff. This scenario presents a neutral or balanced state where we respect each other's property and live with equally restricted freedoms. In cases of both violence or theft, people are consenting to limit their freedoms, consenting to an authority, and consenting to being governed. That is what is important about consent in the context of our conversation.

ML: It seems that a key point is the idea that we, by virtue of being members of society, are understood to consent to and abide by certain rules and norms, to live in society, and to interact with each other. By extension, we are also assumed to consent to the existence of government and all the institutions and practices that uphold rules and respond to their violations.

MM: Yes, and it is the "response to their violations" that is of particular interest to us. But before we tackle the question of violations or theoretical considerations of freedom, we might simply ask: Are we really free to agree or disagree to the current social norms we are born into? Did anyone ask us what our society should be before we were born into it? Are we really giving our free and uncoerced consent when we obey the customs and laws of our "chosen" society? It is like someone has built a ship and set sail, and we are asked to consent to its existence and direction after it has left port. I guess if we do not like the ship or direction, then we are free to jump off the ship and into the water as a legitimate way of withholding our consent. But then of course you would also just drown. We can take this narrative framework and apply it to the issue of law and punishment. For example, if transgressing a rule or law leads to being caught, charged, sentenced, and sent to jail, then the question of consent could be understood to be contradictory. You consent to being tried and you hope to be found innocent, but ultimately you consent to being incarcerated even if you believe yourself to be innocent. So, in this case, the question of consent is not really a complete and utter unproblematic consent but rather a kind of surrender to the system—a surrender to a system that you have virtually no control over. Once you consent to being arrested, then the policing system, the court of law, and the system of incarceration are like these runaway trains that you cannot get off. Even if you consented to being a party to this legal system by not resisting arrest, you never really consented to a whole series of legal and punitive systems that you have no knowledge of. This is a ship from which you cannot jump. I am not saying that I do not believe in law or free will, only that our choices might already be constrained before we are asked to comply or consent.

ML: I like the way you use the analogy of the ship. It invites us to think about both the agency of the passengers, as you say, and also the inertia of big and complex systems—ships that have a set course and lots of momentum behind them. In many ways, the challenge of law reform is similar to the challenge of changing the course of a massive ship that is already underway. But clarify this one thing for me: Are you suggesting that because offenders object to going to prison this then makes the institution illegitimate?

MM: Not exactly. I am glad you are asking for clarification. I can understand how it can be confusing. I am not saying that just because prisoners do not want to go to jail, the system is corrupt or wrong; rather, I am making two points. First, I am arguing that since all or most incarceration involves coercion, it illustrates that our system of prison as punishment is based on the removal of a person's freedom to choose. Second, I am conceptually challenging whether consent—in its purest form—is ever really given in the context of the criminal justice system as it currently exists. No one who is "trapped" in a system ever wants to be there and most feel wrongly done by the system. They hate the system. They do not consent to the way things are.

ML: Nowhere is this more apparent to me than in the documented examples—and there are many—of wrongful convictions. In fact, one of the cruellest aspects of being wrongfully convicted is that because the system is assumed to be operating accurately and effectively, a person's protestations of innocence after a conviction are interpreted by the system as indicators of remorselessness. People who are wrongfully convicted may be released from prison earlier if they consent to the judgment and go along with the process. Consenting to the injustice can shorten the sentence! It would in fact be consenting to a lie or consenting to dishonesty to get a better outcome.

MM: I think your comment follows with a notion of manufactured consent. It supports the notion that we have been captured by a system not of our own choosing—which troubles the idea of consent. What do you think?

ML: What I find interesting about this idea is that we often consider this kind of consent to arise from the inherent reason of individuals and our ability to understand the world we live in and therefore to consent to certain principles and practices. However, there are other scholars who really focus on the idea that consent is manufactured. They suggest it does not arise organically from a free collection of individuals who rationally or dispassionately consider their social conditions and then come to the same conclusion. Rather, they argue that consent is constantly produced, maintained, and reproduced by institutions and that people are often induced or encouraged to consent to arrangements that uphold and normalize significant inequalities. Edward S. Herman and Noam Chomsky's work on manufacturing consent through the news media is particularly instructive here, but I think in the context of criminology there is the idea that police as institutions are actively and directly engaged in producing the consent of communities and in treating those who consent as a resource to be maintained and drawn upon.[2] This brings me to this idea that rather than starting with a concept of active or rational consent, we should instead examine and unpack the institutions and laws or sociopolitical conditions that produce, or shape, consent and examine how institutions play a role in seeding the field for consent.

MM: Yes, and you are implying that consent is in fact not all that freely given or informed. Or that it is not just a notion of "rational consent" because there are many instances of tacit or unspoken consent. For example, in the context of a fight in a bar, if someone struck you and you did not consent to being struck, then that could be seen as illegal. It can be seen as assault. Whereas if you are in a boxing ring with an opponent it would be tacitly understood that you have consented to a "fair fight" with each other under the circumstance of sport. The consent between two friends boxing or wrestling may seem self-evident, but consent can also be much less self-evident. Consent can take on a different flavour when we think about the way police services might use consent to breach the inherent rights people are supposed to possess. For example, we all know that we have the right to privacy, but if a police officer knocks on your door and says, "May I come in?," and you say yes, then you are consenting to the officer searching your home. You may or may not understand that you have consented to search, but that is how the law works because you have now given consent. It does not matter if you understand the meaning of consent or the law. And you may not want the officer to enter, but you also did not know that you had the choice to refuse the request.

ML: This brings up the importance of context when it comes to considering consent. In the scenario you present of the police officer knocking at the door, or at a roadside asking, "Can I look in your trunk?," or any of these other kinds of circumstances, the idea that there is a question implies that the person being asked has the authority to make a decision one way or the other. But in practice, that decision may, or may not, be informed by an understanding of law and is likely to be informed by a perception of the power dynamics at work in the interaction. The decision to either uphold, lay claim to, or grant concession around one's rights is, on the one hand, consensual, but on the other hand, coercive and shaped by considerations other than strict consent. And this is very much built into—as you point out—our laws, for example, around assault, sexual assault, or mischief. The Criminal Code is infused with the word "consent." Let us consider the offence of "Publication, etc., of an intimate image without consent":

> 162.1 (1) Everyone who knowingly publishes, distributes, transmits, sells, makes available or advertises an intimate image of a person knowing that the person depicted in the image did not give their consent to that conduct, or being reckless as to whether or not that person gave their consent to that conduct, is guilty
>
> (a) of an indictable offence and liable to imprisonment for a term of not more than five years; or
>
> (b) of an offence punishable on summary conviction.

Note that whether a given action—that is, the distribution of an intimate image of another person—is a crime hinges entirely on whether the act was consensual. This, and many similar offences, show that consent is very much at the heart of our legal codes. Consent is part of context. And one further point is that this underscores the idea—as we have been discussing—that deviance is not a characteristic of acts or behaviours in and of themselves; rather, deviance arises from the context in which actions occur. The same behaviour in the presence or absence of consent will have very different social implications and can either be considered normal or deviant. Another familiar example is the crime of theft; that is, the act of taking something from someone else without their permission. If I were to give you my favourite coffee cup, and you were to accept it, this would be a gift and regarded as a friendly and social gesture. If you take my coffee cup without my permission, this is of course the crime of theft. So, in this regard, consent is very much at the heart of the way law treats property.

MM: This notion of theft is the clearest example of consent in relationship to possession or dispossession of someone's property. When a person is given permission to take or to receive something it completely alters the act of possession. It is the act of consent that changes the act of giving or taking.

ML: Thinking about permission as a synonym for consent invites us to consider how the concept of consent is also central to our approach to sexual assault and related offences, and indeed to our broader understanding of intimate relationships and autonomy. The Canadian legal system makes use of an "affirmative" consent standard, which means that individuals engaged in sexual activity bear the responsibility of ensuring that their partners consent to that activity.[3] The absence of a "no" is not interpreted as an indication of consent. In other words, no means no, but the lack of a "yes" will likely be regarded by the courts also as a "no." The law also takes into consideration the important issue of capacity—that is, whether age or impairment caused by substances or circumstances makes it impossible for a party to consent to sexual activity. As Robyn Doolittle, the journalist who led *The Globe and Mail*'s Unfounded investigation into police responses to sexual assault complaints in Canada, notes that the legal framework governing sexual assault in Canada is widely regarded as progressive, having been subject to forty years of active reforms.[4]

MM: So, I think this is such an important topic to bring up in relationship to the idea of consent because we know that in this day and age the question of sexual consent is paramount, especially for university students or younger people who are first entering into relationships or who are just first becoming sexually active. The question of consent is very complicated when it pertains to sexual activity. And yet it is not really clarified by our discussion about consent because the way we are talking about consent in relation to sexual activity as assault is much more in the realm of the legal. The way we experience our negotiation of sexual activity with someone else—where we give or withhold our consent—is not experienced as it is in a courtroom or with legal representation; rather, it is experienced in the grey area of interpersonal negotiation. And therein lies the problem of trying to tease out whether consent was given in the context of sexual activity. What do you think about that, Mike?

ML: On the one hand, I agree that consent in the context of intimacy and relationships can be messy and complicated. On the other hand, I think it is important to note that a great deal of coercive and harmful behaviour has historically been enabled by the notion that consent is a vague and undefinable thing. In the current context, there are movements both within and outside the legal field to push for a clearer definition of consent, one that emphasizes the requirements for affirmative and ongoing consent. So, I am cautious about the implications of emphasizing the complexity of consent. From a certain perspective, if consent is unclear in a given situation, then it simply is not present in that situation. If it is not clear, then it is a "no."

You make an important point about the challenge of using the letter of the law as a lens through which we examine a topic like consent. We should take an interest in how these key concepts are operationalized or acted upon by institutions. However, this is not to say that the law is perfectly clear or that it "works" properly for victims. The persistence of stereotypes and "rape myths" throughout the system contributes to underreporting and compounded trauma. This is a good example of the important distinction between "law on the books" and "law in action." It is one thing to note that the principle of affirmative consent is embedded in our legal system, and something else entirely to consider how consent is interpreted, negotiated, and made meaningful in everyday circumstances. We might ask: Does the way our legal system approaches consent protect the interests of victims?

MM: When two people are alone and one of them does not give consent, I am not sure if the law can act in a very protective way at that moment. And that illustrates the limitations of the law in the conjunctural moment of someone not giving consent by saying "no." So, although consent is absolutely vital in any relationship—as we have described throughout this book—and in contracts, or in our relationship to our various social contracts, it is not necessarily a protective concept in the moment of your interaction with someone to whom you express "no." It points to the limitations of the law as a protective instrument of society. It may not protect you in the moment of the act, nor in the moment of legal deliberation after the act.

ML: This is also an important example of why researchers studying crim-inological topics need to situate them in relation to the broader socio-historical context. How we understand and respond to sexual assault in Canada today is interconnected with broader shifts in how we think about gender roles, intimacy, sex, autonomy, and consent, and these shifts are in turn connected to changes in public education, popular culture, and social movements. Consider, for example, the transform-ative impact the #MeToo movement has had on whether and how we talk about sexual harassment, power, and consent. Through coordinated grassroots social media activities and solidarity actions, this movement has shed light on women's pervasive and systemic experiences of non-consensual sexual activity, which range from unwanted and inappropri-ate advances to sexual assault, in work settings and everyday life. It is an example of a large-scale effort to change how we think about and act upon sexual violence.

MM: The notion of consent is not only experienced on the level of the interpersonal—as is the case with sexual assault—or on the microlevel of interaction with police services but can also be understood in rela-tionship to larger state projects like mining. For example, we understand that the Trans Mountain Pipeline goes from Edmonton to Burnaby, but we know that the citizens of Burnaby and even the mayor of Burnaby have resolutely opposed the pipeline. They did not give their consent as a municipality, but the federal government has said that their authority supersedes the municipal authority.[5] Regardless of the lack of consent on the part of the municipal residents, the pipeline has gone through. The pipeline was expanded and built *despite* the organized opposition and active lack of consent of citizens who reside in the jurisdiction where the pipeline is laid.

ML: A more recent example along the same lines is the organized resistance to the logging of old-growth forests at Fairy Creek on Vancouver Island.[6] In this situation, police actively enforced an injunction that supports the rights and interests of a logging company by arresting dozens of people who did not consent to the destruction of these ancient trees. The private logging rights held by the corporation were not secured through the public consent of the people. The debates and the contentious politics around these and other extractive industry projects have certainly turned on this concept of consent, which is often rephrased as social licence, and I think it is instructive and interesting to consider under what circumstances explicit consent is required. We might ask: Under what circumstances is consent politically or legally beneficial but not strictly required? Under what circumstances is consent implied? That certainly is something that comes up in the context of privacy law and the use of people's personal information. For example, do users of the internet actively consent to being tracked by a website that stores and sells their viewing habits—otherwise known as "data"—or is consent indirectly achieved by trickery and software design? And lastly, under what circumstances is it not possible for someone to consent? Are there acts that are beyond the realm of consent when it comes to questions of crime and deviance? For example, even if two parties are mutually committed to a duel to the death, the criminal law prohibits such an action.

All this shows that consent is not very straightforward and highly contextualized. For example, what about some of the institutions and practices in our society that are taken for granted and just assumed to be part of the status quo or the way things are? I am thinking in particular about wage labour. People sign contracts to enter relationships of employment, and those contracts are based on the idea of consent and the right of the worker to freely consent to the conditions of work. But people can also be working in conditions where the alternative is unemployment, lack of food, and lack of housing. Can we consider those kinds of ultimatums consensual or arrived at without threat or coercion? That is, destitution or unemployment looms over a person's "freedom" to choose. What do you think?

MM: That is such a great question. There is quite a lot of immoral and even illegal behaviour surrounding the system of wage labour, but it is never framed as such. In the context of wage labour, we know that it is not considered immoral or illegal to pay someone a wage that is below the living wage. It is not illegal to pay someone a poverty wage. Rather, it is absolutely legal, and in some respects, even morally defendable and smart from a business perspective to secure consent from workers to work for a wage that cannot fully pay their bills. It is a smart employer who pays *the least for the most* work. We might understand that it is illegal, or immoral, to steal, and yet it is not immoral or illegal for an employer to pay someone a wage that might be stealing their labour at a cut-rate price, or for an employer to not properly compensate a worker for their labour at a "fair" rate. So, in this context, it is generally assumed that the worker has entered this labour relation with their eyes wide open and consented to being paid a sub–living wage. In this context, the employer has lawfully sought the consent of the worker in the form of a labour contract and has acted lawfully. But as we have stated here, it appears that this relationship is unjust. It is a clear example of the mechanism of consent being used to support an unjust system. In this regard, we might ask: What is the value of "consent" if it is not freely given? What if consent is just an illusion?

ML: Yes, the example of the worker and their consent to the unfair conditions of employment is a perfect illustration of the illusion of consent. Perhaps we can talk about a very specific kind of work that is often the subject of criminological interest: sex work. At the risk of oversimplifying, we could say that one of the key debates around sex work has been whether it is possible for adults to consent to the exchange of sexual services for compensation and whether society, at a broad level, consents to or permits such transactions to take place. This is an interesting area where questions of politics and morality start to cluster around the conversation about consent.

MM: That is a great question. A key debate surrounding sex work, or prostitution, is the question: Is it really legitimate work? Because some critics would argue it is a form of exploitation and not a true form of labour or paid work. It brings up the question of consent and whether a sex worker freely chooses their work. Do they consent to this lawful act—because according to the Criminal Code sex work is not illegal—or has the sex worker been coerced or forced into a job, and conditions, not of their own choosing? But let us put the question of whether sex work is "real" work aside for a moment and address the primary question: Is the decision between two consenting adults to have sex with one another lawful or not lawful? In the context of dating, no one would bat an eye that two consenting adults who previously did not know each other could easily and lawfully have consensual sex with one another. For illustration we can think of dating apps or hook-up apps that people use today. These are legal and consensual meetings. However, in the case of sex work, once the exchange of money enters the equation, the state responds with the creation of law that says that type of consenting behaviour is not lawful. The law recently changed in the last few years to focus more on the criminalization of the person purchasing sex. So, the law—as it currently stands—is that the sex worker can consent to the sexual meeting and not be out of order or engaged in something unlawful but the person buying the sex is out of order or is conducting illegal behaviour. If the framing of law is put aside for a moment, we can understand that both adults are absolutely consenting in this relationship, and in this sense, we could agree that there is no harm happening. But if there is no harm happening when two adults consent to a sex act between each other, then why has the state prohibited this consenting behaviour? It is because money is exchanged, and our legal system understands this addition of money as deforming the given consent to such a degree that it becomes immoral and unlawful.

ML: This is a good opportunity for us to acknowledge that the prohibition of sex work has historically not been predicated on the belief that it is nonconsensual. It has not even really, until recently, been predicated on the allegation that these acts are harmful. Historically, sex work has been criminalized *despite* its consensual nature because it is regarded as offensive to a very specific but dominant system of moral authority. It has been framed as sinful, degrading, corrupting, and above all, a departure from a vision of sexuality that is closely connected to a particular narrative of family and monogamy.

MM: You are correct. Even the words we use to describe the act are quite telling. In many scholarly and nonscholarly contexts, we have moved from using the word "prostitution" to the words "sex work." And we have done so because we want to move the conversation away from a framing of exploitation to one of legitimate work.[7] In this regard, language matters and is in fact quite political. Using the term "sex work" moves the discussion or the debate into the area of legitimate or lawful work—even though we know prostitution has always been lawful and was never an illegal activity under Canadian law. In this respect you are right; much of our hesitancy about understanding sex work as lawful work is wrapped up with our moral hang-ups or perhaps even Victorian understanding of sex and sexual behaviour.[8]

ML: So, to summarize, the relationship between legality and consent is not straightforward. Another good example is the treatment of drugs by the criminal legal system. The dominant approach to addressing the use, enjoyment, and harms associated with certain substances throughout the twentieth and into the twenty-first centuries has been prohibition. Society has criminalized these substances and directed law enforcement resources to suppress them. We are familiar with concepts like "the war on drugs" and the idea of a black market in narcotics. I am fascinated by this because the very existence of a "market" implies consensual transactions between buyers and sellers. What can we say about the idea of consent when it pertains to substances and their use?

MM: Before we get into the idea of consent as it pertains to buying and selling drugs let us answer a more basic question. What if my friend offers me a controlled substance such as cocaine in the privacy of my home and I consent to taking it and using it to get high? One can argue that there has not been any harm done because it occurs between two consenting adults. The example of cannabis jumps to mind: in the past it was understood that the sharing of cannabis was an illegal and/or harmful act, but since the Canadian law changed to allow for recreational consumption of cannabis this is no longer the case. The sharing of cannabis is now understood as a lawful recreation and not harmful in the way it was morally framed before the change in law. Before the changing of the law, cannabis was formally treated as harmful, but once the law changed it became a legal recreational substance. It is now controlled in the same way as beer, wine, or spirits. I think that is a very good illustration of the notion of harm and consent in relationship to drug consumption. It begs two questions: (1) Is the substance actually harmful, and (2) how should society control substances it believes to be harmful? But I have just sidestepped your initial question because if we use the example of narcotics—like heroin or fentanyl—then I think the parameters of the question of consent and harm in relation to the buying and selling of drugs become rather different because fentanyl can create harm in ways that cannabis cannot.

ML: I think anyone who studies the history of prohibition and law enforcement as it pertains to drugs will come to the conclusion that our laws have not been informed by an awareness of the harms associated with particular substances. For example, you used the scenario of coming over to my home and being offered beer or wine or spirits. These are all legal but controlled substances, and their production and consumption are regarded as extremely important parts of our province's economy. In fact, we have a wine country in British Columbia and the government does a lot to promote its products. And yet, we know that alcohol is a very dangerous substance that is strongly correlated with a range of harmful outcomes, including violence, impaired driving, birth defects, and addiction. No reasonable analysis could arrive at the conclusion that marijuana has comparably harmful effects when it is consumed, and yet cannabis was the focus of a war on drugs in Canada for many years. The conclusion we can draw here is that legality is not tied to consent when it comes to drugs, nor to harm, but to a range of political and moral calculations. It is even the case that consent is *irrelevant*, from the perspective of the state, where certain substances are concerned. On the one hand, we may be prohibited from using a substance to which we consent but which the government makes illegal (e.g., cannabis before it was legalized). On the other hand, we are allowed to consume a substance, which is known to be harmful (e.g., alcohol), because law and society allow for it.

MM: We should also note that many people in Canada did not consent to cannabis being made a legal recreational substance. So, this brings us back to the original question of consent. If some people did not consent to the legalization of recreational cannabis, then were they coerced into accepting this change in law? And if so, how were they coerced? By coercion I do not mean they were intimidated by police or threatened with violence but rather that their values and wishes, which were once in line with the law, are now no longer reflected by the change in law. Is it possible to understand their compliance or acceptance of an undesired law as something that was not freely given or achieved?

ML: These examples really illustrate the grey areas and complexities related to these issues, and this is a good opportunity for us to return to and reconsider the ideas of a social contract or social consensus that we addressed earlier in the chapter and elsewhere in the book. While the idea of a social contract may be a helpful metaphor for the relationship between people, society, and the state, it would be incorrect to suggest that there is a binding social consensus on many matters of law and morality.

MM: OK, so let us review what we have discussed in relation to consent. So far, we have discussed:

- How consenting to a social contract is a mechanism by which we interact and exist with others so that existence occurs without violence, conflict, or transgression.
- How our interactions with police and other state organizations can be based on our active consent, our implied consent, or the absence of our consent.
- How consent is an intricate part of the law and something that is highly contextualized (for example, in relation to property crimes, substance use, and sexual activity).
- How the state can press ahead with large-scale projects without public consent (e.g., how it has taken on the unpopular Trans Mountain resource extraction project and how the Burnaby municipality has resisted and not given consent to the federal government).

ML: That is a good summary of our discussion. If we want to understand law, deviance, coercion, and consent, we need to consider them in relation to context and social relations. So, consent could seem to be one of the most straightforward, black and white concepts—either you consent or you do not consent—but if we are trying to understand this in the context of a conversation about criminology and justice, then the complexity and the role of power and the social context surrounding consent become an essential part of the conversation.

MM: We should mention that in chapter 8: Criminalizing Inequality and Poverty, we will discuss inequality and poverty. The concept of consent is also useful for examining how people are not asked if they want to be born into conditions of wealth or poverty. That is, before you were born no one asked for your permission to be born into favourable or unfavourable conditions. No prior agreement is sought before you are born. No consent is sought. It is truly luck of the draw whether you will have strong social and economic support or poor social and economic support. Similarly, a person does not agree to the country or nation into which they are born and that might have a great effect on their future wealth and success. In this regard, great poverty or great wealth may be entirely beyond our control or consent, especially in the context of family and nation. For example, consider elected politicians like Prime Ministers Justin Trudeau (Canada) and Boris Johnson (UK), who were both born into conditions of great social and economic wealth and capital. It is unlikely that either person would have achieved their leadership roles without the lift or buoyancy afforded to them through the "condition" of their family wealth, stature, and support. Did they consent to having a more favourable starting line in life? The answer must be no. But they have surely benefited from these unearned privileges.

Discussion Questions:

1. The idea of a social contract, popularized by eighteenth-century philosophers, proposes that people voluntarily give up certain liberties (for example, the right to seek private vengeance when wronged) and empower an impartial ruler (the state) to protect individual rights, resolve disputes, and preserve order. The idea is that this hypothetical compact protects the "commonwealth" and general public good. Discuss the merits and shortcomings of this idea.
2. Make a short list of types of actions whose legal status differs depending on the consent of the parties involved. For example, in the chapter, taking a coffee cup can be described as a gift or theft depending on the context.
3. You have probably heard a territorial acknowledgement in which the speaker says something like, "I acknowledge that I live on the traditional and unceded territories" of Indigenous Peoples. What do these things tell us about the role consent plays in the relationship between Indigenous Peoples and the Canadian state?

CHAPTER 7
Systems of Response

This chapter connects our discussion about the ways crime is defined, conceptualized, and produced with an overview of some of the specialized systems and institutions that have been developed to respond to wrongdoing. We open with a discussion of arrest and detention, processes that necessarily involve implied or actual violence. We then consider the court system and the processes that produce judgment in criminal cases, focusing on the tension that exists between official commitments to formal impartiality and the reality that both justice and injustice are messy, complicated, and entangled with social forces that extend well beyond the courtroom. Finally, we consider incarceration and begin to explore the implications of institutions that claim the authority to transform and correct. We conclude with a discussion about how flawed and outdated systems and processes might be transformed in the future.

Michael C. K. Ma (MM): It can be argued that our laws are reactions or responses to things people do in society. For example, if someone steals, then society reacts by creating a rule or a law to prohibit stealing. Why? Because stealing is socially agreed upon to be wrong. But sometimes the prohibition of theft and the criminal legal response to theft does not get to the heart of why someone might steal because the transgression is only met with punishment or arrest. The response is often based on a rigid set of rules and procedures and not flexible negotiation.

Mike Larsen (ML): Another way to think of this would be to say that our system is primarily focused on the symptoms of wrongdoing and disorder (e.g., instances of theft, assault, mischief, as well as issues like visible homelessness, addiction, and mental health crises) rather than on the underlying factors that contribute to these problems. A criminal trial, for instance, is concerned with a specific theft and an alleged offender rather than on overarching issues of property and why relative deprivation exists in society. A consequence we can explore in this conversation is that our legal systems have a limited ability to produce justice or address injustice in a broader social sense. Indeed, contemporary criminological scholars have highlighted the persistence of "wicked problems" that are presently approached as policing matters but are not resolvable through policing and criminal justice. Laura Huey and colleagues, for example, have argued that mental health, substance misuse, homelessness, and missing persons are intractable problems that are regarded as naturally "belonging" to the police, despite the fact that police cannot solve them in any broader social sense.[1] Police are understood as expedient solutions to social problems, particularly when they manifest as emergencies, but our reliance on institutions of security and policing to respond to these problems is actually preventing us from developing much-needed solutions from outside the criminal justice system that address their root causes.

MM: And this relates back to our earlier discussion of what is wrong and/or deviant in society and how these norms are established (see chapter 1). To further support standards, society might create an organized force to enforce the rule and respond to what you refer to as symptoms of wrongdoing and disorder (e.g., police, courts, and prison). In the case of theft, we can understand a process of social reaction as follows:

1. Laws prohibiting theft come into being because society adopts a system of private property.
2. People who take things without consent (see chapter 3) are labelled thieves.
3. Processes that support the production and accumulation of private property are enshrined in law and protected. Acts that transgress private property rights are codified as offences and subject to law enforcement. Courts exist as places where these crimes are debated and adjudicated.
4. Judges are appointed to rule on the law; lawyers are hired to prosecute or defend a case.
5. Prisons are places of rehabilitation and/or punishment; jailers are hired to operate a prison.
6. In summary, society, through the legal system, reacts to theft through naming, criminalization, arrest, prosecution, sentencing, and incarceration.

MM: The devil is in the details. I support the idea of there being a system that responds to crime and keeps people safe. It could be a social service or agency that provides safety or protection from harm, or it could be the adoption of a series of rules or regulations (e.g., laws) that are agreed upon by everyone. It can be both. But the problem of having a social service or a set of rules is that there can always be unintended consequences or unexpected outcomes arising from the creation of such services or rules. Here are two examples of unintended outcomes: (a) Police services have been given powers of detention, arrest, and physical restraint, but these powers can also harm someone (e.g., using a conducted energy weapon, or Taser, to subdue a person). The police service is created to service the public, but what if they harm the public while attempting to ensure public safety? (b) Courts may incarcerate a person facing a charge in pretrial before they face their accusers in court, but if an accused cannot secure surety or bail, then they could be detained before their trial. Their detention could be understood as a violation of human rights because a person in pretrial detention has yet to be found guilty of a crime but must await the pending charge in prison. If they are found innocent during trial, then the time spent in prison cannot be reversed to undo that harm. Both these examples show that the social service (i.e., police, courts, and corrections) that has been created to foster public safety might inadvertently create public harm.

Most things can be worked out between two people, but some things necessitate an outside force or independent neutral party. So, in this chapter, I would like to unpack some of these systems and rules, which are responses to perceived problems in society, that are understood to be needed because the problems cannot be settled through mere interpersonal negotiation.

ML: I agree that many problems can be more productively and effectively responded to by individuals, communities, and processes that lie outside the formal institutions of criminal justice. Indeed, if we reflect on our own lived experiences, we will find that we have navigated many serious conflicts, breaches of trust, and transgressions in our lives without resorting to an external authority. However, this is not always the case. Sometimes wrongdoing involves extraordinary power imbalances and types of harm that transcend our capacity for informal resolution. In these situations, it is important that we are able to turn to institutions and processes that are capable of providing safety, support, and resolution.

For example, family violence was once regarded as a "private matter" to be left to those parties involved, and this locked victims into dangerous cycles of abuse, with few viable exits. The emergence of support services, shelters, and even specialized court processes, coupled with a concerted effort to reconceptualize family violence as a public issue, have helped to provide many victims with solutions that would not otherwise have been available. Another example that comes to mind is exploitation and endangerment in the workplace. Unsafe working conditions, wage theft, harassment, and other forms of workplace wrongdoing are serious and widespread problems, but many workers find themselves in precarious positions that make it difficult for them to individually respond or seek redress. There is a clear structural imbalance in the power of employers and workers. Unions, labour movements, and collective bargaining processes all emerged to respond to these inherent power imbalances and move these problems beyond the individual level and into a collective realm. At the outset of this chapter, then, let us recognize that our exploration of social reaction requires some nuance: to be critical of the role and function of criminal justice institutions does not imply that there is no room for organized responses to social problems.

Arrest

MM: To unpack social reaction let us examine the way society responds to theft with its systems of prohibition, arrest, and control. Here are few rhetorical questions to begin our examination:

> The idea and practice of private property makes it necessary to create rules to protect property from theft. Does the existence of personal private property create the problem of theft? Does private property give rise to the creation of laws against stealing? Is it possible to have a world without theft? Would theft occur in a society where everyone had what they wanted? If no one had unfulfilled desires, would there be theft? If there was no private property, would there be theft? Without theft, would there be a need for property laws or police to protect property? The example of theft demonstrates that responses to crime are a chicken and egg problem. Which comes first, the chicken or the egg?

ML: The above questions are "chicken-and-egg questions" that are important for us to address. The idea is that there is an apparatus, there are these laws, that our system of response to these kinds of deviant acts is taken for granted in a lot of conversations. I am thinking of the work of Jonathan Simon on the idea of governing through crime, and I think he adds something interesting to this conversation.[2] He points out that the criminal justice apparatus—not just the mechanisms in the laws and the formal procedures but also the rhetoric of deviance, the discourse of social control, and the narratives of law and order and security and insecurity that come along with it through the twentieth century—starts to become an increasingly powerful resource. Simon argues that the narrative of crime control starts to be mobilized by a variety of actors who recognize the power inherent in criminalization as a response and seek to use that apparatus or narrative to govern a whole host of different social issues.

The prison might initially be envisioned as a "solution" to the problem of theft or interpersonal violence, both as a deterrent mechanism and a punitive or correctional institution. Once it is in existence, however, it serves as a resource—a way of responding to perceived social problems—that seems attractive because it is regarded as severe and coercive. Prison, and the entire criminal justice system, come to be regarded as a viable solution to any problem that can be described and represented as a product of deviance or wrongdoing.

Another issue worth examining is substance control. Our approach to scrutinizing certain substances as substances worthy of criminalization—through a war on drugs and through prohibition measures—is a good example of this idea of governing. Society governs substance use, and perhaps even the harms associated with substance use, through criminalization. This was so widely accepted without question throughout the second half of the twentieth century that it took concerted efforts from social movements and community activism to challenge the presumption that drug use should be a matter of crime and justice and policing and to introduce a different way of thinking about the issues. For example, many advocates and government bodies now support a public health approach to the issue of harms related to substance use, and this necessarily involves different activities, organizations, and objectives.[3] In a "war on drugs" paradigm, it is not just the drug user who is governed through criminalization, but populations who are deemed to be at risk or potentially involved with drugs are also targeted for intensive surveillance and policing.

MM: You just said that "it is not just the drug user who is governed through criminalization, but populations who are deemed to be at risk or potentially involved with drugs are also governed through the response to crime and the criminalization of drug use." Could you expand on this notion of a social response to a crime exceeding its prevention to become something more? Are you saying it becomes something harmful or counterproductive?

ML: It can indeed, and this can happen despite the best intention of the proponents of the approaches in question. This is an important point for us to recognize. Institutions of public safety can make certain publics less safe. Security services can make people insecure. Justice systems can perpetuate systemic injustice. Put simply, the ways we respond to crime can make things worse. There is ample historical evidence for this.

Let us return to the idea of theft. We have the act of people taking things from other people and we recognize this to be wrong. So, we create a mechanism to address this through the apparatuses of criminalization and law enforcement. But these mechanisms can take on a life of their own and become self-perpetuating and expansionary. When other challenges arise in society, or other forms of wrongdoing or perceived social problems arise, that could have been addressed through other means previously, there is now a recourse to criminalization in terms of both logic and narrative. In cases of both theft and drugs, we have created not just a law but a formal service that enforces the law: the police. And that service somehow begins to grow and expand. In terms of the expansion of the (policing) response, we get things like police in schools to deal with youth disciplinary issues, increasingly intensive policing and surveillance of public spaces where it is not merited, police enforcement of how those spaces should be used, and the framing of migration and refugee issues as a matter of security and crime control when they should be matters of civil society and demographics. The language of response and recourse, and the powers of criminalization, spread into a whole variety of different settings. This is what Simon means by the idea of governing through crime.

MM: So, crimes like theft allow for the creation of a formal mechanism (i.e., police) who then search for other things to control and manage. I think that is right. To push this point further, we can understand that the social practice of creating a system outside the relationships between people, which stands outside their relationship, is a form of alienation. The law or regulation becomes external to people and it codifies the social response into a set of external rules. And once you create a generalist social response mechanism you now must actively find things for it to fix. That is the problem. For example, a series of rules and regulations or laws surrounding theft might not actually be very applicable to something like shoplifting because the act of small retail theft (e.g., stealing batteries at a drugstore) becomes abstracted from the actual social harm or transgression. We have designed one response to many varied social problems. Police are equally the social response to shoplifting and armed bank robbery, even though the danger to the public and the social harms are very different and not proportional. That is one of the problems of creating laws and services in response to something that you want to control. You create a series of rules, regulations, and practices that exceed the crime and may not be proportional to the act or the transgression. The thing that originally brought about the social reaction (i.e., theft) becomes overshadowed by the overmuscular social reaction you have created. It also is now a system that stands outside the relationship between the retailer and the person who shoplifted the item. The system takes it out of their relationship and does not repair it. What if we had a system that mediated and put the two parties into dialogue instead of separating them with a criminal justice system? What are your thoughts about arrest as a social response?

ML: I have a few thoughts about this. My first is that, while I agree with what you have said about the alienating nature of this process, I think it is sometimes the case that victims of wrongdoing—such as the hypothetical retailer in this example—may have no desire to deal with, dialogue with, or repair a relationship with the people they believe have wronged them. The ability to call upon the police and their powers allows for them to step back and let an organization with legal authority resolve the situation, at least in the immediate sense. Do you think it would be preferable for us to emphasize, or even require, mutual participation in conflict and its resolution rather than resorting to the intervention of police?

MM: I think it is reasonable to expect that many people are conflict averse and do not want to enter mediation with the perpetrator of the crime. It is perfectly reasonable to assume that people want a professional force or agency to come in and remove their problem. In this regard, the retailer wants to stop shoplifting. But it ultimately does not serve the interests of the retailer, who probably just wants shoplifting to not exist or to go away. The problem does not go away, and the habitual shoplifter might just enter an endless cycle of arrest, nor does it deter future shoplifters.

ML: You are drawing an important distinction between the idea of an immediate response and a solution to an underlying problem. We have come to refer to many public safety organizations as "first responders," and this connects to our expectation of swift resolution to emergencies and conflicts, but there is a considerable difference between the resources and methods needed to accomplish this and the resources and methods that could meaningfully improve the conditions that give rise to conflicts in the first place.

Returning to the specific practice of arrest, one of the things that comes to my mind when I think about arrest today is how violent arrest is as a process and how this is not necessarily apparent when you think of arrest just as a matter of power and law. When you think of it as a response it almost seems there is this cycle of arrest, arraignment, charge, detention, and/or release. "Arrest" seems to fit into this broader cycle, but it is a very conspicuous and physical exercise of power, and it certainly has come into public debates and discussion recently—largely driven by visible representations of arrest in the media or the new visibility of policing.

For example, the arrest of George Floyd was also the murder of George Floyd, and while this case received extraordinary public attention, it was by no means the only standout example of such an interaction. As we start talking about this, we want to understand that there is a mystification of power that takes place through law, where it starts to seem like this natural, inevitable, and autonomous system. It conceals the fact that at base this is about the application of violence by a state and this violence impacts the bodies of people. I have had the good fortune in my life of not having been subject to routine arrest or even detention. On the other hand, I know people who—both when growing up and as adults—were frequently stopped by police, regularly subject to "random" additional search by border services, and generally experienced involuntary interactions with state officials as a constant feature of everyday life. I think that introduces a level of violence into their relationship to law, crime, and justice issues and that needs to be recognized. A clear example of this that comes to mind is the images from Fairy Creek, where over the course of a year paramilitary police violently arrested over a thousand people who were seeking to protect old-growth forest.[4]

MM: I like your use of the word "violence" because it suggests more than just physical violence but also describes the animosity, tension, and intimidation that exists in such relationships between "peace" officers and the public. The Fairy Creek example demonstrates this violence, but it also happens in the everyday urban environment. So, let us unpack that idea of arrest and detention. When a police officer arrests you on the street they do not need to ask for permission from a judge, a lawyer, or the Crown. The police officer has incredible—maybe even arbitrary—discretion in the case of arrest and detention. I understand the arbitrary nature of being stopped and arrested as an act of violence and harm. It is a violence against your right of innocence because once you have contact with police services and are arrested, then you have been harmed regardless of legal charge, outcome, or innocence. Any arrest can traumatize and do harm to a person. Do you think arrest is violent because the officer has been given unlimited powers to arrest someone, or is it that the system of law is violent because it applies an arbitrary or abstract notion of a "one size fits all" justice onto each and every situation it meets?

ML: I think that is a good question. I think even the most genial, professional, and warm arrest by a police officer is still a violent act. In that sense, I do not think there is such a thing as nonviolent arrest precisely because the concept implies a disregard for consent (for more on consent, see chapter 6). Arrest, by its very nature, implies involuntariness. And we can and should talk about whether this is still necessary or warranted. This happens when people resist arrest, decline to come along, or do not come along "willingly." In this regard, violence is inherent in the apparatus itself as opposed to the specific interactions, which may vary on a spectrum of physical violence. The inherentness of violence in arrest needs to be recognized because that is the entry point into a justice system that is entirely based on the notion of coercion and the doing of justice to people largely against their will.

MM: We should clarify that the word "violence" is a nuanced concept because it can refer to physical or kinetic violence (e.g., being physically forced), but it can also refer to harm or violence being done to your right of innocence or freedom of movement in the context of arrest. "Violence" is not just being used metaphorically here; rather, it is used to describe real damage or harm to the enjoyment of human rights. Is it not interesting that a police officer needs to have a warrant to breach your privacy rights, to search your house, but does not need a warrant to stop you on the street? They possess an infinite power of arrest, and they can exercise that power due to the incredible discretion afforded to police by the law. The police officer can at any moment stop anyone. It is almost a superpower because that search and detention is not governed, for example, by a warrant authorized by a judge, which is necessary in the case of searching your home or property. A warrant temporarily suspends your home privacy rights because a judge has allowed, in this one instance, for that right to be put on hold. When searching a home, the police must ask for permission from a judge, but they do not need permission when searching, detaining, and arresting a person who is standing outside their home.[5]

ML: In some ways I think that the difference between the requirement of a warrant when it comes to a search of a residence or dwelling and the considerable latitude police officers have in terms of detention and arrest reflects the valuation law places on property and its protection. If police want to come into my house, they get a warrant, but someone walking down the street has fewer protections. The rationale for this, at least in law in Canada, has been the logic that police are expected to apply this reasonableness standard—that is, to only use their powers of search in reasonable circumstances—and to be held liable (in theory) for the use of those powers in unreasonable circumstances. But this means that questions of rights and maybe even liberty are often contingent on the perceptions of police officers. Even things like use of force, which is often something associated with arrest, is based on perception. The question of whether somebody was lawfully shot by the police does not hinge on whether they had a weapon but on whether the police *thought* they had a weapon, or otherwise posed a serious threat, at the time of the incident. So, there is this incredible discretion built into that kind of bodily contact aspect of the criminal justice system, and there is always—with any apparatus of policing or security and in every interaction—an implied violence. Even in every polite request, such as police saying, "Can you talk to me for a second?" or "Can you come over here for a minute?," there is always an implied threat until the person being asked says "yes" to consent to the meeting or conversation.

MM: You are totally right. It should be noted that if someone says, "No, I do not want to talk," it is likely the situation will escalate. By not consenting to talking you may have given the police officer the idea that you are not complying and are indeed acting out of order. It may even stimulate a more aggressive posture because you have denied or challenged the authority of the state and the representative acting for the state. Your reaction has now put you in a precarious position. And it has nothing to do with innocence. By not consenting, you have exercised your free right to say "no," unless you are being detained due to suspicious behaviour or "reasonable suspicion." Your ideal rights vs. how they play out on the sidewalk are very different.

ML: Our discussion of arrest and police powers makes me think about Jean Paul Brodeur's work on the policing web and on the question of how police powers are exercised and the role and function of police. One of the things that I take away from his work is this emphasis we have placed on the swift resolution of conflict through police action. It is implied that there is something taking place that ought not to be taking place when police are called to intervene. There is a lot of pressure to resolve things very quickly, which tends to mean yelling orders, an expectation of immediate compliance, and then a swift application of force in case of noncompliance. It is a sad commentary on our expectations that the idea that police could arrive on the scene and a minute later a situation escalates to the point where somebody is killed is unsurprising. We know this both anecdotally and through media reporting.

MM: Yes, this is exactly the opposite of public safety. If the death only occurs minutes after the arrival of police, then we must ask: Did the police precipitate the death? Was the public safer before the arrival of police? Would the person still be alive if the police *did not* arrive? What if the person was a former medical student who boarded a bus and experienced an ongoing mental illness episode (i.e., paranoid schizophrenia)—as was the case of the Edmund Yu shooting?[26] Should they be shot to protect the public?

ML: We might ask if other things could be done, but the notion of that kind of swift escalation is something we take as a "normal" part of how the system functions. This is, in part, a product of our fascination with factual and fictional media products that depict police as action-oriented specialists working in situations of conflict and emergency. Reality TV programming, for example, highlights actions and "encounters" as opposed to the everyday work of police.[7] If we heard that the police arrived on scene and then sat down for coffee with the person for three hours to talk through something or took them for a walk and told their dispatch they will not be on call for the rest of the day because they had a duty to speak with this person and do some things to resolve the crisis, that would strike us as weird. It would certainly be a departure from standard police operating procedure. Our system is invested in this notion of swift resolution backed by force, but it gets us into a lot of trouble, and it locks us into a way of thinking about deviance and social problems that in many ways is counterproductive and dehumanizing.

MM: This cloud of fear follows policing because if you are ever detained on the sidewalk and engaged in a conversation with police services, all of this comes into play. You begin to think: "Am I in trouble? Will this now escalate to a stage of violence? What kind of response can I best give the police to show compliance and de-escalate the situation? How can I show the police officer that I am not a risk or threat?" Through pantomime and acting, you project compliance and respect for police. This fear of harm (see chapter 2: Fear of Harm) immediately puts you on the wrong footing in relation to your rights and entitlements as a citizen. In this regard, this is another aspect of violence, other than in the arrest or in the act of being detained, and that is the violence against your rights as a citizen to always have security of person. You have the right to security of person even in the face of being questioned by police, even while being detained, and even while being arrested. It seems to me that it is not healthy to have a sense of fear of police services when just interacting in a normal everyday way with police services. My fear of police does not make me safer, does not lead to the public being safer, and it does not guarantee that public rights will be well served. Fear should have little or no place in the public's engagement with social services.

Judgment

ML: Let us now move our conversation "off the street" and into the courtroom. When we examine the courtroom, we have the usual cast of characters who would be familiar to anyone, whether they are studying criminology or not. The courtroom is a place to conduct an adversarial process with lawyers, a judge as the arbitrator of facts, and of course the accused party of the case. These are the usual suspects in the courtroom. There are others too, but I want to step back and think about the judge, who is not a party to the dispute between the aggrieved victim and alleged offender. What do we make of the fact that we have this third party who is not only detached from the case but also purposefully meant to be positioned as neutral and disinterested?

MM: I think that is such a fascinating question and is at the crux of the issue. As a response to crime, why should we have a neutral party deciding the culpability or innocence of someone? Would it make more sense to have a system that selects someone who knows the parties involved and can help make judgments and decisions based on this expertise? Why is it that we want to have an outside party who has no prior knowledge of the people or circumstance? Why should we not choose the exact opposite? We could bring the crime (e.g., theft) directly into the small community it has affected as opposed to kicking it up to a provincial or federal court that has no stake in the decision and where the case is heard far away from where the problem occurred. That is something for us to consider. The structure of the court system and the notion of an impartial outside party deciding the facts of the case (e.g., whether someone is guilty or not guilty) is based on whether the argument presented was persuasive; a persuasiveness that is entirely reliant on the quality or expertise of a lawyer. It may not be the facts of a case that sway a judge but the lawyer's expertise in presenting the case. The question of justice—based on the system of courtroom presentation of facts—may not effectively find or reveal so-called truth. If the arguments of a clever lawyer defeat the arguments of an overworked lawyer, is truth revealed and justice served?

ML: The idea of a neutral, objective, impartial, and accurate process is central to the legal system. It is part of what some sociolegal scholars refer to as the "Official Version of Law," or the image that the legal system presents to the public.[8] The legitimacy of the legal system is supported by the notion that it is and should be disinterested. And yet, we know that a variety of extralegal factors influence court proceedings and judicial decisions. Economics, politics, and biases do influence the outcomes of courts. Sometimes this is readily apparent. For example, it is widely acknowledged that the decisions of the US Supreme Court reflect the political leanings of the Justices. When a Republican or Democrat party is in power, they seek to appoint judges to the court whose track records and ideological commitments match those of the party.

Let us return to the important question you posed: Should we support the idea of a disinterested legal system? If matters of justice are deeply connected to the lived experiences of individuals and communities, and if deviance and crime are reflections of inequalities, conflicts, and social problems that require collective solutions, then truly "doing justice" must require recognition and engagement of the public interests at stake.

MM: The issue of disinterest and neutrality is also important when thinking about the sentencing, not just the judgment part of a case. A judge may arrive at a guilty ruling but then must provide a sentence or penalty for the party involved. But in that moment of being a disinterested judge they sometimes have to take into consideration the political interest of the government because there might be, for example, minimum mandatory sentencing[9] requirements that a judge must follow even if they think it is not right or proportional to the offence. It calls into question the independence or the disinterest of a judge who is in charge of rendering the decision and sentence.[10] A judge might have to alter their own judicial opinion about sentencing based not on the facts of the case, which were presented, but on an external sentencing policy.[11] That is a good example of how the court itself is not entirely disinterested and therefore the judge themselves are also not disinterested parties. They may be disinterested in name and concept, but they are not in political and institutional practice.

ML: In some ways you are lifting the curtain and allowing us to peer into the way the system actually functions, moving beyond some of the rhetoric and symbolism of the courts and the law as institutions. We should note that in addition to the issue of objectivity or disinterest, and the challenges associated with this, there are a variety of highly pragmatic forces and considerations that really shape the way things take place in a courtroom. Even if we imagine the perfect judge who sets out to truly act in a detached and dispassionate manner and to base decisions solely on the facts of the case and the letter of the law, we should note that that judge must also deal with systemic delays and backlog in the court process, a shortage of judicial appointments, pressure to resolve cases as swiftly as possible to maximize the usefulness of limited court time, absences or "failure to appear," and complications over parties seeking to delay and postpone hearings. I am often struck by the disconnect between the way we represent courtrooms and trials in popular media and the way they operate in reality. Courtroom dramas show a single judge focusing on a particular case of high importance in a relatively short period of time, with all the parties actively and directly involved throughout and very little in the way of external time pressures or competitions for attention. But, in reality, cases are fragmented things and trials are the exception rather than the rule. Judges must deal with complicated and disjointed processes, and the court emerges as something that is more akin to a messy high pressure bureaucratic institution than a detached forum for producing justice.

MM: As we have demonstrated with our example and discussion about policing and the imagination that police can arrive on scene and fix the situation quickly, we can also understand that in the case of the courtroom there is the imagination, or perhaps fantasy, that if we can just get our case to trial, then we will get a swift resolution or decision that will bring closure to the legal problem. However, that is a fantasy in the case of both the police and the courts because the process of adjudicating the law and rendering justice is a very long, complicated, and drawn-out process.

ML: That is a good summary of what we have explored so far, but I think it is interesting as well that although the courtroom and the legal system are complicated, messy, and bureaucratic, they are also simultaneously infused with ritual and symbolism. This is apparent to anyone who attends and observes court processes. By taking notes and immersing yourself in the courtroom experience you get a sense of what is going on there. I want to draw a distinction between the courtroom as it functions while court is in session and the court building or architectural structure that surrounds it, which I think is something a bit different. What can we learn about the courtroom? For one thing, it is a deeply hierarchal and ritualized space.[12] In the courtroom, you have the elevated position of the judge, you have coats of arms, and often costumes (e.g., robes) and rituals in terms of speech and mannerism. They are anachronistic mannerisms that are seemingly out of sync with what is otherwise a bureaucratic and rule-oriented process. There are not many other situations in day-to-day life where you encounter that kind of ritual and symbolism in what is ostensibly a secular institution. It infuses the court with a symbolic dimension that has a powerful effect. It is also important to consider who is regarded as an essential or central player in the process of justice and how the court is organized around that privileged position. I often give students a diagram of a standard provincial courtroom that shows an elevated place for the judge or justice. The physical structure of the court reflects the adversarial process, really implying that there are directly opposed interests and that justice is something that emerges from a conflict of interests, which is an interesting thing to think about symbolically in and of itself. It implies we do not have a notion of common ground but rather a situation where there is a dispute: the Crown has an entrenched position, and the defence has a position opposite to the Crown.

MM: You have said two interesting things. First, your comment regarding the courtroom giving an impression of two directly opposed and adversarial interests whose arguments will fairly render justice does give us pause to think whether such a system of presentation before a judge can create common ground since it is based on a winner-take-all competition. Does it create common ground or social cohesion? It stands to reason that no one is actually helping the defendant or accuser when they need it the most. There is not solidarity between the accuser, the accused, the lawyers, and the courts. There is no strength of relationship; instead, animosity and dissention is created. In fact, one could call it a kind of highly mediated quarrel. If we go back to the example of a family, we all know that when there is a quarrel between siblings, the parents step in not to adjudicate the fight but to get the two kids to apologize and reconcile because they need to continue to live with each other. The parents do not focus on assessing a winner and a loser and then assign a retributive penalty that damages one child as an award to the other. Second, your comment about clothing and deportment is fascinating. The theatre of the courtroom, the crest, the elevated status of the judge, and the robes. Do you think, as a modern institution, that the system of justice would become fairer if we got rid of those costumes in that theatrical setting? For example, I am thinking of when I visit my family doctor. My doctor no longer wears a white lab coat, and she performs her duties in a kind of bureaucratic way; not at all the way Hollywood movies present a doctor and the healing arts. Healthcare is currently much more like a functional administration of health services. Is that what you are suggesting we could change? If we got rid of the performance of justice in courts, the administration of justice would somehow become more fair?

ML: I think there are examples of ways justice can be done that does not infuse the process with hierarchy and power differentials and is much more focused on reconciliation and consensus, and it is interesting to me that we have not built a court system based on those kinds of principles. But rather than being too prescriptive I think it is important for us to just encourage people to ask what functions are being served by the symbolism, ritual, and organization of courts as they currently are. One observation we could make is that the use of seemingly arcane rituals and very specialized language serves to make the practice of law in a courtroom the province of lawyers in part because those who are not trained are simply unable to navigate the language and the process. Therefore, we are reliant on these professionals and institutions and processes to deliver justice.

MM: In terms of ritual and performance it is easy to show that much of legal representation happens outside the courtroom or the physical buildings the cases are heard in. Many cases involve a negotiation between the Crown and the defendant's lawyer. It is a negotiation happening outside the court. Therefore, much of the justice that is rendered in the court is contingent on these extralegal negotiations. What are your thoughts about that?

ML: Perhaps one of the most important points for us to consider when we are examining the judicial system and court processes is this interweaving or blending and perhaps incompatibility or incongruity between formal and informal processes. Our current system mixes these things together. There are often hurried informal negotiations and almost a trading of concessions during the preparation of a legal case. If those negotiations did not happen—when court is not in session—then the system itself would grind to a halt. I am reminded of Michelle Alexander, who wrote this fantastic short commentary piece called "Go to Trial, Crash the System."[13] Her argument was simply that if everybody who had the right to a fair trial chose to exercise that very important and constitutionally protected right, then the system could not function. It would grind to a crashing halt overnight because the system is not designed to hear each case. I think that tells us something about the system of disincentives that are built into the apparatus of justice and the ways courts are organized to ensure a minimum flow of cases through the system rather than to deliver the best justice possible for each given case.

For example, there is a concept in the study of justice systems called the "trial penalty." The idea is that if you take two cases that are substantially the same in terms of the facts and the nature of the offence, but in one case the accused party pleads guilty and accepts some kind of concession where there is a joint sentencing statement or something like that, whereas in the other case—again, the exact same circumstances—the person exercises the right to a trial, data shows that the person who exercised their right to a trial tends to receive a significantly harsher sentence.[14] That tells us something about how we expect the system of justice to function, and it illustrates some of the disincentives for not pleading guilty. Another disincentive is simply related to the delay embedded in the system, and there are lots of examples of people who are not guilty but who do the math and plead guilty because it is expeditious. Whereas exercising one's right to a fair trial could precipitate a lengthy process during which people are functionally in a position of limbo awaiting the outcome of the case. In some instances, that wait pending a decision can be over a year in duration. That is hard to do, so there are a lot of incentives to get people to do what they are willing to do to expedite the process.

MM: So, are you saying that if you have a good lawyer, and she tells you not to take the risk to go to trial and recommends that you plead guilty, that action skews the notion of justice? That is, if you understand that there could be a long delay in awaiting a trial and that the trial may result in a harsher sentence, then it only makes sense—if you are not a gambler—to not take that risk. If you take the safer option of pleading guilty, then it proves the system of justice is not neutral or impartial because it has pushed the accused in a particular direction. Is that correct?

ML: I think in that situation you just described it is possible that the lawyer is acting in good faith and in what they regard as the client's best interests. Often—especially in the case of state appointed duty counsel as opposed to a private lawyer who you have on retainer—the objective is to achieve the least worst outcome for a client. For example, such a lawyer might be familiar with the phenomenon of overcharging, where the Crown lawyers lay multiple charges (e.g., failure to comply, resisting arrest, assault on a peace officer) in addition to the central substantive charge to increase the pressure on an accused party to plead guilty in return for some dropped charges. A lawyer may also be familiar with the going rate sentence associated with a particular offence and on variations in cases where a party elects to proceed to trial. In this case, it is logical for the lawyer to recommend that you plead guilty because it will lead to a less severe sentence.

MM: The way you describe this sounds like a game or a dance between police, Crown, and defence. Is it all just a game?

ML: I do not think it would be right to say that it is entirely a game, but I think it is fair to say that it is a social and institutional process that has embedded power relations, work arounds, and informalities, or even ways of exerting pressure that are only tangentially related to the substantive case. Just like in any other type of institutional setting, the experienced players understand these things and understand how to work with and around them. It is the inexperienced parties that might be astonished by this.

MM: To recap, we respond to wrongdoing by creating a system that allows for criminalization, law enforcement, judgment, and punishment. However, the judicial system put into place over time begins to create mannerisms, conventions, and habits that are not actually conducive to justice or finding the truth. Rather, the system of justice becomes an arcane administration of justice. Its development happens over a long period of time and through years of accretion and case law. And does the system lead to the repair of said crimes?

ML: Another way we could think about it is to say that some of these court-based institutions were or are meant to be means to the ends of justice, but their functioning and their own logics have become ends in and of themselves.

MM: We began this conversation concerning society's reaction to crime by examining notions of neutrality or impartiality in the court system. We have examined judges and the difficulties that surround rendering neutral, impartial decisions and we have pointed out the presence of extralegal processes in judicial practices and how the legal system may give rise to outcomes that may not provide justice to a legally represented client at the end of the process. Are we saying that our system of justice is illegitimate?

ML: The current system of laws that we have, and indeed any system of laws, functions only to the extent that it is perceived to be legitimate by a sufficient majority of the population. The image of the Court of Justice as being neutral, just, interested but dispassionate, and completely bound by the rule of law helps to reinforce this perception of legitimacy, but it does not take much probing or questioning to find a lot of cracks in this narrative. We must recognize that the system is certainly a legal system, but I think the question of whether it is a justice system is very much open-ended.

MM: What alternative systems could we have for determining innocence or guilt or arriving at a "true" or better justice system? Is it possible to somehow edit or retroactively fix the existing system of judging guilt or innocence?

ML: Maybe we can get at this issue by asking what a just outcome of a case might be. What would it mean for the system to perform as intended; to produce something we could recognize as justice? An alternative system may be designed to be much more oriented towards consensus, reparation, reconciliation, and the resolution of underlying factors that give rise to criminalized acts in the first place. That would require a much more multilateral approach; one that is not based exclusively on the binary of guilt or innocence and the application of the labels that arise from it. It would involve more players and a less adversarial process. Perhaps this is indicative of the fact that we are too ambitious with the idea of a justice system. Maybe it is not possible for a legal system to truly achieve justice in a satisfactory manner. Maybe that role is something that should be distributed throughout other social institutions. What do you think?

MM: There are three ways I can answer your question. First, in our next chapter we discuss inequality and poverty, and I think it might make a good illustration here regarding the limitations of the criminal justice system for delivering justice. For example, if we know social and economic deprivation is at the core of, say, shoplifting of food, then the arrest and prosecution of such a case will not solve the hunger or homelessness that are the real reasons for such crimes. So, this gets back to your comment regarding what other social institutions should be involved in the administration of justice. Housing, education, health services, and social services must also be involved; however, the current criminal justice system does not involve these key social actors.

Second, I think another world is possible, but we should not hold our breath. I do not think the power that has been consolidated and congealed in the form of laws, courts, and the adjudication of justice can be overturned or better "distributed" through other institutions as you put it. Our system of adjudicating guilt or innocence—where we have one judge or a panel of judges—is the initial flaw in the system. In such a system we have externalized both justice-making *and* decision-making onto a combined system that stands outside the relationship of people (e.g., people do not know the judge, nor the law). The law and the judge are external to everyday life, and they are introduced to separate the conflict or problem into two further separate and competing parties; they do not unify the parties involved and they have no stake in the game. Once the case moves through the system, the police, the lawyers, and the judge may never encounter the parties involved again. The result has no direct or long-lasting impact on them. The current system also stands outside their mind and bodies and controls the population or citizenry with a set of arcane rules that few people—other than lawyers—can understand or manipulate. In the current system, justice must be mediated by experts to such a degree that it is normal for everyday people to admit: "I have no idea how the law works."

Third, how can we imagine another world when the current system of judgment and courts is so powerfully ensconced and embedded in current society? How can it change if 99 percent of the population have no idea how it works and are perfectly happy with it being a mystery? As you have suggested, we have a legal system but not a justice system. And I think the naturalness or inevitability of it is too deeply rooted and institutionalized to be altered in any substantive way. It may even be an exercise in fantasy to imagine a different system for adjudicating justice. And for that reason, I am skeptical whether there can be wholesale change, or even partial but substantive change, of the administration of justice in the near future.

ML: This reminds me of the work of the criminologist Nils Christie, and particularly his work on conflicts as property.[15] Christie notes that one of the primary functions of contemporary Western justice systems is the appropriation of conflict. Crime is a type of conflict that arises out of peoples' everyday lived experience and interactions with one another. When these conflicts are taken up by the legal system, and when the police, courts, and criminal law get involved, two things happen.

First, the conflict with all its complexities and nuances and background becomes translated into concepts that are intelligible to the legal system: relevant facts, types of offences, forms of legally recognized harms, questions of standing, and so on. Look at any judicial decision and consider the language used to describe the case, and you will get a sense of how this happens.

Second, and on a related note, the conflict becomes the property not of the original parties involved, or indeed of the broader community, but rather of the professional actors—lawyers, judges, police officials, and so on—who then work on the conflict as part of their formal roles. Even if this is well intentioned, the consequence is that both the conflict and the resolution of that conflict become disconnected from the context it originally emerged from, and the people most directly impacted by it often play little if any formal role in the process. Christie is not naively suggesting that everybody should be involved in identifying solutions to serious conflicts, especially if they are harmed or impacted by these conflicts. But he is suggesting that there is something beneficial, powerful, and transformative in the ability to resolve a conflict and that taking this out of the hands of communities is, in a way, disempowering. The result is that a conflict with deep social roots becomes a case. So, that is something to think about. Perhaps a way forward would be to consider how we can reduce this form of translation, appropriation, and theft of conflict and perhaps a more just and inclusive approach to justice might emerge.

MM: I think this notion of theft of conflict is so important when examining the system of criminal justice that we have because, as you have pointed out, it truly does steal the case away from the parties involved. But let me take up one of the things you mentioned about the actors involved, what you called "professional actors." One of our key problems involves our lack of imagination regarding who comprises this group of legitimate professional actors. We cannot even expand this group of professionals to go beyond those involved with the criminal justice system.

We should be reminded that the criminal justice system is not just the police, courts, and corrections. The criminal justice system also includes the direct participation of agencies or sectors of government we do not naturally associate with criminal justice. For example, we know the Canada Revenue Agency conducts reviews and investigations that are invaluable in cases of financial fraud, but they are not a part of the criminal justice system. We also know that our healthcare sector is involved in treating and assessing individuals with mental health issues when they work with police to respond to individuals experiencing mental health breakdowns.

These institutions are not traditionally understood to be a part of the system and yet they work closely with it. They might be so important that the formal system could not work without their participation. Furthermore, the criminal justice system is not a coherent "system" but is made up of various agencies and levels of state institutions. For example, the police do not consult with corrections to establish policing policy and initiatives, nor vice versa; rather, they work independently and seldom in consultation. We also know that federal police (e.g., RCMP) work independently from municipal and/or provincial police services to such a degree that there are many areas of overlapping and even competing jurisdiction and service. These coexisting agencies are not what most people would understand to be coordinated or systematically and optimally working together. It would be a mistake to describe their work, which does happen in tandem, as a cohesive or coordinated criminal justice *system*. When we start to ask questions like that it blows apart the narrow notion of a highly coordinated system of justice—only comprised of police, courts, and corrections. And it also shows us that maybe we have posed the wrong question. We may not even understand what a change in a justice "system" would entail because our imagination is so tied to the narrow police-courts-corrections model. It might be a much bigger societal reframing of justice that is needed.

ML: It strikes me that this idea of reimagining a justice system must first and foremost involve an exercise in imagination. That is, rather than starting with the existing system and contemplating forms of reform or tinkering or revision or addition, perhaps we need to think seriously about how various structures and institutions in our society reproduce conditions of injustice, and at the same time, what it might be to design social institutions in a way that truly achieved the objective of a just society. This is no small task.

Perhaps, in the final instance, our problem is that we too readily associate the idea of justice as an outcome or as a social good with institutions of judgment and punishment. Courts may be able to achieve something that resembles justice in some cases, but only at a microlevel. That is, at the level of the case and the legally recognized parties directly involved. There is little potential for such moments of judgment to translate into broader social justice. For that, we would need to move well beyond the courts and indeed to the very foundations of our society, particularly in relation to the distribution of wealth, resources, and power.

MM: I think what we are both getting at is that perhaps justice is too important to simply leave to an externalized system of judgment. A system of judgment that—as we have pointed out—has many flaws. I think the system of judgment we have is one designed to turn complex issues into black and white, yes or no, good or bad frameworks. It does try to bring clarity to a situation, but in so doing, the system of judgment fails to acknowledge the grey area of life, the complexity of life, and the fact that individuals may not be entirely responsible for their actions nor their situation in society.

Incarceration

ML: So far, we have talked about some important early phases of the criminal legal system. Let us now turn our attention to the matter of incarceration, and particularly the idea of institutionalized imprisonment as a response to crime. What can we say about the role and function of prison?

MM: Prisons are designed to punish, and they punish prisoners by using force and fear. Force and fear are used to secure obedience so that you behave and comply with the structure of the punishment. Prisons also hide punishment because they are not in the city. They are often in a remote location away from major urban centres. That type of punishment delivers pain, but it is not physical torture; rather, it relies on a form of mental torture. I should mention that my description is not a reflection of how the Correctional Service of Canada (CSC)—who is responsible for the federal prison and parole system—imagines their work, but it does not mean that I am incorrect. Their stated goal is as follows:

> CSC's goal is to assist inmates to become law-abiding citizens. The correctional process begins at sentencing. From the time an offender is initially assessed, through case management and to supervision in the community, there is a team of dedicated professionals working closely with the offender. Correctional programs are offered to help offenders take responsibility for their actions. They are encouraged to learn the skills necessary to help them return safely to the community. A range of motivational strategies are used to help offenders see the value of participating in these programs. The correctional process does not end with the offender's release—it continues in the community. Similar to the dedicated team within the institution, offenders work with a Case Management Team that may include a Parole Officer, health care professionals, volunteers and an entire network of support.[16]

ML: Mike, that is a provocative introduction to this topic, and I think it is provocative because you are not using the words and positions used by contemporary prison systems to describe what they are and what they do. For example, in Canada we typically find prisons described as correctional centres, or even healing facilities. Cells are described as units, solitary confinement is described as administrative segregation, and even though the experience is torturous, officials will adamantly deny that the infliction of pain either psychological or physical is the objective of this system. So, I think you have done us a service by cutting straight to the heart of the matter and avoiding some of our current jargon. Your remarks remind me of the work of Michel Foucault. In his book, *Discipline and Punish*, Foucault argues that the birth of the prison coincided with a shift in the focus of punishments away from the body and towards the mind of the individual.[17] We replaced whippings, hangings, torture, inquisitions, and the guillotine with prison. As he notes, proponents of the current prison, or carceral, system are quick to ask: Are these changes not an indicator of progress? Is this not more humane?

MM: Good point. I think it is important to remember that Foucault did not regard this transformation as necessarily more humane or more progressive. It was just a more clever, stealthy, and efficient form of punishment. The birth of the prison led to the caging of vast numbers of human beings, and it hid the violence away from the public. Although this was initially conceived of as a means to effect change and discipline and promote conformity in the minds or soul of the prisoner, it was still very focused on the body. Prisons are places where human bodies are confined, observed, controlled, and sometimes brutalized. So, yes, it is true that prison may be a mental torture in the sense that society is no longer reacting with the use of flogging or other types of physical punishment, but it may not be less harmful or less bodily-focused. Prisons can also be understood as a form of community-withdrawal punishment because it wrenches the person from their community, socially isolates the prisoner, and withholds social contact. Such isolation—especially in the case of solitary confinement—can lead to great mental anguish and maybe even mental illness. That is certainly one type of force, harm, and/or punishment that the prison produces. The basis of both these punishments (i.e., the individual experience of isolation and the theft of your social connections) revolve around your freedom of mobility, freedom of choice, and freedom of association. The invention and use of prison steals these rights or entitlements from you; that is the crux of prisons. What do you think?

ML: I think you have raised some important points. In particular, the point about prison involving the deprivation of liberty. The prison is not something that has existed in its current form forever. Prisons are in fact modern institutions, and most criminologists will at some point encounter Michel Foucault's work on prisons. In his study on the birth of the prison he connects it to the issue of rights. Foucault argues that the birth of the prison coincides with the idea of rights and liberties as things that are inherent and connected to human values and human experience. Thus, as you point out, punishment involves their deprivation. Prior to this, punishment was much more symbolically embodied in public displays of sovereign power, judgment, and punishment. So, this is an important point for us to acknowledge. I would also say that the contemporary prison is based—as you note—on practices of fear, compliance, and coercion, but it is couched in a language and legal framework of behaviour modification. That is why we call prisons "correctional centres," which I think is an interesting term for two reasons.

First, it suggests that society possesses the authority to "correct" or change those who have transgressed in some fashion. This is an extraordinary claim, and one that invites us to recall our discussion of consent in a previous chapter. It is one thing for a state to claim the legal authority to punish someone and something else for a state to claim the authority to change a person's behaviour.

Second, the term "correctional centre" implies that positive transformations—corrections—can be achieved in a space characterized by fear and deprivation. Having done work with prisoners and on prisons in the past, I think that, to the extent prisons achieve these objectives in terms of any kind of positive change, they generally do so despite its conditions and design and not because of them. The experience of imprisonment is something that must be survived and endured, and many people emerge from prison deeply harmed and dislocated from a society they are expected to return to.

MM: Let me address two things you said: First, prison is characterized not only by fear and deprivation but also harm. For example, if you send someone to prison—so that they are penalized—it harms that person because their freedom is taken away. Their ability to make decisions is taken away and their job is taken away. So, in this sense, the punishment is effective. It harms the person as a punishment. However, another aspect of sentencing and imprisonment is "rehabilitation," but the prison system does little to provide education, employment counselling, skills training, addiction rehabilitation, trauma therapy, job finding postrelease, etc. Prisons fail to rehabilitate or retrain a prisoner. Prisons can be "destructive" because the years spent in prison are not years spent being changed into a better person.

In this regard, the retributive system may not actually provide more public safety after the sentence is served because the person has not been rehabilitated—only punished. Some have argued that the retributive system also punishes the family outside.[18] For example, in some cases, the main income earner is now in prison and children no longer have an active father or mother. In this regard, the retributive system may be found to punish not only the offender but their family and children. The offender exits prison as an unemployed and unrehabilitated person and often exits prison as an indigent (i.e., homeless) person. They might have entered prison as a housed and employed person, but they leave as a homeless and unemployed person. The stated intention of prison was never to continue punishing you after your release nor to create the stigma of being an ex-convict. These are a few examples of the real and continuing harms caused by prison.

Second, let me take up your comment about the licence to change because yes, it is assumed that if you enter a prison and you take your punishment, then you will be changed and altered in a positive way that benefits society. In this regard, prisons are supposed to act in a rehabilitative manner that will dissuade you from future criminal behaviour. But that perspective is in great dispute. There is quite a lot of evidence to challenge whether prisons have a prosocial rehabilitative effect, and I think we could go historically back to the invention of the prison. Some have argued that eighteenth-century Europe had an industrial revolution that brought people from farms into cities, bringing people from an agrarian setting into an urban setting. This migration created new urban social problems (e.g., unemployment) that the state had to address and one of the solutions to that problem was the invention of prisons. Prisons were invented in a specific historical moment of urban growth. Prisons did not always exist and they are rooted in a specific history. For example, in the eighteenth century, the growth of urban centres (e.g., London, England) led to the invention and introduction of institutions like asylums, poor houses, or mental institutions. We can understand that prisons were a part of this moment of invention and that Canada was a recipient of these historical developments. The Kingston Penitentiary in Kingston, Ontario, opened in 1835, was a product of this era. It had observation corridors based on Jeremy Bentham's ideas concerning the use of simultaneous surveillance, isolation, and punishment born of eighteenth-century efforts to use prisons to contain urban social problems. These inventions were not fuelled by rehabilitative or proso-cial intent but rather by the needs of urbanization and the challenges of industrialization in the context of the ascendency of capitalism as the dominant social and economic order.

ML: You raise the important question of whether the prison is simply an anachronism or an outdated institution that continues to function despite its manifest failures. I am reminded of the comments of the Canadian transformative justice activist Ruth Morris who said, "I have nothing against prisons except that they are an expensive, unjust, and immoral failure," and while that is certainly a provocative comment, I would suggest it is also a fully accurate one.[19]

MM: Thank you for that wonderful quote from Ruth Morris and the notion of "manifest failures" because one failure of prison punishment and rehabilitation is that it does not address the question of poverty or low socioeconomic status. As researchers we know that people who are poor, or who have low socioeconomic status, are overrepresented in prisons. We know that many prisoners are unemployed before entering prison, and so there is a correlation between deviance, criminalization, incarceration, and poverty in this equation. Do you think there is a causal relationship between unemployment and crime? Do you think poverty and unemployment are causally linked to crime and imprisonment?

ML: It is always difficult to attribute causation in the social sciences. There is a very high bar for identifying causation—methodologically—but I think in this instance I am going to say yes. And I say this for specific reasons. Maybe the best way to think about this might be to try and encourage ourselves and our readers to disembed ourselves from a lot of the assumptions about crime, justice, and incarceration and to try and think about what the prison would appear to be and what it does from the perspective of somebody who had no familiarity with our society or systems. I think they would quickly draw the conclusion that the prison is an institution primarily meant to house deeply hurt and marginalized poor people and subject them to some regime of coercive control. That interpretation is certainly borne out by the statistics: we know that the demographics of Canadian prisons reflect—and indeed, amplify—all the inequalities and forms of marginalization present else-where in society.

MM: OK, I agree prison is either intentionally or unintentionally targeting poor and marginalized people, but if we know that prisons fail to reduce crime, and we know this through research and statistical proof, then why do you think we continue to use an eighteenth-century European invention?

ML: I do not think there is a single answer to that question, but I think it is a fundamentally important question. On the one hand, we have to recognize the power of inertia when it comes to the way we do crime and justice. There are a lot of examples of practices and institutions related to crime control that seem both ineffective and woefully outdated, but they are also entrenched. I think that has been a significant challenge for those who have been working to decarcerate, to abolish, and to limit the use of prisons. The sheer acceptance of the inevitability of the institution functions as a barrier to the implementation of alternatives. There are a lot of alternatives to incarceration that have been suggested, and many that have been implemented, but they often tend to be absorbed by the carceral. In other words, rather than being something we do instead of incarceration, they become something that is an adjunct to the prison system. Some restorative justice programs and community corrections initiatives have experienced such absorption. Once regarded as alternatives to imprisonment, they have added to the range of processes and institutions associated with the carceral. The prison, as an institution, is remarkably resilient. I will make one further point. Although the official narrative about incarceration is correctional, and although there are many ostensibly correctional components of our prisons, I believe the prison serves also as a vehicle for popular vengeance. If you consider how people talk about prisoners in popular discourse, the language is not one of rehabilitation or transformation but rather of populist punitiveness. We know that we, as individuals, would be harmed by the deprivation of our own liberty. We know that prisons do this, and therefore supporting incarceration—especially calls for longer, harsher, and more austere forms imprisonment—may fulfill a desire for retributive justice. Would you agree? Why do you think the prison continues to exist in the twenty-first century in Canada?

MM: That is a hard question. That is why I asked you first! But if I were put on the spot, I would have to say that there is—as you suggest—an inertia. There is historical inertia, and it is very difficult to change the direction society has been cast in because there are traditions, habits, and social structures that have been built up over centuries that are difficult to overturn. Those habits instruct us to believe that retribution or punishment is either good for social order or a necessary evil. But I would like to take up your comment about popular vengeance because it is so interesting, not just in the context of prisons and detention but also in relation to who is being detained and punished. I am thinking of race and class and how it finds itself reflected in the carceral. It is difficult for us to think about the prison in isolation from other institutions and social structures. In many ways, the prison is a distillation of broader social forces. The processes that produce inequality, marginalization, and hierarchy in society are reflected in our prisons. For example, in the American context, Black Americans are four to five times more likely to be incarcerated than the mainstream population, and in the Canadian context we know that Indigenous Canadians are seven to eight times more likely to be incarcerated than the mainstream population. So why are people who are racialized overrepresented in prisons? That I think is one of the key questions for our generation to answer.

ML: This form of overrepresentation is well acknowledged in various commissions of inquiry that have studied the prison system in Canada for many years. There have been many recommendations for reform but the prison seems resilient and inflexible in producing these kinds of outcomes. I would note that the overrepresentation of Indigenous people in Canadian prisons is even more shocking and outrageous when you consider its gender dynamic. Indigenous women are disproportionately more likely to be incarcerated than just about any other segment of the Canadian population. They also face an intersection of different forms of marginalization both within the prison and in the context of what we can call "community corrections;" that is, the various forms of probation, parole, and community-based supervision that surround the prison as an institution. It is remarkable to me that this highly skewed, highly racialized, and highly classed outcome of prisons for Indigenous women is not sufficient to warrant their abolition simply on principle.

But if I might shift gears a little bit, I think maybe we should also talk about how prisons are not simply or exclusively used for postsentence "correction" in Canada. One of my pet peeves with criminology is the enduring focus on cops, courts, and corrections, which tends to create a set of blinders or blinkers in terms of what we study. For example, in British Columbia there are more people incarcerated while awaiting trial than there are people who have been sentenced.[20] We often do not consider this when we think about who is in prison. We tend to assume that this is the place for the worst of the worst, or that it is a justified outcome or rational tail-end of a criminal justice process. But in fact, the prison is also a vehicle to manage legal, administrative, and political processes. For example, throughout the last forty years one of the fastest growing components of the carceral is immigration detention. This suggests to us that the usefulness of the deprivation of liberty extends well beyond the domain of criminal justice. There are many people incarcerated in provincial prisons and immigration detention centres in Canada who are there not for any criminal transgression or conviction but are part of a broader politics of citizenship and migration control. In this regard, prisons are being used to service immigration policy and not transgressions of the Criminal Code. Do you think it is important for criminology students to consider these aspects of incarceration?

MM: Yes, of course! Thank you for bringing up the issue that not everyone in prison is there because of a criminal infraction or conviction. That is something the public might fail to appreciate. In addition to the issue of innocence and prison, I think we should be honest in our position that we oppose prisons. I am glad you brought up the word "abolition" because I think our hidden perspective is an abolitionist perspective. We do not think prisons should exist; not least of which because it does not satisfy the four principles of sentencing (e.g., denunciation, deterrence, rehabilitation, and protection of the public). First, I think we have shown that it does not protect the public in the sense that prisoners are also part of the public and they are being damaged while in prison. Second, when they are released as unemployed ex-prisoners that also does not satisfy the principle of protecting the public, and in terms of the mandate to rehabilitate there is very little education or skills-building during incarceration. In terms of deterrence, there is the idea that once you go to jail, you will never go back ever again, but that is not borne out by our statistical tracking of re-offending. Prisoners are not deterred from criminal behaviour or further sentencing because of an earlier incarceration. It might be that denunciation is the only principle that is achieved or upheld by the system.

ML: I think you are right to say that there is an abolitionist undertone to our conversation, and I am comfortable with this. There is a lot of merit in taking a stand against the acceptance or inevitability of institutions that appear to be inherently unjust and harmful, even though such a position can strike other criminologists as naive, utopian, or even dangerous. But I wanted to pick up on your comment about denunciation because, on the one hand, by punishing and through the act of a sentence a judge does speak the language of denunciation, but, on the other hand, there is a certain ironic symmetry between the things we are seeking to denounce and the way the carceral system functions. For example, we say it is wrong to hurt people deliberately, take their things, or limit other people's freedoms, but then in response to this, we hurt the criminal person by taking their things and limiting their mobility and freedoms. In so doing, we send a peculiarly inconsistent message about justice. I have always found that to be one of the ironies of imprisonment, where we deprive people of connection and compassion and then expect them to be rehabilitated. We hurt people so they do not hurt people.

What Is to Be Done?

ML: But perhaps it is time to pause. We have been relentlessly critical of the system as it currently exists and of many of its premises and consequences. I think a reader could rightly ask us, "Well, what do you think is to be done if these approaches are wrong or flawed? What should we be doing differently?" The search for solutions is understandable. How might we respond to this question?

MM: I think we have been relentlessly pessimistic and critical of the system, but I do think another world is possible in the sense that we can certainly understand that things have changed in our own lifetime. For example, the decriminalization and legalization of recreational cannabis. I think a lot of people thought that would never happen and that the world was entirely set. But that has been proven wrong; the world is not set in stone; it does change, even when we do not want it to change. The question you have asked is in two parts. On the one hand, you have posed the questions: Should society be different? Should society's response to deviance be different? And should the responses of criminalization be different? Our answer has been clear: Yes! And I think we could offer many ideas about how it should be different. For example, we should not arrest people for being homeless. The police are the wrong service to deploy to correct or solve homelessness. We cynically deploy police just to manage the visible disorder associated with people living in cities without homes. We should not use police services at all to interact with people who are homeless. Rather, we should have healthcare workers and housing placement workers interact with people who are homeless because they can address their immediate and related problems. That would be an easy solution we could implement right now without much thought or planning, but such a shift in response would need strong political will and municipal support that is not currently forthcoming. So, on the other hand, the question you have posed is about political will. How would you have a different criminal response or social response to criminal activity or deviance? That is the $64,000 question.[21] How do you create social change? How do you affect municipal policy? How do you compel politicians to properly represent your interests? How do citizens, social activists, or concerned citizens have agency in altering or changing the social policy or criminal response policy? Those are the real questions. On the one hand, you are asking: "Should we change things?," and on the other hand, you are asking: "How can we turn proposed changes into real policy?" The second part is much more difficult to answer.

ML: It is helpful to break my initial question into the "should things change" and "how do we change" component questions because this helps us to organize both thought and action. Let me add two further complications, or perhaps two additional issues, we should consider. First, I think it is important to note that although we have spoken about the inertia of the existing criminal legal system, it is not as though the system is unchanging. As you have pointed out we have experienced changes in our lifetime. But they have not all been positive. One of the issues is that the criminal legal system and its institutions have been on an expansionary trajectory. More and more aspects of social life fall under the gaze of surveillance systems, under the authority of regulatory and control agencies. Social problems can be subsumed under the auspices of security and criminal justice apparatuses. That is one issue for us to consider. This is—as Christie points out—an industry, and like any industry there is a motivation to expand and accumulate. The second issue I think we should consider is that the system is resilient, and there is a fascinating and perhaps troubling history of reformist ideas and initiatives being absorbed by the criminal legal system or the carceral. Well intentioned efforts to change the way things work, to make the system more humane or more responsive to the needs of communities and victims, can become mere adjuncts to the status quo. In our discussion, I gave the example of restorative justice programs and community corrections, but technological initiatives like GPS ankle monitors for conditional release (house arrest) also come to mind.[22] And this is always challenging for people who want to do things differently, because they must simultaneously envision this other world that is possible and perhaps put it into practice in some way but also guard against the absorbent tendencies of the existing system.

MM: I love the way you have ended by saying "absorbent tendencies." That is a great visual image of society and criminal response. And so, I am cautious about what I want to say because I agree with you that society is so absorbent. But if I were forced to answer the original question, "Is another world possible and what would you do to create that world?," then I would cautiously propose, in relation to homelessness, to have more housing as a way of solving the problem of the unhoused. Or, with respect to prostitution, I would propose that police no longer interact with people who enter consensual sexual relationships, and that would be achieved through the removal of all mention of sex work or prostitution from the Criminal Code. Overall, I would expand and fund social work because so many of people's problems are related to their social situation. As we have stated over and over in this text: people are born into conditions not of their own choosing, so to address homelessness and mental illness, I would propose we deploy more street nurses to help people who have mental illness or other types of psychosocial problems that have intersected with a housing issue. We might have to create an entirely new housing authority to remove the blight and the social problem of people being unhoused in the twenty-first century—an age of incredible wealth and prosperity.

ML: These are important ideas, and we can find promising examples of pilot programs along these lines. The problem is that these initiatives are treated as temporary, experimental, or add-ons rather than as valuable alternatives. Sustained public funding for police organizations and other criminal justice institutions is treated as a given, whereas alternative approaches to social problems—such as street nurses—are supported on an ad hoc and uneven basis. Truly embracing these approaches requires a long-term investment and perhaps a "paradigm shift" in our understanding of causes and solutions.

MM: You use the word "temporary" and "add-ons," and that is very useful. Many innovations are piloted as temporary projects and the core services of the criminal justice system remain unchanged when the experiment ends. With respect to incarceration, I would propose that we change prisons so they are able to rehabilitate people more successfully. For example, it is entirely reasonable for a prisoner to get an education or degree and be discharged with a job. We can avoid discharging prisoners as unemployed ex-convicts. Or I would even go further and abolish prisons or radically redesign their mandate and current configurations. And lastly, I would reduce the police service because I think—as we have argued—police services have been deployed into situations for which it was never designed. It was never designed to solve housing, it was never designed to solve homelessness, or it was never designed to address people with multidimensional social and psychosocial problems like mental health disorders.

I began by saying I agree with you that society is very absorbent. All the suggestions above are blue sky solutions that may be impossible to implement because of society's absorbent nature. Even though we can appreciate the value in having less violence, or responding with less violent measures to social problems, I am still not sure if we know how to politically implement such solutions. I know we can agitate, and we can vote every year, and I know we can be concerned citizens, or even nosy neighbours, and create local solutions, but the problems addressed above are much bigger, macro-social issues that are very difficult to solve overnight by simply having a laundry list of things you want to change, and that I think is the power of your statement about society being absorbent.

ML: You have listed several exciting ideas, ideas that would require a radical revisioning of the way we address social problems. You reminded me of the concept of "justice reinvestment" that has been used extensively by prison abolitionists and police reform advocates in the United

States and around the world. Justice reinvestment involves recognizing that our current system is extraordinarily costly. It is not cheap to put someone in prison and to keep them there. Policing is one of the most expensive things we invest in as a society. So there are tremendous resources wrapped up in the status quo, and justice reinvestment recognizes that fundamentally changing things should involve not simply adding new initiatives, new resources, and new layers to our current system but rather reducing our reliance on these outdated and ineffective institutions and diverting those resources towards community-level solutions that address some of the fundamental or root cause issues that give rise to social problems like homelessness, social inequality, lack of adequate medical services and so on. This is one of the most important observations we can make: serious change, in relation to how our legal system operates, will not come through additive measures but rather through alternatives that reduce the scope of the carceral.

Discussion Questions:

1. When people propose significant changes to the foundational structures of the criminal justice system—for example, radically reducing the use of incarceration or scaling back the powers and resources of police—they often face strong reactions, including claims that these ideas are unrealistic. Do you think it is possible to make sweeping changes in criminal justice system's structure and practice? How can we explain strong negative reactions to proposals to reduce the size and reach of the legal system?

2. Search the web for pictures of provincial courtrooms and the Supreme Court of Canada. Take note of the aspects of ritual, symbolism, and ceremony. How might we explain these features?

3. Everyone has the right to a fair trial and the right to be presumed innocent until proven otherwise. However, the vast majority of criminal cases do not proceed to trial. They end with guilty pleas. Trials are a rarity. Why might people choose to plead guilty rather than exercise their right to a trial? What do you think would happen if the majority of people charged with criminal offences chose to proceed to trial?

4. How might a legal system that focuses on punishment and retribution benefit society? Are there social benefits to our current punitive approaches/reactions? Discuss.

5. A current social reaction to the opioid overdose crisis has been "harm reduction." Harm reduction is based on the idea that if we supervise the consumption of illicit drugs, then we can immediately reverse overdoses if they happen—thereby reducing the harm. Some people think this condones—or even encourages—drug addiction and that a strict prohibitionist approach would better send the appropriate denunciatory message. Supporters of harm reduction argue that "dead people don't detox" and that is why supervised drug use of illicit substances is useful. This is a good example of a controversial social response to the existing problem of extreme opioid addiction. What objectives or values should guide our approach? Discuss.

CHAPTER 8
Criminalizing Inequality and Poverty

In this chapter, we focus on the inextricable connections between inequality, poverty, and criminalization. We return to the theme of causation and explore the relationship between economic forces, the structural conditions that produce and facilitate wrongdoing, and the harms connected with massive and growing inequality. We consider the role of the legal system in the reproduction of a social and economic status quo that is designed to produce vast disparities in wealth, security, and power.

Michael C. K. Ma (MM): When we think about poverty, we often imagine it to be connected with crime. It is common for people to imagine areas where there is more crime to be areas of low socioeconomic status or neighbourhoods that are colloquially understood to be "poor." Poverty is generally understood to refer to a lack of money. Both the general public and scholars alike may imagine poor areas to be incubators of crime, especially street level crime, and official crime statistics do show a correlation between social deprivation and crime. But when we think about poverty we think not just of crime but also low socioeconomic status, lack of employment, lack of education, lack of housing, lack of food security, lack of health services, lack of finances, and/or lack of financial stability.[1] What may be missing when we consider the relationship between crime and poverty is that, at a societal level, it is the economy that determines whether people are engaged with crime or become criminalized. The economic condition of poverty is the thing we must address. It is not the economic "result" of a poor neighbourhood or poor people that should be blamed for crime. We should examine the cause. That is the thing we should address in this chapter. With lower socioeconomic status there may come behaviours that are "deviant" and/or antisocial and which are then criminalized, but what is the origin of these social behaviours? You cannot have one without the other; they are combined or synergistic. Conditions of deprivation, poverty, and inequality come about because of economic conditions that people did not actively choose. The acts of crime and poverty are cocreators. They exist simultaneously. People do not choose poverty, but we assume that people choose crime.

Mike Larsen (ML): It is interesting that when we think about crime there is often an inclination to seek explanations for the causes of crime that are centred on the individual, on individual choices, individual decisions, and individual pathologies. Sometimes a discussion about the relationship between inequality, socioeconomics, and crime involve pushing back against assumptions of crime being caused by criminals who are pathologically amoral or predatory and who tend to congregate in particular kinds of neighbourhoods. For example, assisted and high-density subsidized housing developments, which, by definition, exist in poorer areas, are often assumed to be hotbeds of street crime. We are familiar with the concept of "bad neighbourhoods," and we know that people often avoid these places because of their reputation.

When you think about it, though, we take it for granted that many other phenomena in society are shaped by economic forces. For example, it is easy for us to understand that access to higher education is connected to socioeconomic status. If you cannot afford tuition, then you will find it difficult to attend university and focus on your studies. Here in British Columbia, we have been experiencing an extraordinary explosion in real estate values, and this, coupled with inflation, is giving rise to important conversations about whether it is possible for people who do not have inherited wealth to access affordable housing and make ends meet. Individual choices may play a role in particular cases, but we understand housing prices and inflation to be connected to economic trends that cannot be altered by any one person. However, it can be difficult to get people to use the above framework to think about crime and deviance as phenomena shaped by similar broad socioeconomic factors. This is, in part, because our legal system is designed to focus on individual responsibility and accountability, and in part, because major branches of criminology have historically taken as their starting point the assumption that there is something different or abnormal about individual offenders.

The poverty and crime discussion has been going on for centuries in terms of criminology. What is the relationship between social disorganization, ecology, and crime? This question animated criminological debates in the early 1900s. By contrast, the connections between poverty and criminalization have only been explored comparatively recently and typically by critical criminologists.[2] The central idea here is that our legal system itself is designed in a way that reproduces a particular "status quo"—one that benefits wealthy groups and disproportionately reflects their interests—while maintaining an image of equality and justice. As the poet Anatole France once noted, "In its majestic equality, the law forbids rich and poor alike to sleep under bridges, beg in the streets and steal loaves of bread."[3] I always find that to be a powerful starting point for discussion because it invites us to think about how the contents of criminal law—the content of our statutes, what we criminalize, and how we go about enforcing it—are deeply attached to questions of inequality and poverty.

MM: I could not agree with you more. The rich do not have to choose to sleep under a bridge. It is quite common these days for critics and pundits to talk about the social determinants of health, the social determinants of poverty, or the social determinants of success in society. That is, they agree that social support and social status is intimately connected to what a person is able to choose or act out in practice. If there are social determinants (e.g., lack of income, lower income, or lower socioeconomic status) that help cause criminal behaviour, or the criminalization of behaviours, then it stands to reason we should try to address or fix the cause of lower socioeconomic status as a response to crime. That is, fix poverty and you fix a great deal of crime.[4] And yet, we know police and the courts have no tools to address lower socioeconomic status or solve poverty. If we have crime and it rises and falls based on poverty, then the question for us to ask would be: Why do we continue to deploy police to address the symptoms of lower social economic status?[5] And, in the context of courts, are the courts the right tool to use to solve lower socioeconomic status? Even judges when deliberating on evidence might understand the larger circumstances of a person who appears before the court and that it is their socioeconomic status that has brought them before the courts, and yet there is no mechanism for a judge to use to rectify it except the tool of court sentencing. The crux of the problem is that we do not have the correct tool, agency, or social service to properly address lower socioeconomic status and the behaviours that might go along with it. The law cannot fix, nor was it designed to fix, the socioeconomic determinants of crime.

ML: That is a good point. To return to France's quote, the result is a system that can enforce laws around panhandling, sleeping rough, and petty theft, but cannot meaningfully address hunger, poverty, and lack of housing. Indeed, the former are readily conceptualized as crime and disorder problems and the latter are considered beyond the purview of the courts. We should note that the places where one would expect to encounter panhandling, homelessness, and petty theft are also the places that are routinely patrolled by police and private security whose mandate is to maintain and enforce order. Members of wealthy groups also commit serious forms of wrongdoing, but their actions generally occur in places that are "unpatrolled"—in private residences, corporate offices, and within institutions.

If we are interested in addressing crime as a social problem, then we must understand its intimate connection to marginalization in a variety of ways, including economic marginalization. The challenge is that we understand marginalization to be a problem of social structure and structural problems cannot be "solved" via individualized processes. However, our legal system and its institutions are designed with individualized process in mind. They focus on questions of individual responsibility—on actus reus and mens rea (i.e., did you do it, and are you responsible for it?), and this leads into questions of individual-level sanctions and responses, including rehabilitative and punitive processes. Regardless of the merits of such processes in individual cases, they are fundamentally incapable of addressing the structural problems that give rise to conditions of marginalization. For example, we know we are living in a time of massive and increasing wealth and income inequality,[6] and we know this places extraordinary pressures on a growing class of people who must struggle to make ends meet and who may be one emergency away from losing their housing.[7] We know these pressures can put people in situations of desperation and conflict. The criminal justice system is not designed or empowered to address this problem in any meaningful way, though. In fact, from a critical perspective you could argue that the system was designed to protect precisely this kind of accumulation of wealth and inequality. It is meant to perpetuate such a structure. It is primarily a symptom alleviation mechanism rather than a justice mechanism. There is nothing I can think of that police organizations, judges, courts, and prisons can do to address the determinants of marginalization in society, and yet they are consistently treated and called upon as the key institutions that will best respond to these issues.

MM: Of course, I agree. Being poor, working in a dead-end job, or working for rock-bottom wages is understood to be a choice freely made by free individuals. And yet once we put it like that, it is easy to understand that we are *not* free to choose. On the one hand, France's quote brings up the absurd notion that a rich person could choose to sleep under a bridge but declines and chooses to sleep in their own bed in their own house. On the other hand, it questions why hunger, poverty and lack of housing occur in society. Why would someone sleep under a bridge? Why would someone panhandle or beg for money? What are the social causes of such individual actions? And, most importantly, can the police help someone who is panhandling? The quick answer is no. People who are very poor—and hence hungry or without housing—cannot be helped by police. Police can only help control, further marginalize, or criminalize them. Police cannot feed people or get them housing. The subtitle of this chapter could be phrased as: What causes poverty, and can police, courts, and corrections solve the problem of poverty?

ML: That would be a good subtitle! But it is also a rhetorical question answering its own query. We know police, courts, and corrections have no power to correct poverty and socioeconomic deprivation. So perhaps this is a good time to shift gears. The title of this chapter is inequality and poverty and thus far we have been focusing on the poverty aspect of the equation, and particularly on the relationship between economic marginalization, social structures, and involvement in criminalized activities. However, inequality cuts both ways, and in a society where you have a marginalized class or underclass, you also have powerful corporations and the ultrarich. While poor and working-class communities have historically been the focus of both criminological inquiry (for example, through theories that focus on subcultures and social disorganization) and formal social control efforts, there is a branch of criminology that addresses the crimes of the powerful and, indeed, the forms of injustice, harm, and exploitation embedded in the system itself.

MM: Yes, we should shift gears. You are referring to the study of white-collar and corporate crime, where criminologists such as Edwin Sutherland helped coin the term "white-collar crime."[8] The invention of this term turns our attention from criminalizing the petty criminal to identifying those in positions of social authority and power who may act in an equally deviant or criminal manner. When thinking about this, it is important to bear in mind our earlier discussion about the social and legal construction of deviance. It might help us understand that the powerful have influenced the way the law tends to focus on crimes and deviance in ways that absolve the powerful. We can say that powerful groups and interests have a disproportionate capacity to shape and influence society.

By shifting gears, we can examine how inequality is not just a product of disproportionate poverty but also of disproportionate wealth. When we use the word inequality, or unequal, it refers to people living in poverty and often does not refer to people living in wealth. It is a funny thing about the word "inequality"; our mind immediately goes to people who are at the bottom of the economic pyramid. So it might be fruitful to also investigate wealth as a form of deviant behaviour and social practice. That is, wealth and its pursuit often involve a self-centred pursuit of profit, enriching an individual at the expense of their employees and/or the social environment. But we should bear in mind that "wealth" is not just a reference to the super wealthy. When we examine wealth as a factor of social inequality or unfairness, it is not just those who are extremely wealthy, like celebrities, sports stars, or CEOs of Fortune 500 companies; rather, it also involves examining those who have marginal wealth or middle-class wealth that affords them a significant leg up. Both the very wealthy and the middle class have a significant advantage in terms of where their starting line is in life. Their starting lines in education, health, housing, and social networks are significantly superior to those who do not have comparable wealth. So we might ask the question: Is wealth and economic superiority a kind of deviance since it helps you influence and navigate society in a way that benefits you at the expense of others? Is wealth criminogenic?

ML: These are important points, and it is also important to note that the economic system is a *system* and needs to be understood as such. By this I mean that there is a relationship between a poor underclass living paycheque to paycheque in conditions of precarity struggling to secure housing and a thriving upper class, accumulating exponential wealth and striving to ensure that it is taxed as little as possible. You do not get to be in "the 1%,"[9] as it is often described, without being involved in some degree of exploitation. As you point out, it is easy for us to think about conditions of poverty as being abnormal or problematic (even "criminogenic"), while at the same time admiring or at the very least accepting the existence of billionaires. It is important for us to acknowledge that the social and economic system that we live in creates, and perhaps more provocatively, *requires* inequality. In this sense, poverty is not an aberration but a function of our economic system, and if we understand that criminalization is disproportionately associated with conditions of poverty, this raises some important questions about the justice of our justice system. What do you think?

MM: I cannot agree with you more. Another way to frame this question is with the concept of unearned privileges. People with great wealth are receiving unearned privileges often because they were born into conditions of great wealth not of their own making or "choosing." When we think about great wealth we can cite Thomas Piketty's book *Capital in the Twenty-First Century* regarding inheritance in France.[10] His research demonstrates that wealth is consolidated, funnelled, and congealed into the hands of smaller and smaller groups of people. His work shows that once wealth is passed on through inheritance it continues to increase as you pass it to your children and as your children pass it to their children. Piketty's research is a persuasive historical study showing that wealth becomes concentrated in an unequal manner as time progresses. The wealth is not redistributed through taxation or through some other redistribution mechanism. Piketty's study shows that wealth comes to be held in perpetuity by a very small select group of people.

We can accept that some people will succeed where others fail, but what happens when only a small segment of the population succeeds and passes its success on to its own future generations? That is *exactly* what I would term "economic inequality," and its effects go far beyond the economy. That effect means not only are you economically wealthy, not only are you socially successful, not only are you physically healthier, but you are—as you already pointed out—able to affect which laws, which social programs, which healthcare regimes, and which other social institutions are created. Those systems of social organization will naturally reflect your interests because you and your family have greater wealth as an individual or social unit. Through wealth you have greater social capital and greater economic wealth. You are able to better create, mould, and shape society to better favour you and not those who are weak, poor, or who lack wealth.

ML: We can also note that corporations and economic elites in Canada are able to anticipate that formal institutions of social control will mobilize to defend their interests, especially when these interests are challenged by communities and social movements. In the summer of 2021, we saw police in British Columbia mobilized to arrest over a thousand people who were opposing the logging of old-growth forest at Fairy Creek on Vancouver Island.[11] We also saw police in Toronto aggressively dismantling an encampment of unhoused people that had been set up in a public park. In the latter case, police worked alongside private security to forcibly "clear" the park, arresting or displacing people and destroying or confiscating their property.[12] In both cases, the "legal violence" of the state was directed "downwards," in furtherance of the protection or promotion of the status quo. These are depressingly common scenes. By contrast, think about how extraordinary it would be to wake up and read the news that dozens of police had been deployed to the corporate offices of retail companies that engage in wage theft or to the headquarters of banks that directly benefit from (and enable) housing inequality through the commodification of real estate.

MM: I really like what you say about the legal violence of the state and then also the way this legal violence is disproportionately or unequally served to the public. The legal violence is served, as you say, to protesters but not to those who work in corporate offices. And that would be a question for us to ask: Why is this type of state violence served in a disproportionate manner? Why are police deployed to solve or curtail the problems produced by poverty or inequality? We know that deploying police—and I think we have talked about this in other chapters—is not the best service to deploy if you are trying to solve, say, a housing or mental health problem. Similarly, we also know it is not the best service to deploy if you want to, say, curtail corporate or income tax fraud—which are common problems in Canada and elsewhere. It is telling that the practice of police solves neither the problems of poverty (i.e., street crime) nor wealth (i.e., white-collar crime).

We can also ask why the law criminalizes shoplifting but does not criminalize misstating your taxes or your income. Those offences could be criminal but are understood by law as civil problems. Crimes that are "economic" are often understood as administrative problems that can be solved by noncriminal penalties (e.g., fines, compliance agreements). We can return to our original question: Does poverty cause crime, and can police solve poverty? That is a pregnant and leading question because it points to the bigger question: Are laws, which are created to address crimes linked to poverty, just or fair?

ML: Over time, I have come to the conclusion that our legal system, and particularly the enforcement institutions associated with it, exist and function primarily to preserve and reproduce a status quo. I mean this at a structural level. That is an important point to emphasize. I am certain there are people who go into policing or the practice of criminal law with the sincere intention of reducing injustice in society and protecting vulnerable people. And I am certain there are people in these professions who strive to realize these objectives daily. However, if we pull back and consider the system and its institutions as a whole, it seems apparent that the primary function of the system is to ensure that the way things *are* stays relatively stable (this is the "order" part of "law and order"). It follows that if the status quo—the way things are—is based on an unequal distribution of wealth, resources, and privilege and on the exploitation of certain groups for profit by other groups, this is the order that will be reinforced, normalized, and protected by our institutions.

MM: I like your use of the example of police and lawyers and how they enter their professions in good faith and with good intentions. But this also reminds me of the saying that good intentions pave the path to ruin. That is, at the end of the day we know that neither policing nor lawyering leads to very much social change. When you finish your shift as a police officer, or you close a case you are defending through law, the social structures that surround your work have remained intact and unchanged. So the question we must ask is: What is the purpose of policing, and what is the purpose of lawyering? I submit to you that the purpose of these vocations is exactly to maintain an existing *not equal* or *not fair* system of society. These professions maintain the status quo, as you have suggested. They maintain inequality in society. Therefore they never can solve the problems of inequality that arise because of social economic and structural inequality. You might have good intentions, but those intentions do not solve social structural problems. And the laws, the structure of lawyering, the structure of policing, the institution of policing, and the use of them as state violence—to solve social problems like mental health, unemployment, or housing—are not remediated in any way whatsoever.

ML: We can think about this through the imagery of the tools associated with these institutions. There is nothing in a police cruiser or on a police utility belt, nothing in the sentencing powers available to a judge in a provincial trial court or in the selection of correctional programs available to workers in prisons that will address, or could address, systemic inequality and exploitation. And so, if we understand crime to be correlated with inequality and exploitation, we are left with the uncomfortable conclusion that our system is not equipped to respond to the symptoms of these problems; it is not equipped, by design, to truly solve them at a deeper level.

MM: But to play devil's advocate and to voice what might be on some of our readers' minds, I might ask: Does not policing temporarily alleviate a problem in a positive way? Does not a practice of lawyering temporarily resolve a legal issue in a beneficial way? For example, if you deploy a police officer to a public disturbance (e.g., someone having a mental health episode in a public space) and they are able to stop that disturbance, detain that person, arrest that person, or remove that person, then the public has benefited from the removal of the noise or disturbance. In so doing, they create public good. Similarly, we could ask: Does not a lawyer create more fairness in determining guilt or innocence by representing a client? And cannot a judge—through the use of fair sentencing—create more safety and justice within the confines or limitations of the law? In both cases, policing and the courts have created increased public order or public safety, albeit in a very restricted manner.

ML: Those are good questions. And I would simply answer by saying that these interventions are not true forms of justice and those are not true solutions because they do not solve the much deeper and much more complex social problems that underlie the crimes. We should note that these critical ideas are certainly not exclusive to the two of us. In criminological research on the role, function, and everyday practice of policing, there have been numerous studies over the years that address the gap between the ambition of police officers and the entrenched nature of social problems. Peter Manning, in a famous study, concluded that since police were fundamentally incapable of truly addressing and resolving the root causes of the social problems that had come to define their mandate, their role had subtly shifted to managing appearances and showing that they were actively responding to the symptoms of these problems.[13]

MM: To build on Manning's critique, we can also ask the question: Is the criminal justice system the ideal system to address everyday problems in society? One such everyday problem, if we continue to focus on street crime and justice, is the example of someone who is having a mental health episode or someone committing a petty crime like shoplifting of batteries or cosmetics. If we consider these everyday issues of crime, then it is quite clear that we would not design an overly muscular system of policing to deal with these less significant or less-risk-to-society problems around public safety. We do not need a muscular police force to deal with the repeat offender who keeps stealing batteries at the Shoppers Drug Mart. We might need to have a muscular police force to deal with a bank robbery or deep social emergencies like a hostage situation. In this regard, police organization and training are well set up to deal with hostages or bank robberies, but those forms of crime are so rare that they are akin to lightning strikes. Why should society create and fund a system of response to lightning strikes when they are so rare? Lightning strikes may create fires, but our fire departments were never created as a response to lightning. Similarly, why should we spend precious social resources to create such a response service (i.e., police service) when the design of the service itself is poorly aligned with the social problem at hand? Shoplifting as a "crime" has more to do with economic inequality than it does with public safety. But we know the police service does not address or solve economic inequality.

ML: I think it is helpful for us to use metaphors and analogies when thinking about these issues. Another way to think about this would be through the problem of fire. Historically, massive fires were a commonplace and deeply destructive scourge of early urban environments. The combination of increasing density, flammable materials, and a lack of any meaningful regulation around what could be built—or burned—in particular locations created the conditions of possibility for fires that would engulf entire districts. Most of the City of Vancouver was destroyed by fire in 1886, for example, when fires started to clear brush to make way for development spread out of control. The solution to this problem was not simply more and better equipped firefighters. Rather, it was regulatory, educational, and preventative efforts that were geared towards preventing fires from occurring in the first place. I am thinking of things like building codes, requirements for fire extinguishers, and innovations in alarms and detection systems. We still have and need firefighters, particularly in a context where due to climate change the world around us is burning, but perhaps we can learn something from this more foundational and preventative approach to addressing serious social problems and apply it to our thinking about crime and criminal justice.

MM: I agree. The fire of poverty and social inequality cannot be put out by police, courts, or corrections. And that leaves us with the final question: If you cannot put out the fire of poverty and inequality with our existing criminal justice system, then what is the criminal justice system designed for and what could it be replaced with?

Discussion Questions:

1. What form might a system of justice take if it were able to address systemic injustice as pertains to poverty and inequality?
2. Does the arrest, prosecution, sentencing, and incarceration of someone for petty theft reduce crime (in the long term) and increase public well-being or public safety?
3. Explain the meaning of the quote: "In its majestic equality, the law forbids rich and poor alike to sleep under bridges, beg in the streets and steal loaves of bread."

CHAPTER 9
Racism

In this chapter, we explore how "race"—as a social construct—has been historically used to legitimize hierarchies of power by sorting and dividing people. Most importantly, we highlight how forms of overt, institutional, and systemic racism become enacted and expressed through criminal justice processes and social practice. The chapter demonstrates that race and racism are a multidimensional phenomenon arising from complex historical conditions that must be confronted through our contemporary politics. In discussing race, crime, and criminalization we propose an intersectional framework that links race with other social determinations. We challenge the reader to understand the concepts of race and racism as terms of analysis and not as things in and of themselves.

Mike Larsen (ML): I think people starting to explore criminology in the current context will be unsurprised to learn that there is an active and ongoing interest in the ways racism intersects with law, criminalization, and criminal justice. This is certainly evident to anyone who has been following the news over the last decade. Mike, this is, in fact, your area of specialization. In some ways, the discipline is starting to catch up to you on this! But I suspect you would go beyond acknowledging that there are "intersections" and suggest to us that race and racialization are integrally, inextricably integrated into our legal system and the discipline of criminology.

Michael C. K. Ma (MM): I think racism or even the concept of race is an incredibly complicated subject. We can understand race simply as categorizations of people based on a pseudoscientific notion of human diversity, but often it gets expressed in society as people's colour. So the notion of how people are judged by their colour, skin, hair, the texture of their hair, the shape of their eyes, or the shape of their nose, etc. is much more complicated to examine. How does the shape of your face or the colour of your skin relate to how you experience the criminal justice system? How does the way you are racially understood in society give you certain entitlements if you are white or disadvantages if you are not white? But that is also a very contentious assertion because we can understand that just because you are white does not necessarily make you rich and just because you are not white does not necessarily make you poor. So how race plays into your experience of society, your security, and your experience of the criminal justice system is complex.

ML: These are hugely important questions and the implication is that race and racism are inextricably part of both the legal system and criminology. In other words, it is not only impossible but counterproductive to approach the study of crime, deviance, and law without considering the central role that race plays. Is this correct?

MM: Yes, you are right. It would be a huge mistake not to consider race. For example, we know that people of colour are overrepresented in prisons. We know there are more people of colour in prison than is proportional to the population. According to Statistics Canada, in 2018–2019, Indigenous adults accounted for 31 percent of admissions to provincial/territorial custody and 29 percent of admissions to federal custody despite representing approximately 4.5 percent of the Canadian adult population. A similar pattern can be found in the youth correctional system.[1] So if we do not examine this pattern of significance in incarceration, would we not be willfully denying or avoiding the question of why and how there are more people of colour in prison than is proportional to the population? It behooves us to grapple with this difficult question. A question that can be posed is: How is racial profiling, or bias on the part of the criminal legal system, connected to the socioeconomic wealth or poverty of a person and how is that related to their racialization in society? Questions like this would help us, not hinder us, in understanding how society operates with a racial logic.

ML: This is a good starting point. It is always helpful to unpack and clarify some key terms when we start exploring a topic. I think race is a concept that is simultaneously familiar and complicated. It has certainly been contested. So perhaps this is a good starting point for us. How would you recommend we approach the concept of race as criminologists?

MM: Race is a social invention that is a product of Western European colonization and in a connected manner the product of the transatlantic slave trade. In the fifteenth century, Europeans started exploring and expanding their reach across the globe. In so doing, they "discovered" new worlds and what they perceived to be different types of humans. In that encounter with what was perceived to be an uncivilized world they began to develop certain pseudohistorical and pseudoscientific understandings of how Western Europeans were superior to those they were encountering in the new world. It gave rise to certain types of biological and commonsensical notions of superiority. As critical scholars we want to understand this development of artificially dividing and categorizing humans as a social construct that has very real social implications. But it is important to always keep in mind that it is a human-made and artificial division with no natural or biological basis. The question we must ask is: If race is a flawed social construction, how can we potentially alter or erase the way race currently exists and influences the criminal justice system? How is it being used and how could we alter, remediate, or extinguish its use in the criminal justice system? More specifically, how is racial profiling or racial bias used in policing and can we change it?

ML: This underscores the power of language, discourse, and social construction. We can note that a concept like race, or deviance, is constructed, and even point to the politics and vested interests that have informed its construction. We can acknowledge that this construction has been reified, naturalized, and internalized in ways that are profoundly "real" and consequential. This is something, I think, that is often missed when people initially think about concepts like social construction, which can seem to imply that something is unreal or fabricated. But society itself is fabricated, in the sense that it is organized around ideas and processes that are constructed and given meaning by us as social actors, and this includes some of the most profoundly impactful and taken-for-granted concepts that inform our everyday life, and race certainly stands out as an example.

MM: Yes, I agree. I think we can understand why race is important to the study of crime because we understand that people are identified, categorized, judged, and treated differently because of their appearance or their socioeconomic/racial status. That is, in the North American context, we understand that people are treated differently because they are not white, and we understand that some people who are treated as

white are also treated differently; most often earning and being entitled
to unearned privileges and other types of benefits.[2] So that is why criminology should absolutely grapple with the question of race. We know
that police services and border control, for example, use racial profiling.[3]
We know that when a person of colour who is Indigenous or Black and
who stands before the court is treated differently, whether intentionally
or unconsciously, and that is why it is a matter of importance for the
study of crime.

ML: You mentioned here the example of the person who is Indigenous
and who is treated differently by the system. When we think about
examples of racism in institutional and systemic settings, such as a court
setting, one of the first things that comes to my mind is the historical intersection between racialization and colonialism that occurs long
before the court comes into being. In this regard, I think it is impossible to accurately "unpack" the phenomenon of colonialism without
addressing the role of racism—and particularly the reproduction of
racial hierarchies—in the process. Would you agree? How is race linked
to colonialism?

MM: That is a huge and difficult question but thank you for asking it.
How is race linked to colonialism? It is quite simple. We know that
notions of race were produced because of the encounter with the new
world and with the colonization of these new territories. And that colonization had to have a repressive state apparatus like police. In the
Canadian context, we invented and deployed the RCMP in concert
with the introduction of a legal system (e.g., British law—or French
law in the case of upper/lower Canada). The legal and repressive state
apparatus was introduced as a method of controlling and reterritorial-
izing the new world in the image of Western European society. There
was an introduction of European rationalism, science, the rule of law,
custom, religion, and so forth as European countries such as England,
France, Spain, and Portugal began to discover, conquer, and colonize
the Americas.

ML: So, if I understand correctly, the idea is that the process of colonization was facilitated, from the perspective of the colonial powers and
their publics, by the ability of those people to understand themselves
to be racially and categorically different from the people who were the

subjects of colonization. And, not just different, but by virtue of race, naturally superior.

MM: Yes! I think another way to think about or examine this notion of colonization and the development of racial categories is also to understand the colonizer's position. We should understand that even the colonizer's own self-imagination—as a people or society—was created in their confrontation with the new world. The entities we know as England or France came into a kind of racial being in this moment of contact. Their own identity as white came into being as a language and pseudoscience of race began to be developed to help discuss and imagine their difference and racial superiority. Ideas of superiority were developed in the moment of contact with North and South America, the Indian subcontinent, Africa, and Asia. All this contact gave rise to a Western European imagination and application of pseudoscience that created the concept of a "white" race that was superior to the populations of these other continents. Therefore, the process of colonization can be understood to be a process of "civilization" and an extension of Western European logic, science, and law. That is why the question of colonization matters when we are examining the criminal justice system, because it has direct connections to the laws, policing, and incarceration structures we have in the present era.

ML: These are excellent points, Mike, and of course they immediately bring to mind the treatment of Indigenous Peoples by Canadian institutions including law, courts, and policing. The lengthy and in some ways ongoing processes of displacement, dispossession, and marginalization accomplished through colonial institutions like Indian residential schools and indeed the Indian act itself were justified and rationalized by a Eurocentric rhetoric of a civilizing process and by instruments like the Church-issued Doctrine of Discovery, which provided religious, legal, and moral justification for the claiming of Indigenous land.[4]

MM: Yes, Indigenous Peoples have suffered in this long-drawn-out encounter with Western European society. An excellent illustration is the creation of the RCMP by Prime Minister John A. McDonald. At the time of its invention there was a need to continue to expand the colonization and settlement of North America into the western provinces. The RCMP is a paramilitary force that was created to subjugate and control First Nations in the West.[5] So we can understand how the origins of a federal police force was connected to the political practice of colonization and the need for the Canadian state to have a repressive paramilitary organization tasked with dispossessing Indigenous Peoples of their land, social structures, religion, language, and cultural practices. A paramilitary force was created to enforce the Indian act; an act that was passed through Parliament to control, relocate, and dispossess Indigenous Peoples of their treaty rights. We also know that the RCMP was important in helping maintain both the reserve system and the pass system that were created through the Indian act. We also know they were involved in helping support the residential school system. They intervened and were useful in taking children away from families and helping put them into residential schools, and they were also useful in returning students who ran away from residential schools.[6] Some readers may think that this is ancient history because current RCMP are no longer involved in arresting and detaining children and returning them to residential schools, but history matters, and our understanding of the origins of our police service informs how we understand their current structure and their current mandates.

ML: History does matter, and of course it matters not just in the sense of understanding the events of the past but also in understanding the history of our present. It is particularly important to acknowledge that antiracist struggles in Canada—for example, struggles against slavery, officially sanctioned forms of discrimination, the repression or exclusion of certain peoples, both historical and recent—have involved people fighting against the status quo and indeed institutions backed by the force of law. I think that is a very important point. Forms of institutionalized and systemic racism do not exist despite our legal system but because of it and through it. And so again we see that understanding these issues is of central importance to us as criminologists.

MM: I should also mention that it is not just understanding the origins of the RCMP but also understanding why they were created and deployed in the service of the colonization of Canada. They were created because there was Indigenous resistance to the dispossession of Indigenous land and their treaty entitlements to the land. So there was a constant social, political, and physical struggle and resistance against colonization. We can understand ourselves now in the post–94 Calls to Action world as uninvited guests but historically we can clearly see we were more than uninvited guests.[7] We were interlopers, colonizers, and violent political actors who were doing great harm to Indigenous Peoples and to their way of life. So that relationship extends to the current period. That relationship has not been amended or repaired. That is why the origins of the RCMP and why they were deployed is important for us to understand. It is important for us to understand that the presence of a harmful and violent racism was perpetrated on the part of the state by law, the courts, corrections, and police.

So, to summarize: First, the colonizing power invents a distinction to separate themselves from the population they seek to control. Second, the idea that colonized peoples are different and inferior types of humans allows for them to be treated in a subhuman manner. Third, this distinction justifies control over the new territory and the colonizer's understanding of their presence in the new world as a civilizing and positive force.

ML: This is a succinct summary. I think it is important to recognize the role that social, economic, and legal institutions play in manufacturing and reproducing historically specific understandings of race. Law plays a particularly important role here. How often do we hear statements like, "I don't like it, but it's the law," or appeals to the neutral and apolitical nature of the legal system. Embedding racist and colonial ideas and processes in the law helps to "launder" and naturalize them. What are some specific examples of this in relation to settler-colonialism?

MM: A British criminal system of law was imposed through its empire to establish that Indigenous practices were barbaric and uncivilized. For example, in India there was a British criminal system of law that helped establish the laws to prevent dowry because it was considered to be uncivilized. In Canada we had legislation that banned Indigenous practices such as potlatch or Sundance and other systems of trade that were understood to be uncivilized.[8] We can understand laws themselves as tools to be used to subjugate social practices that were constructed as uncivilized or detrimental to the social and capitalist expansion of Western European powers. We also know that many laws were introduced to prevent nonwhite Canadians, such as Chinese Canadians or Indigenous Peoples in Canada, from enjoying their rights, enjoying the ability to vote, enjoying their ability to own property, to enjoy their ability to run a business.[9] Laws themselves were very important in creating a system of racism that is embedded in the history of Canada.

ML: These are important points. It is the case that the same processes that are used to designate certain groups as "others" and to prohibit their practices also construct a powerful sense of what it means to be normal, natural, and superior. Processes of exclusion also function to reify notions of who and what is to be included and protected. In other words, the mechanisms that legally and socially construct the racialized other also, and by direct implication, shape the status and perceived legitimacy of members of dominant colonial groups.

MM: Yes. To be specific, in the context of England and France, the colonizer did identify their Western European social practices as being superior to those of the Indigenous population. So that produced a particular kind of identity for the colonizer and their own imagination of their social cultural and biological difference and how that was attached to their own nationhood. English people began to imagine the English nation as distinct, and French people, or French colonizers, also began to imagine their French state or institutions as being specifically superior and unique to their nationhood. In other words, a sense of nationalism began to be fomented and created in this golden era of colonization. One can even say we would not have the nations of England or France today if not for the practices of colonization and territorial expansion during this period of North American colonization and resettlement.

ML: The idea that there are inherent differences that constitute racial categories is so central to everything we have been talking about here, and I think it is important to note that these ideas did not simply emerge organically during the process of colonization. Ideas like racial categories were constructed by specific actors and through particular forms of knowledge. So this is a good opportunity for us to briefly consider the role of scholars and intellectuals in creating the categories and concepts that gave these forms of racism a sense of naturalness and legitimacy. What are some examples of this?

MM: You are right to remind us that scholars themselves were incredibly important in the imagination and creation of languages to describe Western European superiority. One such scholar was Johan Friedrich

Blumenbach, who was doing research in the eighteenth century.[10] He was very influential in creating categories of race and racism—in particular the imagination of "Caucasian" peoples as white people, or Western European colonizers as a race of humans who are distinct from everyone else. He measured skulls and skeletons, collected remains, and categorized people under five categorizations of humans: Caucasians, Mongolians, Ethiopians, Americans, and Malays. These are categories that have long been discredited and are no longer in use, but they help us understand how an imagination of "race" became misrepresented through of a pseudoscience of race—although it is interesting that "Caucasian" is still (mis)used today. Colonizers of North America assumed that the people they encountered or "discovered" were inferior and therefore in response began to produce harmful institutions like the RCMP or residential schools to control this racially inferior population.

ML: We can see the parallels between Blumenbach's work and the work of early biological criminologists like Cesare Lombroso.[11] In both cases, observable biological differences were presented as natural indicators of deep and profound—and incontrovertible—meaning. And, in both cases, the academic expertise and implied legitimacy of this empirical knowledge served to justify and legitimize practices of marginalization and forms of hierarchy.

MM: What is important about what we are saying here is that we now understand Blumenbach's scientific method and his discredited findings as mere pseudoscience. The current scientific community no longer understands his pseudoscientific categories to be legitimate categories of race. In fact, much of the study of genetics and the DNA of ancient peoples show us that "race" is a social imagination and is not reflected in the genetic code of humans. We may have different heights, different shades of colour, different languages, different foods, and different cultures but that does not mean humans have different races. That type of conceptualization has been discredited and described as historical artifacts arising out of a history of colonization. And you are right to point out that it is not just Blumenbach; we can also examine Lombroso's work. Lombroso was invested in using empirical understanding, which is achieved through scientific method, to understand how the world evolved—in the Darwinian meaning of the word. He examined the natural world, but also directed his attention to the area of deviance and criminal behaviour. He is most famous for proposing that criminals are atavists or beings who retain a vestigial and earlier DNA or human trait belonging to prior human ancestors. According to Lombroso, deviant behaviours were understood as the product of a more primitive stage in human development. Today, his work has been discredited by contemporary science. But both the examples of Blumenbach and Lombroso's scientific, or pseudoscientific, research have shown us that race is not a scientific category; rather, it is a social imagination and construction. It is a false categorization that was instrumentalized by nations like England and France during a golden era of Western European expansion and colonization. And these practices of racialization had an incredibly powerful and detrimental effect on the peoples and the territories they encountered.

ML: I think one of the important takeaways from this conversation for me is the reminder that the development of social scientific knowledge involves the testing and rejection of outdated notions based on contemporary techniques and research, but this can be inconsequential in some ways for the institutions and systems of belief based on these outdated ideas. So, hundreds of years after Blumenbach and Lombroso, we are still dealing with belief systems and institutional practices that reify ideas of inherent inferiority, born criminality, and "natural" racial traits. It is a good illustration of the power of institutionalized knowledge. This has been a fascinating conversation about the history of race and its connection to law and colonialism, but perhaps this is a good opportunity for us to segue to a more contemporary context. So far, we have talked about race in relation to processes of categorization, "social sorting," and the reproduction of hierarchies. Race is also something that is enacted on a day-to-day basis, though. What are your thoughts on this?

MM: You are right to point out that we have so far focused on the historical and institutional practice of Western European colonization of the new world and how race and racism was fomented and created in that moment. But we have not talked about how it is practised in the current day. It is important to tackle this. I think we can understand race as an everyday happening or as in everyday operation. We can understand race, racism, or racialization as a verb or as something that we do to somebody else. As a verb we can understand it as a common mental shortcut; we use a person's physical appearance as a stand-in or a marker of their intelligence, their thinking, or their potential actions. So we can understand racism as an action and as a mental shortcut, where you create potential stereotypes or artifacts to represent someone, or stand-in for someone, instead of interacting with them as they are. Instead of understanding people as they are, you use a mental shortcut that helps you imagine who they should be in your imagination of them. Your imagination might use their appearance to arrive at a set of conclusions or prejudgments or prejudices. In this sense, race is something we do to other people.

ML: I think that is a helpful and straightforward way to understand race and its connection to everyday practices. It invites us to think about how we consciously or subconsciously engage in racialization or are subject to it. In the context of criminology and the criminal legal system we can certainly see how this kind of mental shortcut or heuristic social sorting can have profound effects on the people who are encountered by the system. What are some examples?

MM: An excellent example of the way a state institution might use mental shortcuts or engage in racialization, or what we commonly refer to as racial profiling, is the use of race by border control. Border control uses people's race, religion, skin colour, place of birth, the language they speak, their surname, and the type of passport they use to control and judge their entry into a country. That is not contentious. It is a practice that border control officials would freely admit to using as a form of social sorting—as you call it. And yet if we think about the history of race and racialization, which we have just discussed, we can understand that the use of the practice called racial profiling by border control is in fact a practice of harmful racism that is directly connected to the origins of colonization and the dispossession of Indigenous territory in the new world by Western European countries. There is no other way to interpret our history of colonization. The concept of "Caucasian" arose in the moment of contact with non-European peoples. Current racial profiling at borders continues to use these categories and are an extension and product of that history. Some use of race at the border may not be direct criminal profiling, but to be categorized as Asian, Black, or Middle Eastern is to be categorized as non-Caucasian or other. Being nonwhite directly connects your categorization to all the damaging history that we spoke of earlier.

ML: That is a good example. There are clear connections between the reproduction of racial categories and official notions of who is suspicious or what constitutes suspicious behaviour. We see this in other aspects of the legal system as well, where race plays a role in how certain people or groups are interpreted as being out of place and dangerous, or conversely, normal, unproblematic, and innocuous. And it is the case that these conceptual shortcuts can very quickly change the dynamics of an encounter between a given person and a representative of the legal system. If, for example my first impression upon seeing you is that you are a threat, I—as a hypothetical police officer—will almost certainly approach you differently. The question for us as criminologists is why and how certain people are subject to these forms of perceptual prejudice.

MM: That is an excellent point, and it calls into question whether we can even call it a "conceptual" shortcut because that suggests high order thinking or reasoning. Maybe it is more like a habitual and unquestioned shortcut that is well hidden from the user. Some may even call it an "unconscious bias." The very legitimacy of racial profiling—on the part of border services—allows a border agent to justify the racialization of the customers or clients who pass before them. It allows those mental shortcuts to express themselves, it allows for that type of biased social sorting to happen, and that could be detrimental to people's public safety or their ability to cross the border. But let me pivot to something even more benign. We can consider Statistics Canada and their use of the national household survey. The long form survey asks respondents to self-identify as twelve potential choices. Those choices include White, South Asian, Chinese, Black, Filipino, Latin American, Arab, South Asian, West Asian, Korean, Japanese, or Other—asking you to specify what type of other. I bring up this example because this benign survey, which is used institutionally to understand the demographic composition of the country, is asking participants to self-declare their race or racial identity. And that is both problematic and complicated. For example, we can see how it would be complicated if, say you had a parent who is Chinese and a parent who is not Chinese. Do you then check the box for Chinese or the box for Other? This hypothetical situation gives rise to many questions that we can ask about the legitimacy of even asking racial questions. It throws into question the accuracy of the survey instrument and the data it collects. That is, is there such a thing as a half-Chinese person from the perspectives of biological race or

Canadian demographics? Is there a dominant half? Could there be disproportional racial-biological halves? Could products of miscegenation be conceived other than as an even 50/50 split (e.g., 90/10)? What gives rise to such uneven racial compositions? Or how should a person self-identify if there are more than two "races" in their ancestry? Statistics Canada is asking Canadians to unproblematically insert themselves into this kind of racial sorting without acknowledging the history and misuse of racialization. As a side note, I should point out that the categorization of "White" used in the Statistics Canada survey forms is interesting because "white" itself is not a racial category in as far as the other non-white categories such as Chinese or Black or Asian are understood to be biological or racially coded.

ML: Absolutely, Mike, and it is worth noting that a similar survey conducted fifty years ago would have used different categories. And a survey conducted twenty years in the future might also be quite different. It might be tempting to conclude that this entire exercise of pursuing racial self-identification is inherently flawed and fraught with bias and error. However, it is interesting to note also that some Canadian institutions, and particularly police institutions, have deliberately resisted calls to collect and track race-based data. Some of the people calling for the collection of such data are criminologists who are deeply concerned about issues like profiling and racism and who are aware of the history and social construction dynamics we have spoken about. Why do we see the call for the collection of this kind of information?

MM: I think I can answer that question. First, we call for the collection of this information simply because it is understood to be everyday normal police practice. We know when you are arrested or detained by police services, the police will enter your information into a database. So we want to understand this practice of race tracking. Many municipal, federal, or provincial police services will enter racial information. For example, the Vancouver police uses the categories of Asian, Black, Caucasian, Hispanic, Indigenous, Middle Eastern, South Asian, Other, and Unknown. The system of sorting demands officers to put the person they are interacting with into a particular racial box. The officer has no choice, the officer must comply. It is not an option to not racialize. It is an institutional requirement of their job. Hence, it would be useful to know how police services are racially sorting the population that it serves. Second, from a critical perspective, it might tell us that certain populations may have more interaction with the police than is warranted. It might help point out areas where there are problems that need to be addressed.

ML: In other words, there is a call for the collection of race-based data because there is an understanding that racial categories are actively used by police and other legal system institutions. By collecting and analyzing this data, we can come to a better understanding of the nature and extent of different and disproportionate interactions based on racialization. And yet many police services regularly refuse to share this information for fear of being challenged on the question of racial bias. Anecdotally, it is both fascinating and extremely frustrating to me that conversations about forms of institutional bias and racism in Canada consistently return to questions of whether and to what extent something problematic is indeed happening. For example, earlier debates over racial profiling in Canada consistently returned to this issue of whether people's lived experiences were merely anecdotal or symptomatic of a broader trend. It was only when researchers—including criminologists and journalists—accessed and began to systematically analyze police contact information that the experience of communities subject to discriminatory policing were taken as empirically valid. Unfortunately, that is also an explanation for the pursuit of race-based data in the criminal legal systems. Policymakers and officials seem reluctant to accept the lived experience of racialized groups as valid unless it is backed by quantitative data.[12]

MM: Mike, are you saying that it is not useful to have race-based data regarding arrest, detention, incarceration, and so forth, or, are you saying that using race—as a social sorting mechanism—is a flawed practice and hence open to misuse?

ML: You are putting me on the spot, Mike, but I have an answer for you. Insofar as we understand the use of race as a conceptual shortcut by legal system institutions, I think it is important for us to problematize this. Implicit, I believe in our conversation so far, is a critical perspective on these practices. Put differently, it is unjust, discriminatory, and harmful for institutions of law and justice to treat people differently according to assumed racial categories. And I think we would both agree that these practices should be challenged and changed. But simultaneously, since we understand that racialization and the use of race-based categories informs the activities of institutions, the collection and analysis of race-based data based on these institutional practices, however flawed the categories may be, reveals something about how these institutions operate.

MM: OK, so let us consider racial profiling as an example of the practice of race and racism. We know racial profiling is the use of race by police or border security to select certain people for surveillance, monitoring, investigation, detention, denial of entry, or arrest. For example, we know through an examination of racial profiling studies that being stopped by police for a motor vehicle violation—like having a broken taillight or not fully stopping at a stop sign or other types of moving violations—might involve people of colour at a greater rate. In both the Canadian and the American context, Black people are overrepresented in those police stops. But there is a debate in the scholarship about racial profiling around whether it is a form of racism. Some scholars believe there is a damaging racist practice happening in racial profiling, while others argue that as a form of criminal profiling, racial profiling is not racist because it simply uses race as a legitimate social sorting mechanism and not in a racist manner.[13] Racial profiling and the debates about whether or not it is racist is a good illustration of this conundrum of trying to understand the use of race as an identifier and/or sorting mechanism.

ML: Towards the start of our conversation we talked about the importance of unpacking some of the concepts and terms we were using, especially given their simultaneously complex but also everyday nature. Since then, we have mentioned several specific terms I think we should unpack further. For example, we have talked about institutional racism, systemic racism, and overt bias based on race. How should we distinguish these, and why is the distinction important? Perhaps we can begin with what I think is the most straightforward example, and the one that people often think about when we talk about racism, which is overt racism. How can we understand this?

MM: I think overt racism is very easy to understand. Overt racism is racism or bias experienced interpersonally between two people. It is experienced when somebody uses a racist term or a racist word or a racist epithet or a biased or racist idiom—and the effects are transparent. It is overt racism when there is no misunderstanding of what or how racist remarks are used. They are meant to hurt, and they are meant to elicit a response from the other person. If somebody mocks you and your ethnic, social, or racial background and then follows up that mocking with a physical assault, I think you could say that assault was motivated by overt racism because the connection between the harm and the speech act are transparent.

ML: So, would it be fair to say that in situations of overt racism the actions of the person behaving in a racist manner are a direct reflection of their internalized racist beliefs?

MM: I think you can never know what people are really thinking. But in the case of someone yelling something that is racist and then hitting you, I think it would be fair to say that they have internalized racist beliefs. In that sense, that is an easy illustration of overt racism. But as we know, not all racisms are so easy to identify or to call out.

ML: You are absolutely right, and maybe it would be helpful for us to pose a more complicated example of overt racism. What about a situation where a person in a position of authority specifically chooses not to hire or even to interview an applicant for a position because of racist beliefs?

MM: If an employer goes on record with racist reasonings for not hiring someone, then I think there is something you can do about it. If there is documented racist beliefs that are then expressed as racist actions—such as not hiring someone based on their race—then you have something that is actionable. But I believe not all cases are so clear-cut. Often an employer may have racist or biased beliefs, but they are smart enough to not reveal those thoughts or go on record with those thoughts. In such cases, a racist outcome can happen undetected and without any recourse.

ML: Let us move beyond the context of interpersonal and direct interactions. People are part of, work in, and interact with institutions, and institutions can engage in racism as well. Indeed, people can enact racist practices within institutions without individually holding racist beliefs. Can you talk about institutional racism?

MM: Sure. A very famous case of institutional racism is the case of Viola Desmond. In 1946 in New Glasgow, Nova Scotia, Viola Desmond wanted to see a movie at a theatre; however, the theatre owner had a policy that Black people could not sit in the lower orchestra seating. And Viola Desmond was a Black woman living in Halifax. She asked the ticket seller to sell her a downstairs ticket for the orchestra seating, but the ticket seller said, "I'm sorry I can't sell you a ticket, it is the policy of this theatre that Black people have to sit upstairs in the mezzanine." Viola Desmond famously disregarded the theatre rule. She specifically paid for a downstairs ticket, refusing to receiving the change for a lower-priced upstairs ticket, and proceeded to sit in the downstairs seating. Soon after taking her seat, she was thrown out of the theatre by the theatre owner and the police, who acted in concert. This is an example of institutional racism because it was not necessarily perpetrated by a racist person; we can understand that the ticket seller did not have to be racist to enact the racist policy. The ticket seller could say, "I'm not racist, I'm just following the policy of this theatre. It's not my fault I can't sell you a ticket." This is an excellent illustration of racism that is perpetrated or practised through a rule or an institutional edict. Hence the term "institutional racism."

ML: That is a good example, Mike, and I think it does an effective job of illustrating the distinction between overt racism and institutionalized forms of racism. A key distinguishing factor is the relative role of individual internal beliefs versus ideas embedded in rules and systems. And this brings us to still another form of racism, systemic racism. This is a concept that has gained greater resonance in the popular imagination and discourse recently, particularly in relation to active social movements opposing systemic racism in, for example, policing. How can we define systemic racism?

MM: Great question, Mike, not least of which because systemic racism as a concept is so poorly understood. It would be a pleasure to help clarify this important concept. Systemic racism is different from the other two forms of racism in that it is not a form of racism that is experienced between two individuals; rather, systemic racism is a way to refer to how nonracial aspects of society, such as employment, housing, education, and health, intersect with race to create the outcome of bias or reduced social wealth or income. Another way to name or express the notion of systemic racism might be to call it multidimensional disparity or multidimensional economic and income disparity.[14] What do I mean by that? I think it is easy for us to understand that individuals might have lower wealth not simply because of the colour of their skin but because of their lower education, their poverty, their inadequate housing, or because of conditions not of their own choosing, such as the wealth or poverty of their parents. We can understand that there are many factors other than overt racist beliefs and actions that might impinge or affect your ability to prosper in society. This shows us that racist outcomes are not just a product of racist beliefs or racist actors but could be interlocked with—to continue the example of Viola Desmond—the behaviour of the ticket seller who said, "I'm just following the rules." It might be interlocked with the realtor who says, "I was told not to show the house to anyone who wasn't white," or with education, where a teacher with an unconscious bias against nonwhite students does not spend the time or energy or effort to engage nonwhite students. That is an example of systemic racism. Systemic racism is a very complicated form of bias and discrimination in society, and it is not easily identified because it interlocks or intersects with many other social institutions and practices.

ML: This is such an important concept. In the case of institutional racism, we can locate racial bias in the rules and formal functioning of a particular institution. In the case of overt racism, we can observe racial bias and enmity in action at the interpersonal level. With systemic racism, the discrimination may be more subtle and harder to pinpoint but still profoundly impactful in its implications. For example, institutions and organizations like educational or policing institutions play an important role in reproducing forms of systemic racism but simultaneously have and actively advertise official policies of antiracism. And this gives rise to situations where we see both patterns of systemic racism and extreme resistance on the part of institutions to acknowledge their role in the perpetuation of these patterns. I think this is one of the reasons it is so difficult to challenge systemic racism.

MM: Yes, absolutely. I cannot agree with you more, Mike. I am thinking of the example of studies that have shown that Toronto public schools prepare Black students not to graduate and not to attend university and to be streamed into vocational training. That is not because there is a policy at the Toronto District School Board to do so. It is not because teachers themselves are actively and intentionally reducing opportunities for Black students; rather, it occurs because there are certain mechanisms within the education system that hold back students and do not empower them to succeed and go onto higher education or professional forms of employment. In this example of Toronto schools, it is the system of instruction and the school system that acts in a biased manner, without requiring overt racism. Systemic racism can express itself in many forms.[15]

ML: OK, so systemic racism can be understood as operating in concert with other institutions and practices. This might be a good opportunity for us to also speak about the very important concept of "intersectionality." As the term implies, intersectionality concerns the ways people are constituted as subjects through the intersection of a variety of aspects of their identity. So, for example, while we have been speaking about the ways people are treated differently according to ascribed racial categories, they are also treated differently according to their gender, sexuality, disability, and class. Do you want to elaborate on this concept and its importance?

MM: Intersectionality is such an interesting concept that I am surprised it did not formally come into focus until Kimberlé Crenshaw and others in her reading and scholarly debate group invented the term in the late 1980s.[16] Crenshaw coined the term to describe how race is intersected with other social categories like class, gender, and sex and until she and her group invented the term it was somewhat submerged or unclear. Intersectionality is so easy to understand today because it is so easy to understand that race does not exist by itself, that it is not experienced in isolation from other social factors. For example, a Black woman who feels that she is experiencing bias or discrimination might find it difficult to ascertain whether it is because she is a woman or because she is Black. A Black woman's experiences are at the intersection of anti-Black racism and patriarchy, or antiwomen bias, simultaneously and the two cannot be extricated. This is what is meant by intersectionality and why Crenshaw and others argue that a holistic examination cannot just have a racist perspective or racist analysis. A more complete analysis of race must also include an understanding that race intersects other social factors like bias against women, social economic class, employment, housing, education, and so on and so forth. That is what is meant by intersectionality. Race has never existed by itself, but in creating the term "race" and the discourse around race we have forgotten that it has always intersected with these other socioeconomic factors. In this sense, it is very similar to a notion of systemic racism because it is also multidimensional.

ML: If we return to our earlier discussion about race and hierarchy, we might say that there are a variety of constructed statuses that are used to sort and categorize people, distributing privilege and disadvantage. People occupy—or are placed in—more than one category at a given time; therefore, peoples' experiences of marginalization, empowerment, privilege, and oppression are also and necessarily shaped by complex intersections of identity and status.

MM: I think this discussion has demonstrated that race and racism is in fact a multidimensional problem that comes about through a variety of historical and contemporary conditions. These conditions are things you do not choose but rather things you are born into. And I think our discussion has shown that racism is interlocked with other social factors. We can understand that we cannot simply analyze racism isolated from all the other social factors. It is so interlocked or interlinked with other social factors that perhaps we should not even have a word for "race" but instead a word for "race-class-gender-ability-housing-education-health-employment." But of course, it is not so easy to just change it through some force of will.

ML: You point to the difficulty of creating substantive, enduring change. I agree—especially with regards to the challenge of systemic racism, which persists despite official rhetoric espousing equality and antidiscrimination. We are also living in a time where we have ample evidence—online and on the streets—of social movements that are overtly racist and xenophobic. I am heartened by the fact that it seems impossible for people such as ourselves to write a book about criminology in the current context without including a serious discussion of race, racialization, and intersectionality. This, to me, is a cause for hope. Although the problems we face are very real and deeply entrenched, there seems to be a greater willingness to name them as problems and to pursue structural solutions.

Criminology and Decolonization: What Is to Be Done?

ML: One of the things we can say definitively about our experience in recent years is that there has been an intensified public conversation about the concept of systemic racism. This issue is not new, but the conversation has become far more mainstream, and it is starting to shift consciousness and shape policy. I think it is fair to say that students who are starting to study criminology now will be more likely to have encountered the concept of systemic racism than many of their predecessors and past cohorts. I think this gives us a good opportunity to think about or talk about what systemic racism is and why it is increasingly recognized as the topic that ought to be central to the study of criminology. What do you think about that?

MM: That is an excellent question. I think the term "systemic racism" is simply a way to refer to a social structure that is biased or is damaging people because of the way they have been imagined or the way society has framed them as being "not-normal." That is important for us to think about in relationship to criminology because—in some respects— we are always studying what is not normal or what is deviant. What is not normal is that society is dominated by white subjectivity. It can be argued that nonwhite people are understood to be not-normal or deviant because of their appearance or where they live. We can understand systemic racism as a system or structure that may not even have racists in them. Some might argue that structural or systemic racism is simply racism without racists—which is quite provocative because how can you have a racist practice or racist system without racists? Well, it can be very easily illustrated with an example of a hypothetical club that has a "white-only" policy governing membership. There is no need for any racists in the club; it is simply the structure that tells us we cannot allow certain people to be members. That is an example of how you can have racism without racists.

But let us return to the context of 2020 or 2021. When we are thinking about Black Lives Matter or about defunding the police, we are thinking about racial profiling, carding, and street checks; we know all of those things are absolutely tied to race. It is a practice of othering by police services.[17] But police services often respond to such accusations by saying: "We do not act in a racist way because as officers we are not individual perpetrators of racism; we are simply doing criminal profiling, not racial profiling."[18] This is another good illustration of systemic racism. The police themselves, or the court, are saying they are not racist because as individual subjects they are not individually racist. However, it is impossible for us to agree that there is no racism or bias in policing because the statistics for arrest or incarceration show that people of colour are overrepresented. The unanswered question in the room is: What would explain that imbalance in the data? There must be a system of bias operating or occurring that is creating these disproportionate numbers.

To be antiracist we must examine the way discrimination and racism have been carried out in a historical and institutionalized fashion. We have to examine how race and racism are activities that are human-made, artificial, and created but appear to us as if they are natural categories and real material things. "Race" is a verb, not a noun. Race is not a thing; it is a practice. We racialize ourselves and we racialize other people. *This is what we want our examination to reveal.* But of course we are not studying ourselves specifically but rather the society into which we are born. We want to examine the histories, institutions, and social practices that comprise society. It is through social practices that we come to racialize people. And police, courts, and corrections are one such mechanism by which race is systemically or socially expressed.

ML: I think you have laid a strong foundation for this discussion. When I reflect on a lot of the conversations that took place in 2020–21 there was this recognition of systemic racism with serious problematic effects for communities of colour in the United States, Canada, and around the world. There were calls for change, there were movements and mobilization for social change, and there was a clear recognition that the status quo was intolerable, deeply problematic, and required immediate action. But shifting the status quo and transforming systems that have embedded systemic forms of racism is no small task. It is not as if the many people who fed and grew these systems and institutions ten or twenty years ago went in with the intention of perpetuating forms of racism—at least most did not. And yet here we are today dealing with many of the same patterns that have been evident for decades. The legacy of colonialism, anti-Black racism, and anti-Asian racism have deep historical roots. What is it about institutions associated with the criminal legal system that makes it so difficult to transform them in ways that address systemic racism?

MM: You are right, Mike. It is a tall ask but it is an excellent question. I think we are deploying the wrong public service to fix a social problem. We deploy police because we believe there are types of crime they can fix or stop. In particular, street crime in poorer or lower socioeconomic status neighbourhoods. We know that economic status is interlocked, or as Crenshaw says, intersected with race, gender, and class. In Canada there is more kinetic policing or street policing happening in neighbourhoods that have lower socioeconomic status or are poor. If it is the case, then we are trying to use police to fix poverty, and this is something police were never designed to fix. That is the real problem. Many community activists want to defund police because they want to reallocate the police budget to social services or municipal or community services that can better address poverty.[19] That is a beautiful example of how systemic bias—and let us not even use the word racism—could be fixed—by a reallocation in the way we deploy resources. We could begin to address systemic inequality in society, which of course is intersected with race and the economy, by designing new or different services that address the questions of public safety in neighbourhoods that find themselves interlocked with issues of poverty.

ML: It is interesting to note that, as you so eloquently put it, you cannot use the police to fix poverty has been recognized in the sociology of policing literature for quite a while. There are some classic contributions in that literature, and I am thinking of Peter Kay Manning's work on the mandate of policing going back to 1995. [20] Manning and colleagues pointed out that the police had very deliberately positioned themselves as these jacks of all trades who could take on and respond to essentially any kind of social problem. In so doing, they increased their mandates beyond—let us call it—core crime prevention and law enforcement into a whole range of public order type work, information gathering and brokering type work, management of populations, and so on. Manning points out that because this mandate is impossible for any institution to take on as a sole institution, what ends up happening is the police shift gears and start managing appearances; that is, appearing to be doing as much as possible, appearing to be active, appearing to be engaged and dedicated rather than dealing truly efficaciously with these kinds of problems. They simply do not have the capacity to alleviate some of these deeply embedded structural issues.

Manning's point really intersects with the current critique of policing as it pertains to systemic racism. Simultaneously, you have an institution that is characterized by a history of colonialism and violence and associated with racist violence in its modern iteration trying to engage in all this social order policing it is fundamentally ill equipped for. It is very hard for us to imagine things, institutions, differently. If we say that systemic racism is a problem, and clearly there is a mass movement mobilized to call attention to this, it is difficult for many people to get beyond the idea that our current institutions are natural and inevitable. People might just default to the position that there must be police (as it currently exists), that there must be courts (as it currently exists), and of course that we have to put people in prison. This is just how you do criminology and crime control. Shifting this thinking is a prerequisite to really addressing the systemic racism in the current system.

MM: It is depressing to think we cannot fix racism, or that racism is escalating in the age of divisive politics illustrated by the presence of Donald Trump and others on the political landscape. I think we have to fight despair, and one thing that gives us hope is, for example, the movement to decolonize, which comes out of and has been encouraged by the 94 Calls to Action arising from the residential school Truth and Reconciliation process. It is a process that occurred over the course of many years in Canada and culminated in the Truth and Reconciliation Commission reports and the 94 Calls to Action.[21] It does give us hope because we see organizations attempting—not least of which our own university—to integrate or include the ideal of decolonization into its mandate. What does decolonization mean? Decolonization means to self-examine our sociopolitical history of colonization in Canada and its destructive force, its colonizing force, its violent force, and the way that force tried to destroy an entire society, culture, and political structure in Canada.

We are now called upon to think of how current society can reverse or rectify some of those problems. An important first step towards decolonization is recognizing and acknowledging that you are on unceded or stolen land. It is important for the study of criminology because if we are decolonizing in this wider social manner, then the potential for us to decolonize policing, the courts, and in prisons also exists. It is aspirational, and it is possible because we are seeing a real and legitimate attempt to rethink what it means to be a settler within a antiracist framing. For myself, as an immigrant, I also must think about the way I have been racialized and how I fit into the larger white settler-colonial history of Canada. How does a nonwhite immigrant fit into a white settler-colonial framework? As we begin to think our way out of colonization and a white landscape of history, we must also think about how race is interlocked with our criminal justice system.

ML: It is possible to think differently and there does seem to be an appetite for a different vocabulary and different lenses for many of these issues. That is something hopeful in the largely pessimistic twist we have spun. But it is also important to bear in mind that the status quo is deeply valued by many people; not just those who have a direct material interest in its maintenance but also by people who connect to the symbolic or ideological aspects of the way things are currently done.

One of the things we can say about legal systems and institutions is that they are deeply symbolic. I mean, there are uniforms, there are badges, there are rituals of standing before the judge—"all rise" and all the ritual built into the system of justice and law—and it has this deeply connected symbolic dimension. Look at the image of the Mountie in the Red Serge that is sold and laminated on key chains and for purchase in any airport in Canada. It depicts the police as a national symbol. We should not take that lightly. It tells us that there is this attachment to order and the status quo that is connected to certain visions of identity. When these things are challenged, when there are calls for reform especially and when there are arguments around deeply entrenched systemic problems biases and racism, there is a strong effort to push back and defend the status quo; to protect it from any kind of meaningful change.

We see it happen in the context of calls to defund police. It is inevitable any movement for social change will have to contend with the attachments people have to the status quo. There is defensive or even revanchist kinds of impulses that are not necessarily rooted in commitments to racism or individual bias. Such rootedness may be more connected to an image or an idea of institutions as being natural, proper, and existing in perpetuity. But beyond that—perhaps as a final point— there are deep material interests associated with the status quo. When I think about the factors that have driven racialized mass incarceration there is no way to talk about that without considering the war on drugs and the policing apparatus associated with that war. The war on drugs has been a deeply racist endeavour. It has often been that prohibition is connected to racialized politics of othering and discrimination, but it is also connected to massive budgets and the expansion of criminology—as a field of study—but also policing in terms of powers and practices. Those budgets are threatened directly and materially by efforts to defund the police. It is important to say that these practices and policies are not only not working but that they are causing harm and need to be shifted radically and transformed. This challenge affects the bottom line of institutions and people who work in them, and we must bear that in mind going forward.

MM: If I were to put on my pessimist hat, I would also agree that attacking the racism within and decolonizing the criminal justice system is no small task and will be very difficult to achieve. For example, I believe police services will continue to argue that they are not engaged in racial profiling but rather criminal profiling. In so doing, they will present a difficult institutional obstacle to decolonization. Police services might continue to state that the use of the racial identifier of, for example, "Black male of this height and build" or "an Indigenous man of this height and this build with this type of clothing" is an indispensable tool of policing, but it does not address the problem of race or racialization. It will be very difficult to get rid of racial profiling because it can be framed as a tool of criminal profiling or as a technique of policing. This is a good illustration of the difficulty of pursuing any kind of antiracist project within the criminal justice system. The very fact that police services can and will use race as an identifier is already the first obstacle to this pursuit of decolonization.

ML: This chapter has sought to demonstrate how race and racism is a multidimensional problem arising from a complex set of historical conditions into which people are born. These conditions are not of our choosing and therefore they are also not within our power to simply change or erase through a force of will. We can understand overt racism as expressing itself in the form of interpersonal bias or stereotyping that occurs between unique individuals. And we can understand institutional racism as a form of racism that arises due to an institution adopting a set of rules that are biased or based in prejudice. However, it is the question of systemic racism that is the most difficult to understand. In the case of systemic racism, this chapter has demonstrated that racism can occur without the presence of overt or institutional forms of racism. In fact, it does not need individual racists at all. Racism without racists is both possible and commonplace.

In our discussion of border control, we argued that the border acts in a racist manner, but it does not need racists to create or maintain the racism. The border is not a person who is acting in an overt racist manner because the border is inert and inanimate, but the border can produce racism through its systems of examination and control. At the border, there is no overt race-based rules instructing border guards to act in a prejudiced or racist manner because people from the Middle East, those who have a non-Western name, who are not white, who are Muslim, or who come from the Global South are instantly—without prejudice—under scrutiny. The social and historical trajectory of Canada and its neighbour, the United States—as products of settler-colonial enterprises arising from Western European expansion—has helped create state border control services that are more interested in those with a non-Western European background or heritage. Thus, the practice of racial profiling at the border is not "officially" racist because it does not overtly recommend to its border guards to be more interested in examining people of colour. The suspicion is not only based on race, but on the assumed intersections of nationality, religion, employment, wealth/poverty, and whether someone comes from the Global South. But invariably these factors of suspicion get interlocked with race and colour and can be experienced as racial profiling. From the perspective of the border guard it is not racist, but from the perspective of the person being examined or detained it can be experienced as race-based interrogation.

MM: That's a great wrap-up of some of the key points of this chapter. Similarly, in the context of the criminal justice system, and in particular the police service, we have discussed how police interact with Indigenous or First Nations Peoples at a rate higher than their interactions with the general public. Is that racist? No, it is not a form of overt racism on the part of police. However, this higher interaction with police is a socio-political product of settler-colonialism because Indigenous Peoples find themselves with higher levels of poverty, poor health, poor education, poor housing, and poor overall care. These forms of poverty are due to the Western European conquest and occupation of the new world. It is these sociohistorical attributes that expose Indigenous Peoples to higher rates of interaction with police services, courts, and corrections.

The chapter has demonstrated that because social forces are inter-locked and catalytic in operation, the existence of racism can be made invisible or naturalized. However, through an effort of critical thinking, it is possible to reveal it and see it as a social conglomeration, or as a set of domino effects, or intersecting social conditions, that lead to racial disparity (e.g., how history, housing, schooling, policing, border control, and racial profiling may all be interlocked). This is the pernicious power and complexity of race and racism.

Discussion Questions:

1. The Roseland Theatre ticket seller—who would not sell Viola Desmond a downstairs ticket—claimed she was "just following the rules." Was the worker passively following the rules of her work or was she actively being racist? Is she innocent of racism because she followed the rules of her employment and the general practices of society in New Glasgow, Nova Scotia, in 1946?

2. Black high school students in Toronto are more likely to be streamed into special classes and vocational programs, more likely to live with a single female parent, more likely to drop out, more likely to be suspended, and more likely to have interactions with police than the average Canadian person. What does this tell us about race and racism?

3. Without the assistance of the RCMP, the Indian residential school system would not have been possible. Were the RCMP just doing their job and acting to enforce the social norms and practices of this period, or are they guilty of a historical wrongdoing or crime? If the RCMP were once involved in the enforcement of Indian residential schools, are present-day RCMP historically responsible for such past acts? If the RCMP helped remove children from their families and helped track down and return school runaways, were they "party to a crime"?

4. Using your own experience or current events, think of examples that illustrate the presence and practice of overt, institutional, and/or systemic racism.

CHAPTER 10
Troubling Criminology

In this final chapter, we examine various critical perspectives on crime and deviance, and in so doing, we challenge the assumption that crime has an objective nature and argue that it is a social construct. We query the notion of individual agency and the freedom to choose, suggesting that social structures and conditions significantly influence behaviour. We review how fear, harm, and media representations shape our understanding of crime and justice while highlighting the flaws in traditional approaches to causation that might miss the impact of social and economic structures on individual choices. We also review the limitations of counting crime and deviance and revisit the issue of underreporting and overrepresentation in official statistics. By presenting a critical perspective on crime and deviance, this chapter encourages readers to challenge commonly held assumptions and consider the influence of social constructions in the field of criminology. We conclude the chapter with an exploration of the complexities inherent in understanding crime, critiquing traditional approaches to causation and re-evaluating the role of social and economic structures in shaping individual choices and behaviour.

Mike Larsen (ML): As the title of our book implies, we set out to trouble some of the taken-for-granted assumptions that often come along with thinking about and acting on questions of crime, deviance, and criminality. At the outset, we troubled the notion that there is an objective or obvious nature to crime and deviance. Rather, these things are best understood as social constructions, and that means we must always think about how and why certain things come to be defined as wrong, or indeed as right, as we are thinking about how society responds to these things. We also raised at the outset the question of obedience or compliance—and by association our freedom to choose—because we propose that all thinking about deviance must necessarily encompass some consideration of what is normal and how deviance is defined in contrast to it. Why is it so important for a discussion of crime to involve a discussion of liberty or the freedom to choose at the outset?

Michael C. K. Ma (MM): The question of liberty is important because if you go back to our first chapter you will see that we talk about this notion of liberal humanism. The Western European notion of liberal humanism is one in which individuals enjoy specific rights and where society is based on a concept of individuals choosing to act according to specific shared rules. But then we cast a critical eye on this assumption and ask whether we freely choose our destiny or behaviours. Maybe it is the case that we are coerced to choose something. Liberal humanist thinking presents a convenient picture where individuals have the freedom to decide whether they choose this or that path in life. The liberal humanist perspective suggests that we all have freedom of choice and that freedom means we have complete and ultimate control over our destiny. The idea of freedom is critical to liberal humanism and its framework of laws, rules, and rights. If you do not behave, do not follow set rules, or deviate from those laws, then the state can enter your life and discipline or punish you. It is assumed that individuals are always free to choose.

Throughout the book we have been troubling these ideas of agency and freedom and whether individuals truly possess control over their lives. If you are born into conditions not of your own choosing, it must mean that some decisions are already premade for you before you were born. That is what is troubling. The notions of right and wrong and our freedom to choose which side of the law to be on is the logic behind liberal humanism. The logic is that we are free to comply, but if we do not comply then we will be punished. And the criminal justice system is the mechanism by which you enforce the rule. But in our discussion, we advanced the argument that this logic is based less on consent than it is on coercion.

Thinking back to the first chapter, we discussed the seminal figures of John Locke and Thomas Hobbes. Their intellectual debate frames the concept of people's ability to come into a contract, or "social contract," with one another. If somehow that social contract is breached, that is when the application of the law comes into effect. We troubled that question in this book because we question whether people really comply with laws because they are afraid of the punishment that can arise from transgressing the law. Do we really consent to being in this relationship of law and order or right and wrong? Do we really agree or give permission to the state to both enforce and create systems of repression or control to surveil our behaviour? Do we give consent to this? What do you make of our discussion of consent?

ML: I think this notion of consent and our willingness to comply with rules and systems is directly connected to the themes we explore in our second chapter on fear and harm. Implicit in liberal humanism and classical theory is the notion that liberty has limits, and one of those limits is on behaviour that harms others. Harm, fear of harm, and risk of harm are central to a lot of criminological thinking and legal system practices. In our second chapter, we trouble the idea that what we consider fearful, frightening, and harmful are obvious or natural. We raised the question of who benefits from our fears and how systems may be both designed to respond to fear of harm and an opportunity to provide services or products—or perhaps more provocatively, to cultivate certain fears to allow for such services. Such systems produce official fears to shape consciousness and perpetuate certain ways of responding to social problems. By "certain ways" I mean the system of police, courts, and corrections. We raised the idea that the kinds of fears that are widely accepted in relation to crime and fear of crime tend to be individualized in nature. That is, it is perfectly acceptable for people to fear interpersonal harm or victimization by strangers and both private and public sector institutions exist to respond to such fears. However, as we take up later in the text, larger social fears (e.g., fear of unemployment, poverty, illness, or precarity) are generally not regarded as being within the domain of crime and deviance—despite the disproportionate amount of harm they cause to society. There is a fundamental disconnect between the level at which criminal justice systems conceptualize and respond to harm and the level at which the greatest harms of our age manifest.

MM: I think the main value of our second chapter concerning harm and the fear of harm is our discussion of how our fears are monetized and how they are used to create systems of control, surveillance, monitoring, punishment, and so forth. Our fear of harm, which might also have been constructed for us, allows for the funding of these systems. Our fear of harm has created or allowed the state to create a system of policing, courts, and corrections. Our fear of harm has allowed for the creation of systems that promise to prevent potential harm through repressive systems of surveillance, monitoring, and the kinetic force that we call police. It is useful to name the police as a kinetic force because they project order through intimidation and they act as an embodied force of the state. And we have conceded to the police—if you will—these superhuman powers no one else possesses in society. They can do the things they do to us without any of the restrictions that curtail everyday people. As individual agents of the state, they exist outside the social contract because they represent the state, but at the same time, they also exist as individuals like you and I. But unlike you and I, they can act in ways that are outside systems of control like the *Charter of Rights and Freedoms*. Our rights, at our moment of contact with police, cannot be enjoyed or enforced because it is the state itself (e.g., the police) that is breaching them. Our rights are not necessarily upheld in our interactions with police. And maybe that itself is harmful. Fear of harm is monetized and is absolutely used to create systems not of our own choosing (e.g., systems of control, systems of policing, systems of judgment, and systems of incarceration). The conceptual value of our second chapter discussion allows us to see that fear of harm is perhaps doing us more harm than the solutions that we allow for.

ML: Well put. I think what we are troubling in that chapter is the very idea that the apparatus of crime control wants us to not be afraid. This continues a fairly disruptive line of thinking throughout the text where we are questioning and encouraging readers to question some of the axiomatic ideas embedded in our thinking about crime and justice. We continue this in our discussion of media representations, which focuses on the ways our shared understanding of crime and justice issues is constructed and mediated. We draw attention to the selection and production of stories by news media, the operation of news values, filters, and frames, and the importance of sources and language. These topics are important for us to understand because, as we note, much of our knowledge of crime and justice is derived from our constant engagement with media. By developing media literacy and thinking critically about the social production of news, we can become more attentive to how certain assumptions about crime, criminals, and justice come to be normalized and to how and why certain voices come to be treated as authoritative.

Our disruptive efforts continue in our chapter on causation, which encompasses a review of many different ways of thinking about what causes crime. We trouble the idea of a quest for any kind of singular causal explanation, not only at the level of theory or paradigm but indeed in relation to individual people and individual instances of transgression. We argue that the quest for singular causes is a pitfall of traditional criminological thinking. We also raise some important questions about why criminology is so concerned about causation. Setting aside the general pursuit of understanding of the social world, which indeed does motivate much criminological scholarship, we note that in criminology the quest for causation has been conjoined with the development of systems of reaction, response, intervention, and control. We also trouble the level of analysis that tends to be associated with questions of causation and motivation, as there has been a great deal of emphasis on explanations that function at the level of individuals. Why is this atomistic approach problematic?

MM: I think social structure causes behaviour. That does not mean I, as an individual subject with agency, cannot decide to stand up or sit down whenever I want. Individuals do have a lot of agency over certain things they can or cannot do. But as an individual I do not have that much control over, for example, the wealth or lack of wealth into which I was born. As an individual I would have very little agency over what type of house, or lack of house, I was born into. As an individual I would have very little control over what type of school my parents did or did not put me into. Therein lies the conundrum of causation: Does an individual have the will to power and the free will to decide their complete behaviour and their destiny in life? Or do social structures or socioeconomic structures (e.g., housing, education, and health) determine behaviours? Or let us be even more bold about it: Do outside conditions give rise to or limit the decisions you and I can make? I think in this chapter on causation we have absolutely made the conclusion and provided quite a lot of proof that socioeconomic structure does limit your choices. And that gives rise to the question: If social structure causes behaviour, or limits behaviour in the sense of what you can or cannot do, then what is the purpose of police? Police exist to create more public safety but we know police are unable, for example, to solve poverty, to solve homelessness, to solve health problems, or to solve the lack of education. If we accept these assertions to be true, then we are in a conundrum. If we only consider cause and effect in the limited sense of individual causal decisions, then we have addressed nothing. For example, in the case of shoplifting, the logic of our system is to arrest that shoplifter but never address the real cause of petty theft. The social response to that behaviour is flawed. That is the main takeaway from this chapter. Some of the mechanisms and systems by which we judge causation are flawed and the systems by which we respond to what we believe to be individual decisions are flawed. That is the main thrust of our conversation regarding causation.

ML: One of the ways we can explore or demonstrate this idea of social structure playing a determining factor in transgression, deviance, and crime is by considering the information we gather about who is being processed through our systems, and this is what we take up in our chapter on counting. We note, first and foremost, that insofar as crime and deviance are social constructions, the quantitative impulse to count them in some objective manner must always be regarded critically. Nonetheless, we also note that the ways we currently systematically count crime and deviance, cases, incarceration rates, and other crime and justice phenomena reveal something about who the system of counting encompasses. It reveals how factors beyond the choices of individuals lead to disproportionate levels of representation for certain groups.

MM: Another desire for counting is to have perfect information. The desire to count how many crimes are occurring in society is based on the desire to have a perfect picture of what types of transgressions or deviance are occurring in society. Possessing perfect information means you can design and deploy meaningful solutions to solve those problems. So, counting or assessment arises out of a desire for accurate measurement or perfect information. Yet we know that is impossible. First, we have demonstrated in our discussion that there are many crimes that are undercounted. The most easily accessible example of this is the crime of sexual assault against women. We discuss the underreporting of sexual assault because women may hesitate to report it to police or engage with police services. Women underreport because they fear not being believed or fear that the reporting will achieve nothing. This example demonstrates that there is undercounting. So, although there is a desire to have perfect information, even police services must acknowledge that they do not have perfect information on which to base the delivery of their service. That is the most important thing about the question of counting that we unpacked in that chapter. Second, we also unpacked the question of overrepresentation in the issue of counting because there can be great value in existing statistics even if they are not perfect information. For example, criminal justice records demonstrate that certain populations in society (e.g., people of colour, people who are Indigenous, and people who are Black) are overrepresented in our criminal justice system. Overrepresentation gets our attention because it means there is a disproportionate number of arrests, sentences, and incarceration of people of colour. It tells us that there is an imbalance or error in our response to crime and deviance. So, the question of counting gives us these two important issues to unpack: (1) The desire for perfect information and how that information may be flawed and (2) the question of overrepresentation and how our systems of response may be out of balance.

ML: This is a situation where I think we advise readers to embrace the troubled nature of the issue. That is, there is utility in counting, as you say, and our statistics reveal a great deal about the nature of our institutions and the types of people in cases they focus on. However, all of this must be interpreted through a lens that recognizes the partial, problematic, and socially constructed nature of both deviance or crime and our social reaction to these things. We do not suggest that official measures of crime are lies or fabrications, but that they are absolutely distortions. I suppose our message is "use with caution."

MM: To jump off this idea of "use with caution," we can also see that our conversation about consent revolves around similar issues. We have troubled the idea of consent by suggesting that consent is useful because it allows people to agree on something. For instance, how to be peaceful or collaborative. Consent allows us to give permission to police to search us. Consent is also useful when we want something like natural resources. We might want to get permission to drill in a particular place or cut down a particular type of tree. In that sense, consent is important for the day-to-day practices of everyday life; however, we have also suggested that maybe the permission we give to police, or permission we give to websites, or consent that we give to mining corporations to cut trees or drill for oil may be consent that is not arrived at in the pure and ideal imagination of consent. The ideal is that we give permission without being coerced or without being fooled or tricked into giving permission. That I think is the value of our discussion about consent, because our conversation demonstrates it is not necessarily arrived at without coercion. What do you think?

ML: I think this is a concept that has been underexamined in criminology, and when we start to think about it, we recognize that it is and should be central to thinking about rulemaking, social interactions, transgression, and indeed everyday life. We have mentioned before that a lot of our thinking about criminology needs to connect with the idea that we are predominantly operating in a liberal humanist paradigm and, since this paradigm emphasizes the idea of the individual, rational, choosing actor, it follows that questions of consent (e.g., Who consents to what? When is consent informed? How is consent coerced?) really ought to be central. So, I find our conversation about consent to be exciting. It is exciting not just because it is important but because it is a scalable concept. We can talk about consent at the level of interpersonal interactions, where we often refer, for example, to consent when discussing things like sexual encounters or the use of certain substances, and we can talk about consent—as you have so importantly mentioned—on a much larger social scale when examining the legitimacy of resource extraction. On this larger scale, we can discuss notions of rights and power and whether the consent of communities to industry and capital are arrived at through free, prior, and informed consent. In part, we are engaged in this book to help craft a toolkit for thinking about crime and criminology in relation to consent and to think seriously about consent when it is present, when it is implied, and when it is coerced. These are important tools in the kit.

MM: Maybe we should have named the chapter consent and coercion because it is perhaps more bald to admit that with consent there is always coercion, or if not coercion, then certainly some type of persuasiveness or pressure to give permission. It need not be overt because that pressure could also be quite invisible. For example, in our discussion, we gave the example of how social media or the internet often asks for our consent to give up our information and privacy so that we can access a website. This would be an example of this very innocent and invisible consent that we are always giving up. That is an example of the quiet coerciveness of systems beyond our control and their manipulation of our consent or our permission. Our next chapter also talks a little bit about how the concept of consent could be attached to this idea of social reaction. Social reaction is the name we give to the process of arrest, judgment, and detention that we named in chapter six. What are your thoughts about this notion of reacting to deviants or reacting to everyday life and the systems that have been created to do so?

ML: There is so much to say about social reaction and the institutions and processes involved in it, and we cover a lot of ground in our chapter on this. I think one of the main points that we want to convey with this chapter is that just as crime and deviance are social constructions so too are our reactions and responses to crime and deviance also not natural inevitable or unproblematic. They are reflections of the ways we think about matters of crime and justice, and they are shaped by power and vested interests. Institutions and processes of social reaction are informed by implicit understandings of the nature and causes of deviance. For example, we have noted throughout the text that one of the major aspects of thinking about crime and justice that we want to trouble is the individualizing nature of our ideas and our responses. This is something we see very actively with our systems of social reaction that translate complex, multifaceted, and historically situated social problems and their symptoms. In cases that involve accused persons and named victims I think it is fair to say that we are skeptical and even pessimistic about this approach to crime. Since our systems are so reliant on an individualizing lens it gives us reason to question whether the criminal justice system can ever (a) adequately respond to crime and social harm or (b) produce anything recognizable as justice on a larger scale. So, I think this might be our most troubling chapter in a book about troubling criminology. What do you think?

MM: You said it best when you said there is so much to say about social reaction and that is because, in essence, the study of criminology is the study of social reaction to deviance, crime, or things that are out of the ordinary or not normal. As critical criminologists our investigation has shown two things. First, it has shown how deviance and "not normal" is always contingent on many social and political factors. For example, what is illegal today might not be illegal tomorrow. The issue of cannabis illustrates how we are capable, as a society, of shifting from illegality to acceptance. Second, we have discussed how a system of response to deviance (i.e., the police/courts/law), which was created to produce public peace, can then become much larger than its creators designed. It can become the default system that we use to respond to all things deviants, criminal, or out of order. It can then be the same system we deploy to address deviance in schools, in hospitals, in relationship to immigration and refugees, to sex workers, to intimate partner violence, to drug addiction, to corporate crime, to terrorism, but also to shoplifting. The magnitude and scope of police/social reaction to these deviant practices or things that are out of order are so broad that it suggests the system has overreached its mandate and that its original design can no longer fit the new mandate; a mandate of policing everywhere. And that gives us pause. That is the value of this discussion about social reaction—it helps us understand that maybe the system we designed to react to crime, things out of order, or deviance is now misshapen or perhaps is misaligned with its original intention.

ML: Or, perhaps more provocatively, it is performing precisely as intended. The institutions that give rise to inequality, marginalization, the concentration of wealth, climate collapse, colonization, and exploitation are largely peripheral to the institutions that are supposed to respond to harm and injustice. This is not by accident. We have persisted with an approach to questions of harm and transgression that emphasize the interpersonal and the individual. Indeed, efforts by communities and groups to challenge some of these much larger structural forces and their main beneficiaries are actually met with criminalization. We see this with the response to land defence actions in Canada, for example, and in responses to efforts to push back on extractive industries around the world. So, perhaps our system is functioning as intended, and perhaps that is the central problem people who are starting to think about criminology in the current context will need to grapple with going forward.

MM: Another way in which social reaction, police, courts, and prisons are deployed is in relationship to inequality in society, to poverty. So, we have also discussed how police are deployed to try to cure or create solutions to problems of inequality, lack of wealth, low socioeconomic status, or poverty. And we have argued that they are the wrong public service to deploy to fix poverty, the lack of housing, the lack of health, or the lack of education. We have repeatedly used the phrase "people do not choose the conditions into which they are born" to illustrate the idea that whether a person is poor or wealthy, those conditions exist external to them before they are born into this world or before they are thrown into this world. So, police have no ability, by their very design, to address those issues of inequality and low socioeconomic status, or for that matter high socioeconomic status. Police are not designed to fix social inequality and yet they are dispatched to try and maintain public peace. So, in some respects, the police have been given an impossible mission. Or perhaps they have been deployed in the wrong manner to solve social problems that cannot be solved by the tools and training they have been given. That is why social inequality or poverty are key issues for criminologists to examine and unpack when they are discussing public safety and social cohesion.

ML: You remind me of our earlier exchange about trying to create a toolkit for thinking about matters of crime, justice, and injustice. Fundamentally, the tools in our toolkit of social reaction are not the tools needed to address the root causes of many of the large-scale injustices we face. I think this is actually—upon examination—not a very controversial claim. However, it raises some serious questions about how and why we respond to injustice in certain ways. In our discussion of poverty, we talk about the idea that in a late modern neoliberal capitalist society inequality is not accidental or even, from a certain perspective, problematic. That is the way we have organized our society. Our institutions create and sustain a certain order. It is an order that benefits certain vested interests and classes of people at the expense of many others. It is the others, those in precarious positions, those on the margins, those left behind by productive forces, who are disproportionately the people of interest for the criminal justice apparatus. So, when we talk about law and order, this is the order we are speaking about. And once again I think we are called to trouble this notion of a natural order or status quo.

MM: I love that you mentioned "people who are disproportionately the people of interest for criminal justice apparatus" because that immediately makes me think that the system is biased or is—as you suggest—disproportionately interested in particular types of people. And that leads us to the question of race and racism. I think one of the strengths of this conversation is that we have tried to take on very difficult subjects that are not easy to unpack and the question of race is one of them. We have sought to show that racism is a social system that arises out of particular historical developments. Our discussion about race demonstrates that it is linked to a history of Western European expansion, where culture, social practices, and laws were exported and imposed onto the new world. And those social practices and that history are still present in our current day police, courts, and corrections. We know there is an overrepresentation of people of colour who are in contact with this public safety system. And if there is this overrepresentation of people of colour then this must suggest something is out of balance. We cannot say that it is simply the product of individual racists or individuals who have bias; rather, it is more accurate to say that the imbalance is also a systemic or institutional product. That is the value of our discussion; we have identified racism, racial profiling, or bias in policing, courts, and corrections as a systemic problem. We take great pains to unpack and discuss how that system is also intertwined with issues around economic inequality, inequality in education, inequality in housing, inequality in nutrition, and so on and so forth. We have sought to show that it is a multifaceted and multidimensional problem. These various factors are intertwined to such an extent that the identification of race or racial issues cannot be so simply extracted from all these other socioeconomic factors. That is the value of our discussion regarding race and racism and how it is expressed through our criminal justice system.

ML: I think that is a very successful summation of our main ideas in that chapter. We always need to think about race in an intersectional way, connecting it with a range of other registers of identity, status, and inclusion or exclusion. So, when we say our systems and our ways of thinking about crime and justice are infused with and perpetuate systemic racism, we need to also think about how this intersects with marginalization on the basis of class, gender, sexuality, and indigeneity. I think attempting to tackle many of these issues in isolation, without consideration for their interconnected nature, sets us up for failure.

Asking to address systemic racism as it exists in these "systems" is monumental, but we did end our discussion in that chapter on a hopeful note, worth reiterating here. That is, we are acutely aware that people who are beginning to study and think about criminology, in our experience, recognize, care about, and regard as central to this kind of inquiry a serious discussion about race and racism. The refusal of people to treat these as peripheral issues opens up possibilities to imagine different kinds of institutions, different kinds of approaches, and truly fundamental change, which is precisely the kind of change that is necessary.

MM: As a final comment and reflection on our conversation, which has been so fruitful, I think what we are doing concerns questioning and interrogating the existing criminal justice system. In our conversation we have tried to unpack and discuss what is right and wrong. We have discussed why we might not comply and conform to rules and regulations. We have discussed our fear of harm and how our fear of harm and fear of policing might pattern our responses in society.

We have discussed how society and the criminal justice system understand and react to the mechanisms or the acts causing crime and we have pointed out their shortcomings. And we have interrogated how consent and coercion are intertwined in the types of social control, policing, law, courts, detention, and incarceration we have created in response to crime. And I think we have really tried to say that the questions of poverty, inequality, socioeconomic status, and race are never properly addressed by these responses. In future projects and in future conversations, the question criminologists, and all of us, need to grapple with is: What is to be done?

Notes

Points of Departure

1   Sam Levin, "The Movement to Defund Police Has Won Historic Victories Across the US. What's Next?," *The Guardian* (London), August 15, 2020; Health Canada Expert Task Force on Substance Use, *Report 1: Recommendations on Alternatives to Criminal Penalties for Simple Possession of Controlled Substances and Recommendations on the Federal Government's Drug Policy as Articulated in a Draft Canadian Drugs and Substances Strategy* (CDSS), Health Canada, 2020.

2   Ryan Patrick Jones, "The Police Budget Is One of Toronto's Largest Expenses. Here's What You Need to Know About It," *CBC News*, October 21, 2022, cbc.ca.

3   Katie Hyslop, "How to Resist the War on LGBTQ2S+ Kids: An SFU Panel on Misinformation and Parents' Rights Suggested Ways to Make Society Safer by Seeking Common Ground," *The Tyee*, February 26, 2024, thetyee.ca; Rafferty Baker, "B.C. Court of Appeal Decision a Mixed Outcome for Trans Teen and Disapproving Father," *CBC News*, January 10, 2020, cbc.ca.

4   The Truth and Reconciliation Commission, *Canada's Residential Schools: Missing Children and Unmarked Burials*, Vol. 4 of *The Final Report of the Truth and Reconciliation Commission of Canada* (McGill-Queen's University Press, 2015), exactdn.com.

Chapter 1: Right and Wrong

1   Jared J. Wesley, "Beyond Prohibition: The Legalization of Cannabis in Canada," *Canadian Public Administration*, 62, no. 4 (2019): 533–48, doi-org.ezproxy.kpu.ca:2443/10.1111/capa.12348.

2   Louis Althusser, *Lenin and Philosophy, and Other Essays*, trans. Ben Brewster (Monthly Review Press, 2001).

3   Roger Cotterrell, *The Sociology of Law: An Introduction* (Oxford University Press, 1992).

4   William J. Chambliss, "Toward a Political Economy of Crime," *Theory and Society* 2, no. 2 (1975): 149–70, jstor.org.

5   Kitty Calavita, *Invitation to Law and Society: An Introduction to the Study of Real Law*, 2nd ed. (University of Chicago Press, 2016).

6   Susan C. Boyd, and Connie I. Carter, *Killer Weed: Marijuana Grow Ops, Media, and Justice* (University of Toronto Press, 2014).

7   Peter Kropotkin, *Mutual Aid: A Factor of Evolution* (Heinemann, 1902); Murray Bookchin, *The Ecology of Freedom: The Emergence and Dissolution of Hierarchy* (Cheshire Books, 1982).

8   Jean-Paul Brodeur, *The Policing Web* (Oxford University Press, 2010).

9   Brodeur, *Policing Web*.

10   Cotterrell, *Sociology of Law*.

11   Antonio Gramsci, *Selections from the Prison Notebooks* (International Publishers, 1971).

12   Michel Foucault, *Discipline and Punish: The Birth of the Prison* (Vintage Books, 1977); David Graeber, *The Utopia of Rules: On Technology, Stupidity, and the Secret Joys of Bureaucracy* (Melville House, 2015).

13   Michel Foucault, Graham Burchell, Colin Gordon, and Peter Miller, eds., *The Foucault Effect: Studies in Governmentality: With Two Lectures by and an Interview with Michel Foucault* (University of Chicago Press, 1991).

14   See BC Civil Liberties Association, *The Arrest Handbook*, 2023, bccla.org.

15   Susan A. Bandes, "Remorse and Criminal Justice," *Emotion Review* 8, no. 1 (2016): 14–19, doi.org/10.1177/1754073915601222.

16   Steven Keith Tudor, "Why Should Remorse Be a Mitigating Factor in Sentencing?," *Criminal Law and Philosophy* 2, no. 3 (2008): 241–57, doi.org/10.1007/s11572-007-9044-z.

17   Chloé Leclerc and Elsa Euvard, "Pleading Guilty: A Voluntary or Coerced Decision?," *Canadian Journal of Law and Society / La Revue Canadienne Droit Et Société* 34, no. 3 (2019): 457–78.

18   Nicole R. Fleetwood, "Racist Police Practices Like Mug Shots Normalize the Criminalization of Black Americans," *NBC News,* August 6, 2020, nbcnews.com.

19   Julian Van Der Walle Law Corporation, "Does a Person Have a Reasonable Expectation of Privacy in a Police Mugs?," 2020, criminallawyervernonbc.com; Andreas Bernard, *The Triumph of Profiling: The Self in Digital Culture* (Polity Press, 2019).

20   Jon Ronson, *So You've Been Publicly Shamed*, 1st Riverhead trade paperback ed. (Riverhead Books, 2016).

21   We will examine Thomas Hobbes's work in relation to John Locke in more detail in the next chapter.

22   Michael R. Gottfredson and Travis Hirschi, *A General Theory of Crime* (Stanford University Press, 1990).

23   Louis Althusser, "Ideology and Ideological State Apparatuses," in *Lenin and Philosophy,* 121–176.

24   Egon Bittner, *The Functions of the Police in Modern Society* (National Institute of Mental Health, 1970).

25   Calavita, *Invitation to Law & Society*.

26   C. Wright Mills, *The Sociological Imagination* (Oxford University Press, 2000).

27   Lynn Hunt, *Inventing Human Rights: A History,* 1st ed. (W. W. Norton, 2007).

28   James C. Scott, *Against the Grain: A Deep History of the Earliest States* (Yale University Press, 2017).

29   Enrique Dussel, *The Invention of the Americas: Eclipse of "the Other" and the Myth of Modernity* (Continuum, 1995); John Borrows, "Sovereignty's

Alchemy: An Analysis of Delgamuukw v. British Columbia," *Osgoode Hall Law Journal* 37, no. 3 (1999): 537–96.

30 Shiri Pasternak, "Jurisdiction and Settler Colonialism: Where Do Laws Meet?," *Canadian Journal of Law and Society / Revue Canadienne Droit et Societe* 29, no. 2 (2014): 145–61.

31 Larry Chartrand, Kanatase Horn, and Canadian Electronic Library (Firm), *A Report on the Relationship Between Restorative Justice and Indigenous Legal Traditions in Canada*, Department of Justice Canada, 2016.

32 Jean-Jacques Rousseau, *Discourse on the Origin of Inequality* (Oxford University Press, 1994); Charles Taylor, "The Politics of Recognition," *Multiculturalism and the Politics of Recognition*, ed. Amy Gutmann (Princeton University Press, 1992), 25–74.

33 Robert Agnew, "Foundation for a General Strain Theory of Crime and Delinquency," *Criminology* 30 (1992): 47–87; D. Dario Melossi, *Controlling Crime, Controlling Society: Thinking About Crime in Europe and America* (Polity Press, 2008).

34 Eduardo Bonilla-Silva, *Racism Without Racists: Color-Blind Racism and the Persistence of Racial Inequality in the United States* (Rowman & Littlefield, 2006); Joe R. Feagin, *Systemic Racism: A Theory of Oppression* (Routledge, 2006).

35 Susana Borràs, "New Transitions from Human Rights to the Environment to the Rights of Nature," *Transnational Environmental Law* 5, no. 1 (2016): 113–43.

36 Elizabeth Comack, ed., *Locating Law: Race, Class, Gender, Sexuality, Connections*, 3rd ed. (Fernwood Publishing, 2014).

37 Eve Darian-Smith, *Laws and Societies in Global Contexts: Contemporary Approaches* (Cambridge University Press, 2013).

38 *Canadian Charter of Rights and Freedoms*, Part I of the *Constitution Act, 1982*, being Schedule B to the *Canada Act 1982* (UK), 1982, c 11, s 91(24).

39 Office of the Privacy Commissioner of Canada, et al., Joint Investigation of Clearview AI, Inc. by the Office of the Privacy Commissioner of Canada, the Commission d'accès à l'information du Québec, the Information and Privacy Commissioner for British Columbia, and the Information Privacy Commissioner of Alberta, PIPEDA Findings #2021-001, 2021, gc.ca.

40 Dimensions of Poverty Hub, Statistics Canada, 2024, statcan.gc.ca.

41 Mills, *Sociological Imagination*.

42 Ian Taylor, Paul Walton, and Jock Young, *The New Criminology: For a Social Theory of Deviance* (Routledge, 1996).

Chapter 2: Fear of Harm

1 George W. Holden, Tricia Gower, Sharyl E. Wee, Rachel Gaspar, and Rose Ashraf, "Is It Time for 'Time-In'?: A Pilot Test of the Child-Rearing Technique," *Pediatric Reports* 14, no. 2 (2022): 244–53, MDPI AG, doi.org/10.3390/pediatric14020032; Elizabeth T. Gershoff, Gail S. Goodman, Cindy L. Miller-Perrin, George W. Holden, Yo Jackson, and

Alan E. Kazdin, "The Strength of the Causal Evidence Against Physical Punishment of Children and Its Implications for Parents, Psychologists, and Policymakers," *American Psychologist* 73, no. 5 (2018): 626–38, doi-org. ezproxy.kpu.ca:2443/10.1037/amp0000327.

2   Erving Goffman, *Stigma: Notes on the Management of Spoiled Identity.* (Simon & Schuster, 1963; repr. Penguin, 1990).

3   Micheal Chapman and Carolyn Zahn-Wexler, "Young Children's Compliance and Noncompliance to Parental Discipline in a Natural Setting," *International Journal of Behavioral Development* 5, no. 1 (1982): 81–94; Martin Hoffman, "Moral Development," in *Carmichael's Manual of Child Psychology,* 3rd ed., vol. 2, ed. Paul H. Mussen (Wiley, 1970); Daniel J. Siegel and Tina Payne Bryson, *No-Drama Discipline: The Whole-Brain Way to Calm the Chaos and Nurture Your Child's Developing Mind* (Bantam, 2014).

4   Michel Foucault, *Discipline and Punish: The Birth of the Prison* (Vintage Books, 1977).

5   David Lyon, *Surveillance Society: Monitoring Everyday Life* (McGraw-Hill Education, 2001); David Lyon, *The Culture of Surveillance: Watching as a Way of Life* (Polity Press, 2018).

6   Richard Ericson, *Crime in an Insecure World* (Wiley, 2007).

7   Stephen Spielberg, dir., *Minority Report*, starring Tom Cruise, Twentieth Century Fox, 2002. Based on the short story by Philip K. Dick, "The Minority Report," *Fantastic Universe* (1956).

8   Mark Garrett Cooper, "The Contradictions of *Minority Report*," *Film Criticism* 28, no. 2 (2003): 24–41.

9   Nicole R. Fleetwood, "Racist Police Practices Like Mug Shots Normalize the Criminalization of Black Americans," Think, *NBC News*, August 6, 2020, nbcnews.com.

10   "SFPD Chief Bill Scott Ends the Release of Most Booking Photos, Saying New Reform Aims to End Bias, Affirm Procedural Justice," San Francisco Police, July 1, 2020, sanfranciscopolice.org.

11   Kathleen McGrory and Neil Bedi, "Targeted," *Tampa Bay Times,* September 3, 2020, tampabay.com; John Romano, "Pasco Sheriff's Irresponsible Use of Crime Fighting Tactics," *Tampa Bay Times*, September 10, 2020, tampabay.com.

12   Ericson, *Crime in an Insecure World.*

13   Rafael Prieto Curiel and Steven Richard Bishop, "A Metric of the Difference Between Perception of Security and Victimisation Rates," *Crime Sci* 5, no. 1 (2016): 1–15.

14   Sandra Walklate and Gabe Mythen, "How Scared Are We?," *British Journal of Criminology* 48, no. 2 (2008): 209–25.

15   Mike Maguire, Rod Morgan, and Robert Reiner, *The Oxford Handbook of Criminology* (Oxford University Press, 2002); Zygmunt Bauman, *Liquid Fear* (Polity Press, 2006).

16   Nicole E. Rader, *Teaching Fear: How We Learn to Fear Crime and Why It Matters* (Temple University Press, 2023).

17   Chris Linder and Marvette Lacy, "Blue Lights and Pepper Spray: Cisgender College Women's Perceptions of Campus Safety and Implications of the 'Stranger Danger' Myth," *Journal of Higher Education* 91, no. 3 (2019): 433–54.

18   Yvonne Jewkes, "Online Child Pornography, Paedophilia and the Sexualized Child: Mediated Myths and Moral Panics," in *Understanding and Preventing Online Sexual Exploitation of Children,* eds. Ethel Quayle and Kurt Ribisl (Routledge, 2012), 116–32.

19   Rafael Prieto Curiel and Steven Richard Bishop, "Fear of Crime: The Impact of Different Distributions of Victimisation," *Palgrave Communication* 4 (2018): 46.

20   Susan C. Boyd and Connie I. Carter, *Killer Weed: Marijuana Grow Ops, Media, and Justice* (University of Toronto Press, 2014).

21   Dan Werb, Greg Rowell, Gordon Guyatt, Thomas Kerr, Julio Montaner, and Evan Wood, "Effect of Drug Law Enforcement on Drug Market Violence: A Systematic Review," *International Journal of Drug Policy* 22, no. 2 (2011): 87–94.

22   Rader, *Teaching Fear.*

23   Bauman, *Liquid Fear.*

24   Bauman, *Liquid Fear.*

25   Adam Curtis, dir., *The Power of Nightmares: The Rise of the Politics of Fear,* BBC, 2005.

26   Richard V. Ericson and Kevin D. Haggerty, *Policing the Risk Society* (University of Toronto Press, 1997).

27   Melanie S. Seabrook, Alex Luscombe, Nicole Balian, Aisha Lofters, Flora I. Matheson, Braden G. O'Neill, Akwasi Owusu-Bempah, Navindra Persaud, and Andrew D. Pinto, "Police Funding and Crime Rates in 20 of Canada's Largest Municipalities: A Longitudinal Study," *Canadian Public Policy* 49, no. 4 (2023): 383–98.

Chapter 3: Media Representations

1   Daniel Romer, Kathleen Hall Jamieson, and Sean Aday, "Television News and the Cultivation of Fear of Crime" *Journal of Communication* 53, no. 1 (2003): 88–104.

2   Mirka Smolej and Janne Kivivuori, "The Relation Between Crime News and Fear of Violence," *Journal of Scandinavian Studies in Criminology & Crime Prevention* 7, no. 2 (2006): 211–27.

3   Chris Greer and Robert Reiner, "Mediated Mayhem: Media, Crime, Criminal Justice," in *The Oxford Handbook of Criminology,* 5th ed., eds. Rod Morgan, Robert Reiner, and Mike Maguire (Oxford University Press, 2012), 245–78; Ray Surette, "New Media and Social Constructionism," in *Media, Crime, and Criminal Justice: Images, Realities, and Policies,* 5th ed. (Cengage Learning, 2015), 30–56.

4   Yvonne Jewkes, "The Construction of Crime News," in *Media & Crime,* 3rd ed. (SAGE, 2015), 43–79.

5   Jeff Ferrell, Keith J. Hayward, and Jock Young, "Cultural Criminology: An Invitation," in *Cultural Criminology: An Invitation*, 2nd ed. (SAGE, 2015), 1–30.

6   Liam Kennedy, "'Whenever There's Trouble, Just Yelp for Help': Crime, Conservation, and Corporatization in Paw Patrol," *Crime, Media, Culture* 17, no. 2 (2021): 255–70.

7   For more on incel cultures, see Lewys Brace, "A Short Introduction to Involuntary Celibate Sub-Culture," Centre for Research and Evidence on Security Threats, August 26, 2021, crestresearch.ac.uk.

8   Stanley Cohen, *Folk Devils and Moral Panics: The Creation of the Mods and Rockers* (Routledge, 2002).

9   See commonsensemedia.org.

10   Matti Vuorre, Niklas Johannes, Kristoffer Magnusson, and Andrew K. Przybylski, "Time Spent Playing Video Games Is Unlikely to Impact Well-Being," *Royal Society Open Science* 9, no. 7 (2022), doi.org/10.1098/rsos.220411; see also Matti Vuorre, Niklas Johannes, Kristoffer Magnusson, and Andrew K. Przybylski, "Major New Study Finds Little Evidence for Causal Connection Between Well-Being and Video Game Playing," News Release, Oxford Internet Institute, July 27, 2022, ox.ac.uk.

11   Anthony Scott Cunningham, Benjamin Engelstätter, and Michael R. Ward, "Violent Video Games and Violent Crime," *Southern Economic Journal* 82, no. 4 (2016): 1247–65.

12   Andrew John Goldsmith, "Policing's New Visibility," *British Journal of Criminology* 50, no. 5 (2010): 914–34, doi.org/10.1093/bjc/azq033.

13   "Dash Camera Shows Moment Philandro Castile Is Shot, *New York Times*, July 20, 2017, nytimes.com.

14   "On This Day: Camera Rolls as Rodney King Beaten by LAPD," *CBS News*, March 2, 2016, cbsnews.com.

15   See a reprint of the 1979 *Montreal Star* article: "Allo Police Is 'Must Reading' – Information for Cops, Robbers," theresaallore. com, March 27, 2016, theresaallore.com; for more about Allô Police see Wikipedia, s. v. "Allô Police," last modified December 9, 2023, 11:25, wikipedia.org.

16   See thesocialjusticecentre.org.

17   Marshal McLuhan, *Understanding Media: The Extensions of Man* (New American Library of Canada, 1964).

18   Guy Debord, *Society of the Spectacle* (Soul Bay Press, 2009).

Chapter 4: The Quest for Causation

1   Behaviouralism—as an analytic framework rooted in psychological theory—tries to understand criminal behaviour as something that arises out of environmental influences or learning processes shaping an individual and/or their individual conduct.

2   Karl Marx and Daniel De Leon, *The Eighteenth Brumaire of Louis Bonaparte* (International Publishers, 1898).

3   For more, see Mark M. Lanier, Stuart Henry, and Desire J. M. Anastasia,

"Capitalism as a Criminogenic Society," in *Essential Criminology*, 4th ed. (Routledge, 2015), chapter 10.

4 Don Mitchell, "The Annihilation of Space by Law: Anti-Homeless Laws and the Shrinking Landscape of Rights," in *The Right to the City: Social Justice and the Fight for Public Space* (Guilford Press, 2003), 161–94.

5 Paolo Mazzarello, "Cesare Lombroso: An Anthropologist Between Evolution and Degeneration," *Funct Neurol* 26, no. 2 (April-June 2011): 97–101.

6 Nell I. Painter, *The History of White People* (W. W. Norton, 2010).

7 Gresham M. Sykes and David Matza, "Techniques of Neutralization: A Theory of Delinquency," *American Sociological Review* 22, no. 6 (1957): 664–70.

8 György Lukács and Rodney Livingstone, *History and Class Consciousness: Studies in Marxist Dialectics* (MIT Press, 1971).

9 Gary Becker, "Crime and Punishment: An Economic Approach," *Journal of Political Economy* 76, no. 2 (1968): 169–217.

10 Stanley Cohen, "Footprints in the Sand: A Further Report on Criminology and the Sociology of Deviance in Britain," in *Crime and Society: Readings in History and Theory*, eds. Mike Fitzgerald, Gregor McLennan, and Jennie Pawson (Routledge and Kegan Paul, 1980), 183–205.

11 Louis Althusser, "Ideology and Ideological State Apparatuses," in *Lenin and Philosophy and Other Essays* (New Left Books, 1971).

12 C. B. MacPherson. *The Political Theory of Possessive Individualism (Hobbes to Locke)* (Oxford University Press, 1962).

Chapter 5: The Counting Conundrum

1 For more information see Criminal Code 265.1-, gc.ca.

2 Jing Hui Wang and Greg Moreau. "Police-Reported Hate Crime in Canada, 2020," *Juristat*, 2022, 1–40.

3 Note: The terms "hate," "dislike," or "extreme bias" are very broad in meaning. How strong does a dislike have to be to constitute "hate"? The Criminal Code does not concern itself with this question. The code does not define "genocide" nor does it define the concept of "hatred," even though both these concepts are described in Section 318 and 319.

4 Crime rate is a measurement of the amount or quantity of reported crime relative to the size of the population. We often get crime rates via the news. Another common measurement used by governments is the crime severity index. This is a variation on the crime rate. Instead of counting all crimes as equal, the crime severity index assigns a weight to offenses based on the average sentence handed down in the courts. This weight is then used to measure the severity of crime in a given jurisdiction over a given period of time. The intention is to ensure that high volume but less serious crimes, like the theft of a chocolate bar, do not obscure important patterns related to very serious but uncommon crimes, like aggravated assault.

5 Jim Rankin, "Singled Out," *Toronto Star*, October 19, 2002; Carol Tator

and Frances Henry, *Racial Profiling in Canada: Challenging the Myth of "a Few Bad Apples"* (University of Toronto Press, 2006).

6   Jeffrey H. Reiman and Paul Leighton, *The Rich Get Richer and the Poor Get Prison: Ideology, Class, and Criminal Justice,* 11th ed. (Routledge/Taylor & Francis, 2017).

7   Robyn Doolittle, "Unfounded: Police Dismiss 1 in 5 Sexual Assault Claims as Baseless, Globe Investigation Reveals," *Globe and Mail,* February 3, 2017, theglobeandmail.com.

Chapter 6: Consent

1   Thomas Hobbes, *Leviathan* (Penguin Books, 1968); John Locke, *The Second Treatise of Civil Government and a Letter Concerning Toleration* (B. Blackwell, 1948).

2   Edward S. Herman and Noam Chomsky, *Manufacturing Consent: The Political Economy of the Mass Media* (Pantheon Books, 1988).

3   Readers may find it helpful to review Part V of the Criminal Code of Canada, which deals with "Sexual Offences, Public Morals and Disorderly Conduct." The concept of consent is used throughout this part of the code: gc.ca.

4   Robyn Doolittle, *Had It Coming: What's Fair in the Age of #MeToo* (Penguin Random House, 2019).

5   For more information, see: "Why the City of Burnaby Opposes Kinder Morgan's Proposed Pipeline Route," Pure Souls Media, YouTube video, 21:57, youtu.be.

6   Arno Kopecky, "Three Days in the Theatre of Fairy Creek," *The Tyee,* June 1, 2021, thetyee.ca.

7   Elya M. Durisin, Emily van der Meulen, and Chris Bruckert, *Red Light Labour: Sex Work Regulation, Agency, and Resistance* (University of British Columbia Press, 2018).

8   Magaly Rodriguez García, A. F. Lex Heerma van Voss, and Elise van Nederveen Meerkerk, eds., *Selling Sex in the City: A Global History of Prostitution, 1600s-2000s,* Vol. 31 of Studies in Global Social History (Brill, 2017).

Chapter 7: Systems of Response

1   Laura Huey, Lorna Ferguson, and Jennifer L. Schulenberg, *The Wicked Problems of Police Reform in Canada* (Routledge, 2023).

2   Jonathan Simon, *Governing Through Crime: How the War on Crime Transformed American Democracy and Created a Culture of Fear* (Oxford University Press, 2007).

3   See the Government of Canada's policy document outlining substance use as a health issue: *Strengthening Canada's Approach to Substance Use Issues,* Health Canada, July 9, 2019, canada.ca.

4   Michelle Gamage and Zoë Yunker, "Bombshell Decision: Judge Ends Fairy Creek Injunction," *The Tyee*, September 29, 2021, thetyee.ca.

5   R. *v.* Mann, [2004] 3 S.C.R. 59, 2004 SCC 52. In this case, the court clarified the limits of police powers regarding lawful search incidental to a detention, as compared to the more comprehensive powers of search associated with arrest.

6   For more information on the Edmund Yu Shooting, see Wikipedia, s. v. "Shooting of Edmond Yu," last modified January 27, 2025, 11:58, wikipedia.org.

7   Jeff Ferrell, Keith J. Hayward, and Jock Young, "Cultural Criminology: An Invitation," in *Cultural Criminology: An Invitation*, 2nd ed. (SAGE, 2015), 1–30.

8   Elizabeth Comack, ed., *Locating Law: Race, Class, Gender, Sexuality, Connections*, 3rd ed. (Fernwood Publishing, 2014).

9   For more information, see Government of Canada, *Mandatory Minimum Penalties in Canada: Analysis and Annotated Bibliography*, Department of Justice, January 20, 2023, gc.ca.

10 For a critique of minimum mandatory sentencing see the positions taken by the Canadian Criminal Justice Association and LEAF: Canadian Criminal Justice Association, "Mandatory Minimum Sentences," n.d., accessed May 22, 2025, ccja-acjp.ca; Women's Legal and Action Fund (LEAF), "Submission to the Standing Committee on Justice and Human Rights Re: Bill C-10," November 20, 2006, leaf.ca.

11 For more, see R v Ellis: A New Frontier for Sentencing Drug Trafficking Offences. pivotlegal.org; Haley Hrymak, "A Bad Deal: British Columbia's Emphasis on Deterrence and Increasing Prison Sentences for Street-Level Fentanyl Traffickers," *Manitoba Law Journal* 41, no. 4 (2018).

12 Douglas Hay, "Property, Authority and the Criminal Law," in *The Social Organization of Law: Introductory Readings*, ed. A. Sarat (Roxbury Publishing, 2004), 75–83.

13 Michelle Alexander, "Go to Trial: Crash the Justice System," *New York Times*, March 10, 2012, nytimes.com.

14 Miko M. Wilford, Gary L. Wells, and Annabelle Frazier, "Plea-Bargaining Law: The Impact of Innocence, Trial Penalty, and Conviction Probability on Plea Outcomes," *American Journal of Criminal Justice* 46, no. 3 (2021): 554–75, doi.org/10.1007/s12103-020-09564-y.

15 Nils Christie, "Conflicts as Property," *British Journal of Criminology* 17, no. 1 (1977): 1–15.

16 Government of Canada, *Correctional Process*, Correctional Services Canada, last modified April 24, 2014, gc.ca.

17 Michel Foucault, *Discipline and Punish: The Birth of the Prison*, 2nd Vintage Books ed. (Vintage Books, 1995).

18 Rachel Condry and Shona Minson, "Conceptualizing the Effects of Imprisonment on Families: Collateral Consequences, Secondary Punishment, or Symbiotic Harms?," *Theoretical Criminology* 25, no. 4 (2021): 540–58, doi.org/10.1177/1362480619897078.

19   Ruth Morris, *Stories of Transformative Justice* (Canadian Scholars' Press, 2000).
20   Jamil Malakieh, *Adult and Youth Correctional Statistics in Canada, 2018/2019*, *Juristat*, Canadian Centre for Justice Statistics, December 21, 2020, gc.ca
21   Wikipedia, s. v. "The $64,000 Question," last modified April 17, 2025, 11:05, wikipedia.org.
22   Mike Larsen, "Indefinitely Pending: Security Certificates and Permanent Temporariness," in *Liberating Temporariness?: Migration, Work, and Citizenship in an Age of Insecurity,* eds. Leah F. Vosko, Valerie Preston, and Robert Latham (McGill-Queen's University Press, 2014), 76–96.

Chapter 8: Criminalizing Inequality and Poverty

1   David Levinson, *Encyclopedia of Crime and Punishment* (SAGE, 2002), 1212–15.
2   For example, see Peter B. Edelman, *Not a Crime to Be Poor: The Criminalization of Poverty in America* (The New Press, 2019).
3   Anatole France, *The Red Lily* (J. Lane, 1910).
4   Kostadis J. Papaioannou, "'Hunger Makes a Thief of Any Man': Poverty and Crime in British Colonial Asia," *European Review of Economic History* 21, no. 1 (2017): 1–28, doi-org.ezproxy.kpu.ca:2443/10.1093/ereh/hew019.
5   For more, see "Canadians Living in Low-Income Households More Likely Than Those from Higher Income Households to Report Socially Disruptive Conditions in Their Neighbourhoods," Statistics Canada, November 30, 2015, gc.ca; Mathieu Charron, *Neighbourhood Characteristics and the Distribution of Police-Reported Crime in the City of Toronto*, Canadian Centre for Justice Statistics, Statistics Canada, 2009, gc.ca; Min-Jen Lin, "Does Unemployment Increase Crime? Evidence from U.S. Data 1974–2000," *The Journal of Human Resources* 43, no. 2 (2008): 413–36, jstor.org.
6   *Canada Inequality: Is Canada Becoming More Unequal?*, Conference Board of Canada, 2011, conferenceboard.ca.
7   *Public Good or Private Wealth?*, Oxfam Canada, 2019, oxfam.ca.
8   Edwin Hardin Sutherland, *White Collar Crime* (Holt, Rinehart and Winston, 1961).
9   For more, see Alexandre Tanzi and Mike Dorning, "Top 1% of U.S. Earners Now Hold More Wealth Than All of the Middle Class," Wealth, *Bloomberg*, August 10, 2021, bloomberg.com.
10   Thomas Piketty, *Capital in the Twenty-First Century* (Belknap Press, 2014).
11   The Canadian Press, "RCMP Make 27 More Arrests at B.C. Old-Growth Logging Blockades," *CBC News*, September 12, 2021, cbc.ca.
12   "Toronto's Promise for Permanent Housing Ends Standoff in Trinity Bellwoods Park, Advocate Says," *CBC News*, June 22, 2021, cbc.ca.
13   Peter K. Manning, "The Police: Mandate, Strategies, and Appearances," in *Policing: Key Readings*, ed. Tim Newburn (Willan Publishing, 2005), 191–214.

Chapter 9: Racism

1 Jamil Malakieh, "Adult and Youth Correctional Statistics in Canada, 2018/2019," *Juristat*, Canadian Centre for Justice and Community Safety Statistics, 2020, gc.ca.

2 Adam Cotter, "Perceptions of and Experiences with Police and the Justice System Among the Black and Indigenous Populations in Canada," *Juristat*, Canadian Centre for Justice and Community Safety Statistics, 2022, gc.ca.

3 For more information, see BC Civil Liberties Association, *A Special BCCLA Report on Racial Profiling in Canada*, 2010, bccla.org.

4 Peter McFarlane and Nicole Schabus, eds., *Whose Land Is It Anyway? A Manual for Decolonization*, Federation of Post-Secondary Educators of BC, 2017, fpse.ca; Shiri Pasternak, "Jurisdiction and Settler Colonialism: Where Do Laws Meet?," *Canadian Journal of Law and Society / Revue Canadienne Droit et Société* 29, no. 2 (2014): 145–61, doi.org/10.1017/cls.2014.5.

5 Andrew Graybill, "Rangers, Mounties, and the Subjugation of Indigenous Peoples, 1870–1885," *Great Plains Quarterly* 24, no. 2 (2004): 91.

6 M-E LeBeuf and Royal Canadian Mounted Police, *The Role of the Royal Canadian Mounted Police During the Indian Residential School System*, Royal Canadian Mounted Police, 2011.

7 For more information, see Truth and Reconciliation Commission of Canada, *Truth and Reconciliation Commission of Canada: Calls to Action*, 2015, gov.bc.ca.

8 For more information on Potlach and Sundance, see potlatch6767.com.

9 Timothy Stanley, "John A. Macdonald, 'the Chinese' and Racist State Formation in Canada," *Journal of Critical Race Inquiry* 3, no. 1 (2016).

10 N. I. Painter, *The History of White People* (W. W. Norton, 2010).

11 Cesare Lombroso, *Criminal Man* (G. P. Putnam's Sons, 1911).

12 Carol Tator and Frances Henry, *Racial Profiling in Canada: Challenging the Myth of "a Few Bad Apples"* (University of Toronto Press, 2006).

13 Thomas Gabor, "Inflammatory Rhetoric on Racial Profiling Can Undermine Police Services," *Canadian Journal of Criminology and Criminal Justice* 46, no. 4 (2004): 457–66.

14 Nicholas Rohde and Ross Guest, "Multidimensional Racial Inequality in the United States," *Social Indicators Research* 4, no. 2 (November 11, 2013): 591–605.

15 Beverly-Jean M. Daniel, "Troubling and Disrupting the 'Cradle to Prison Pipeline': The Experience of Black Youth in Ontario," in *Diversity, Justice, and Community: The Canadian Context* (Canadian Scholars' Press, 2016).

16 Kimberlé Crenshaw, "Demarginalizing The Intersection of Race and Sex: A Black Feminist Critique of Antidiscrimination Doctrine, Feminist Theory and Antiracist Policies," *The University of Chicago Legal Forum* 1989, no. 1 (1989): 139–67.

17 British Columbia Civil Liberties Association, *Open Letter: Immediate Municipal and Provincial Ban on Police Street Checks*, 2020, bccla.org; Scot Wortley and Akwasi Owusu-Bempah, "The Usual Suspects: Police Stop and Search Practices in Canada," *Policing & Society* 21, no. 4 (2011): 395–407.

18 Gabor, "Inflammatory Rhetoric"; Tator and Henry, *Racial Profiling in Canada.*

19 Ryan Patrick Jones, "The Police Budget Is One of Toronto's Largest Expenses. Here's What You Need to Know About It," *CBC News*, October 21, 2022, cbc.ca.

20 Peter K. Manning, "The Police: Mandate, Strategies, and Appearances," in *Policing: Key Readings*, ed. T. Newburn (Willan Publishing, 2005), 191–214.

21 For more on the Truth and Reconciliation Commissions, see nctr.ca; for more on the Calls to Action, see gov.bc.ca.

Index

Michael C. K. Ma is a faculty member in the Department of Sociology at the University of Victoria, British Columbia. He works in the area of social justice, community advocacy, anti-racism, and harm reduction. His current research is in the area of drug use. He is a founding member of The Social Justice Centre. In the past he was very active with the Chinese Canadian National Council - Toronto Chapter and the Metro Network for Social Justice. His academic training is in sculpture, art history, and social/political thought. He lives in Victoria, BC.

Mike Larsen is a faculty member in the Criminology Department at Kwantlen Polytechnic University in Surrey, British Columbia. He lives on the unceded territories of the Coast Salish peoples, including the Katzie, Kwantlen, and Semiahmoo First Nations. Mike teaches courses on criminology, law and society, crime and media, and surveillance and privacy. His research deals with access to information, privacy, and security practices. He is the current President of the BC Freedom of Information and Privacy Association.